Land of Extremes

LAND OF EXTREMES

A NATURAL HISTORY OF THE
ARCTIC NORTH SLOPE OF ALASKA

Alexander D. Huryn

John E. Hobbie

University of Alaska Press
Fairbanks, Alaska

University of Alaska Press
P.O. Box 756240
Fairbanks, AK 99775-6240

Support for this book was provided by the
    Thomas Saunders English fund

ISBN 978-1-60223-181-8 (paper)
ISBN 978-1-60223-182-5 (electronic)

Library of Congress Cataloging-in-Publication Data

Huryn, Alexander D.
  Land of extremes : a natural history of the North Slope of Arctic
Alaska / Alexander D. Huryn, John E. Hobbie.
     p. cm.
  Includes bibliographical references and index.
  ISBN 978-1-60223-181-8 (paper : alk. paper) — ISBN 978-1-60223-
    182-5 (electronic)
  1. Natural history—Alaska—North Slope. 2. Extreme environments—
Alaska—North Slope. 3. North Slope (Alaska)—Environmental con-
ditions. I. Hobbie, John E. II. Title.
  QH105.A4H87 2012
  508.798—dc23
                        2012005967

Cover design by Matt Simmons
Cover photo: Lupine over Kongakut, © John Schwieder

This publication was printed on acid-free paper that meets the minimum requirements for ANSI / NISO Z39.48–1992 (R2002) (Perma-
nence of Paper for Printed Library Materials).

Printed in the United States of America

Dedications

For Eugene, Maria, Alexandra, and Vivian, and
all other students of nature.
—Alexander D. Huryn

For my wife, Olivann, lab and field assistant during
our 1960–1961 winter in the Brooks Range.
—John E. Hobbie

Contents

Arctic Small Tool Tradition (~5,000–2,400 Years BP) 248
Kavik Athapaskan (AD 1500 to 1800)   249
The Maritime Eskimos: Birnirk, Thule, and Iñupiat
     (1,600 Years BP to present)   250
**Appendix: Guide to Natural History Along the
Dalton Highway: Atigun Pass to Deadhorse   255**
Introduction   255
     Four Notes of Caution Before Traveling
          on the Dalton Highway   255
The Road Log   257

     Endnotes   *281*
     Sources   *287*
     Index   *301*

Acknowledgments

Many people contributed to this book in many ways, some knowingly, some not. E. C. Pielou provides an example of the latter. Her excellent *A Naturalist's Guide to the Arctic* (University of Chicago Press, 1994) provided the initial inspiration as well as a model for our more regionally focused book. Among the former are many, many friends and colleagues who generously contributed time, knowledge, specimens, and photographs. First and foremost we would like to acknowledge Jake Schas and Brian Barnes. Without Jake's dedication to the study of the natural history of the Toolik Lake region and his excellent field skills, this book would have suffered greatly. Brian Barnes, the director of the Institute of Arctic Biology (IAB) at the University of Alaska Fairbanks, provided essential encouragement in the early stages of our project. Others who provided significant information include George Batzli, Jon Benstead, Syndonia Bret-Harte, Malcom Butler, Robert Golder, Laura Gough, Anne Hershey, Cody Johnson, Mike Kendrick, George Kling, Michael Kunz, Chris Leuke, Jeff Lozier, William Morris, David Murray, Dave Norton, Stephanie Parker, Heidi Rantala, Brendan Scanlon, Donald Walker, and John Wingfield. Eugene, Maria, and Alexandra Huryn dissected snowy owl pellets. Photographs are central to this book; many individuals graciously contributed wonderful examples. These include Andrew Balser, George Batzli, Jon Benstead, Breck Bowden, Julie Deslippe, Jason Dobkowski, Cody Johnson, Mike Kendrick, Jen Kostrzewski, Michael Kunz, Chris Leuke, Cameron Mackenzie, Edward Metzger, William Morris, Larry Moulton, Stephanie Parker, Jake Schas, Emily Weiser, and John Wingfield. Assistance with taxonomy was provided by Bernard Goffinet (lichens), Chris Leucke (zooplankton), David Murray (plants), Peter Ray (plants), Brendan Scanlon (fish), Jake Schas (birds), and Dale Vitt (lichens, bryophytes). Individuals who read all or portions of the book and provided critical comments for improvement include Brian Barnes (entire book), George Batzli (mammals), Malcom

Butler (invertebrates), Vivian Butz Huryn (entire book), Laura Gough (vascular plants), Erik Hobbie (mushroom madness), Olivann Hobbie, Michael Kunz (archeology), Rich McHorney (geology), William Morris (fish), David Norton (entire book), Brendan Scanlon (fish), Jake Schas (birds), and John Wingfield (birds). Jason Stuckey (IAB) and Randy Fulweber (IAB) produced the maps. Access to much of the information and many of the photographs included in this book would not have been possible without the support provided by the Toolik Field Station (TFS) operated by the IAB. Members of the TFS staff who provided essential assistance include Mike Abels, Chad Diesinger, Jake Schas, and Thom Walker. A grant from the National Science Foundation (NSF) to ADH and Jon Benstead (ARC 0611995) provided year-round helicopter transport to the Ivishak River in the Arctic National Wildlife Refuge, which greatly enhanced the quality and depth of the content of this book. Similarly, several decades of continuous funding from the NSF Long Term Ecological Research (LTER) to JEH and colleagues (DEB 0423385) for scientific and logistical support of the Arctic LTER project at the Toolik Field Station were also essential for our success. Finally, the University of Alabama provided a sabbatical leave for ADH during the autumn of 2010, during which much of the original manuscript was prepared. Although many individuals assisted us in numerous ways, we alone are responsible for any inaccuracies or errors that may remain nestled amongst the pages of this book.

Preface

The natural history of the North Slope is well documented, with detailed scientific papers and books on every conceivable topic, from geology to biology to archeology. In this book we bring together the fascinating stories of how animals and plants interact and survive in the harsh arctic environment. We have written it for visitors to the Arctic and the North Slope—those who are interested in natural history in general, in a specific topic such as mammals or birds, in a specific region such as the coastal plain around Barrow or the Arctic National Wildlife Refuge (ANWR), or in finding out more about the last American wilderness. The authors of this book, active researchers working on the North Slope, have also written and edited many scientific papers and books. In text and photos we identify many of the natural history features and describe interesting life histories and adaptations for survival in the Arctic. We have chosen to identify, interpret, and explain only what the visitor will actually see. We avoid scientific jargon and vocabulary and define the relatively few words that are necessary and new to naturalists, such as aufeis, active layer, frost boil, thaw pond, and pingo.

More than half of the book is devoted to descriptions of organisms. Major species or groups of organisms are illustrated with color photos; migrations, feeding habits, and reproduction strategies are also described. A brief list of papers is given as a guide to more information on each topic (see Sources). Coverage is as complete as is practical, with emphasis on intriguing elements of the story such as hibernation, migration, and food webs.

The North Slope extends from the crest of the Brooks Range in the south to the Arctic Ocean in the north. The progression of geological features is similar along the entire Brooks Range, so that a transect from south to north in the east North Slope is similar to one in the west. For example, the Lisburne Limestone, named for Cape Lisburne at the west end of the Brooks Range, is found at the surface along the entire Brooks Range. The vegetation and animals are also similar in the same geographic sense: a natural history transect from the crest of the Brooks Range to the Arctic Ocean in the west passes through mountains, foothills, and a coastal plain while similar geology, plants, and animals are also found along a transect in the ANWR in the east. Because of this similarity, we include, as a typical transect, a detailed description of the arctic section of the Dalton Highway. Along the highway, at sites identified by mile markers, we describe important natural history features like bedrock geology and evidence of permafrost, as well as streams, lakes, plants, birds, mammals, fish, and insects. This transect extends along the Dalton Highway some 275 km (170 miles) from the crest of the Brooks Range to Deadhorse near the Arctic Ocean.

Finally, the book includes short sections on the ecology of the ecosystems and the various habitats found on the North Slope. A visitor to Barrow should be aware of how the vegetation and animals of the coastal plain differ from those of the foothills and mountains. There are also interesting differences in how whole ecosystems operate in the three major habitats of the North Slope: mountains, foothills, and coastal plain. Exhibits about the natural history of the region's national parks and ANWR (http://arctic.fws.gov) can be seen at the Arctic Interagency Visitor Center at Coldfoot on the Dalton Highway.

Introduction

The North Slope

The North Slope, also known as the Arctic Slope, is that part of northern Alaska where rivers drain into the Arctic Ocean north of Point Hope (Map 1). It is enormous, with an area equal to Nebraska or South Dakota (about 200,000 km²) and extending from about 68°N to 71°N at its greatest width. The North Slope contains three major physiographic regions: the Brooks Range, Arctic Foothills, and Arctic Coastal Plain. These are arranged as east–west trending bands parallel to the arctic coast, with the Arctic Coastal Plain most northerly and the Brooks Range most southerly. Each region has characteristic plant and animal communities due to differences in geology, topography, and climate. Nevertheless, they are all considered tundra. There are two types of tundra. Alpine tundra refers to mountain habitats *above* the tree line. Arctic tundra refers to habitats *beyond* the northern tree line. This book is an introduction to the natural history of the North Slope, the only arctic tundra in the United States.

Why the "Arctic"?

The Arctic is precisely defined as that part of the Northern Hemisphere where the sun is visible above the horizon for 24 hours during the summer solstice (around June 21) and is hidden below the horizon for 24 hours during the winter solstice (around December 22). The lowest latitude at which this occurs is about 66°33′N, which marks the position of the Arctic Circle and delimits the southern boundary of the Arctic. As one moves north from the Arctic Circle, the period of continuous daylight ("polar day") or darkness ("polar night") lengthens. At the southern North Slope village of Anaktuvuk Pass (68°8′N) in 2010, for example, the sun rose on May 25 and did not set again

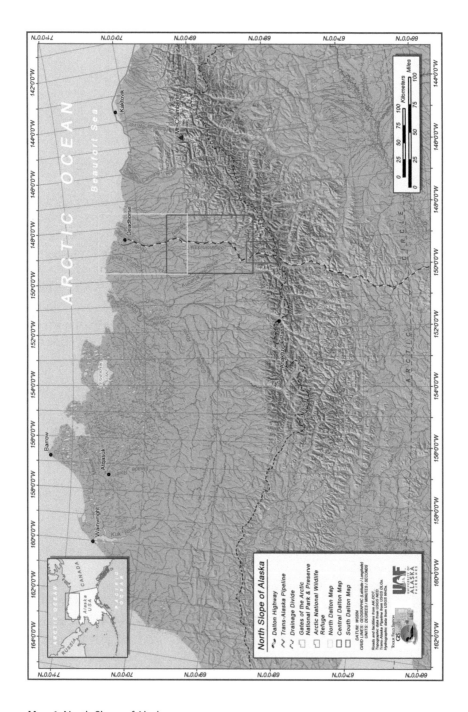

Map 1. North Slope of Alaska.

until July 18 (a 54-day polar day), while the polar day for the northern North Slope town of Barrow (71°17′N) lasted from May 11 to August 1 (82 days). Conversely, the polar night lasted from December 7, 2010, to January 4, 2011 (28 days), at Anaktuvuk Pass and from November 19, 2010, to January 21, 2011, at Barrow (63 days). Those unfamiliar with the relatively low arctic latitudes of the North Slope may have the impression that polar day and night are relatively constant periods of light and darkness. This is not so. During the polar day there are noticeable declines in light and temperature even on the summer solstice because the sun strikes the ground at a low angle during the early morning hours. During the polar night, even on the winter solstice, there is sufficient midday twilight to perform outdoor chores without a headlamp or lantern.

Having provided this pleasingly precise definition of the Arctic, it is important to point out its shortcomings. First, its precision is illusory. The Arctic Circle is not fixed but varies over about 2° during 40,000-year cycles caused by wobbles in the angle of the Earth's axis. Consequently, the location of the famous monument marking where the Dalton Highway crosses the Arctic Circle is only an approximation. Second, it does not adequately delimit the distribution of ecosystems containing communities of organisms adapted to arctic conditions. For example, no biologist would argue that the western shore of the Hudson Bay near Churchill, Manitoba, is not a typical arctic ecosystem, complete with polar bears, arctic foxes, and collared lemmings. Yet Churchill (58°45′N) is clearly south of the Arctic Circle and thus experiences no midnight sun. To accommodate such discrepancies, it has been suggested that the Arctic be defined to include areas of the Northern Hemisphere that have mean July temperatures of 10°C or less. The "10°C July mean-temperature rule" roughly determines the northern limit of tree growth[1] and the southern limit of continuous permafrost.[2] This definition is ecologically sound because it is based on a single key attribute that underlies the structure and function of all arctic communities: a long annual period of deep, dark cold.

Low Arctic versus High Arctic

The Arctic is often subdivided into the "high Arctic" and "low Arctic." The high Arctic includes habitats relatively close to the North Pole (e.g., greater than 75°N). With the exception of limited sedge meadows near streams and below lasting snowbanks, these are best characterized as rocky barrens populated by relatively few plant species (e.g., fewer than

150 vascular plant species). The low Arctic includes habitats closer to the Arctic Circle. These generally have comparatively lush vegetation and high plant diversity (more than 250 vascular plant species). Although all this may seem to be an exercise in hair splitting, it is important to be aware of the large differences between these subdivisions because much of what has been written about arctic ecosystems is based on the high Arctic and may not directly apply to the low Arctic. The North Slope, the focus of this book, provides an excellent example of a low-arctic ecosystem.

Climate

Temperature

The average annual temperature of the North Slope is about –12°C. The warmest month is July (mean near arctic coast = 5 to 8°C, mean in foothills = 12 to 13°C). The coldest is February (mean near arctic coast = –29 to –27°C; mean in foothills = –30°C) because the Arctic Ocean becomes completely covered by ice at this time, dramatically decreasing the transfer of heat from the relatively warm ocean. The major variation in temperatures across the North Slope is related to the distance south of the arctic coast. Coastal regions have warmer winters and colder summers, and interior locations have colder winters and warmer summers. For example, long-term climate records show average July high temperatures of 8°C for Barrow (coastal) to 19°C in Umiat (interior) and average February low temperatures ranging from –30°C at Barrow and –35°C at Umiat. To put all this in perspective, the summer freeze-free period at inland locations can be as much as 30 days; the freeze-free period at Barrow, however, is only 10 days. Needless to say, summers are short everywhere on the North Slope, a place where snowfall can be expected any day of the year!

Precipitation

Precipitation on the North Slope is highly influenced by seasonal patterns of freezing of the Beaufort, Chuchki, and Bering Seas. As continuous sea ice develops, atmospheric moisture is reduced and, as a consequence, precipitation on the North Slope is low from November through April. On the other hand, the lack of near-shore sea ice results in relatively high amounts of precipitation during July and August. Annual precipitation measured on the North Slope ranges from a minimum of 150 mm/yr near Barrow to 550 mm/yr in portions of the Brooks Range (North Slope annual average = 250 mm, or about 10 inches). There are problems with these estimates due to the difficulty of sampling blowing snow, but they nevertheless indicate low precipitation by any measure. To provide perspective, a common definition of a desert is a region receiving less than 250 mm of precipitation annually. By this definition, the North Slope is surely close to a desert—but a very strange one. During summer, the soils of much of the foothills and coastal plain are water saturated and often covered by thick, spongy layers of sphagnum moss. This is because the shallow layer of soil that thaws every summer—the "active layer" (0.3–1.0 m deep, or about 12–39 inches deep)—is sealed by the continuous layer of watertight permafrost below. In low-lying, poorly drained habitats, the water released as the active layer thaws simply has no place to go! The occurrence of water-saturated soils is further facilitated by low rates of evaporation and transpiration (water loss through plant tissues) due to cool summer temperatures. As a consequence of this conspiracy between a shallow active layer, a continuous layer of underlying permafrost, and cool summer temperatures, pools of standing water, extensive wetlands, ponds, lakes, rivers, and streams are all common features of the North Slope landscape. These features defy traditional definitions of a desert, to say the least.

Seasonality

It has been suggested that the traditional concept of the four seasons— winter, spring, summer, autumn—is not useful for the Arctic. There is good reason for this because the calendar dates that define the seasons of temperate regions are of little relevance here. The arctic year can be divided more usefully into a short warm period and a long cold period. The warm period is delimited by the consecutive days centered on mid-July when the *mean* daily temperature is above freezing (usually 10 to 30 days, although frost may occur on any day). The concepts of spring and autumn are reduced to brief seasons ("spring" from mid-May through mid-June, and "autumn" from mid-August through mid-September). The cold period begins in September when soils and surface water freeze ("freezeup") and lasts until they thaw ("breakup") in May. This concept of a "warm season" and a "cold season" makes sense ecologically and is similar to the concept of tropical seasonality, where the year is divided into monsoon and dry seasons, rather than the traditional four seasons.

Snow

The North Slope is blanketed with snow for almost nine months each year. Consequently, the ecology of plants and nonmigratory animals living here cannot be fully appreciated without some knowledge as to how they are affected by this. Snow performs four major ecological roles. First and foremost it provides *insulation* that maintains moderate soil temperatures even in the depth of winter. Second, high *humidity* within the snowpack reduces desiccating effects of dry winter air on buried plants and animals. Third, it provides critical winter *habitat* for small mammals (e.g., lemmings and voles) while simultaneously hampering foraging by the burial of food sources used by some larger animals (e.g., Dall sheep, caribou) and birds. Finally—although this role occurs only during the spring thaw—the melting snowpack provides a spatially variable water supply that is critical in determining the distribution of tundra plant species.

Insulation

Snow provides excellent insulation. Once a snow layer reaches a depth of 20–80 cm (about 8–31 inches), an uncoupling of air and ground temperatures occurs.[3] The depth at which this occurs is called the "hiemal threshold." The wide range in snow depths at which the hiemal threshold occurs is due to differences in the amount of insulation provided by different types of snow. Low-density "new snow" (about 0.1 g/cm³) provides the highest insulation because it contains many dead-air spaces; high-density "old snow" (about 0.4 g/cm³) provides less insulation due to few dead-air spaces. As new snow becomes old snow a predictable process of structural metamorphism occurs, resulting in the difference in dead-air volume. As snow falls, it forms a layer of the familiar lacy snowflakes (new snow). Within a short time (hours to days depending upon factors such as snow depth, temperature, and wind packing), the snowflakes are compacted into a layer of tightly packed grains (old snow) and the volume of trapped dead air declines while the snow's strength and ability to support weight increase. Regardless of age or state of metamorphism, the insulation value of a snow layer approaching 40–50 cm (about 16–20 inches) is sufficient to maintain relatively constant ground temperatures. When insulated by 50 cm or more of winter snow, ground surface temperatures in the foothills, for example, rarely fall below –4 to –10°C (about 25–14°F) even though air temperatures of –30°C (about –22°F) or less are frequent and long lasting.[4] The insulating effect of snow across the vast distances of the North Slope varies because the winter snowpack is relatively deep inland but relatively shallow near the coast due to wind. Consequently, mean winter ground surface temperatures range from about −6°C in the southern foothills to −20°C on the northern coastal plain.

Humidity

A thick snow layer maintains relatively high levels of internal humidity. Following the relatively rapid conversion of new snow to old snow, further structural changes occur that are related to the temperature gradient that forms within the snow layer. The top of the snow layer, which is in contact with the atmosphere, is usually colder than the bottom, which is in contact with the ground. The relatively warm temperature of the ground causes a high rate of sublimation[5] of the ice grains in the bottom of the snow layer. The water vapor produced contributes to high levels of relative humidity (e.g., 100 percent) within the air spaces of the snowpack. Such high levels of humidity greatly enhance the ability of buried plants to avoid desiccation during winter.

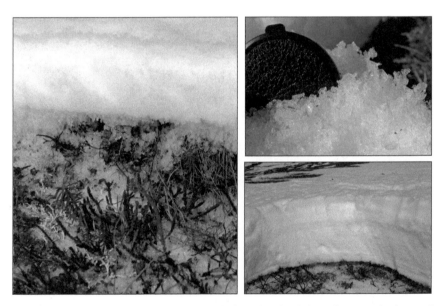

Fig. 1.1. The easily navigated space provided by the depth hoar layer at the base of the winter snowpack is used for habitat by lemmings, voles, shrews, and weasels. *Left:* Detail of depth hoar layer (about 5 cm deep) showing the loose, nonadhesive crystals formed by vapor produced by sublimation of the snow layer adjacent to the ground (Dalton Highway, MP 355, ADH). *Upper right:* Detail of ice crystals forming depth hoar (Atigun Pass, ADH). *Lower right:* A 4 cm deep layer of depth hoar formed at the base of a 33 cm snowpack (Atigun Pass, ADH). The depth hoar layer was lightly brushed to remove the loosely packed crystal layer to better show its extent and location.

Habitat

A thick snow layer provides space near the ground that allows construction of runways and nests by voles, lemmings, shrews, and weasels. This space results from the redistribution of water from the bottom of the snow layer to the top. This process is driven by the diffusion of vapor produced by sublimation at the bottom of the snow layer to the colder top of the snow layer. Here it refreezes and becomes incorporated into a "snow-ice matrix." The snow grains near the top of the snowpack thus increase in size and density at the expense of snow grains near the bottom. As a consequence the bottom of the snow layer is converted to a relatively open matrix of large, brittle, nonadhesive crystals known as "depth hoar" (Fig. 1.1). It is the open space provided by depth hoar that is used as habitat by lemmings, voles, shrews, and weasels, all of which remain active beneath the snow during winter.

2

Bedrock Geology

Suspect Terrane?

Most large landmasses are formed by the fusion of distinct blocks of continental crust ("terranes") with different geographical origins. Consequently, each terrane has a unique combination of rocks and fossils.[1] Alaska consists of at least 13 terranes, with one of the largest being the North Slope. The North Slope is considered a "suspect terrane" because it was joined to the northern Alaskan landmass after migrating from an uncertain ("suspect") location. Information based on the fossil record, however, indicates that the North Slope terrane was always part of North America—it just changed location. The most credible explanation of how the present-day North Slope came to be involves the rifting (splitting) of a large chunk of land from northernmost Canada, followed by a jackknife rotation centered near the Mackenzie River delta, and then a final collision with the north coast of ancestral Alaska. The rifting and subsequent rotation was caused by seafloor spreading during the Early Cretaceous (145–112 million years ago, or mya). Consequently, much of the very old geologic features of the North Slope, including the deposition of the oil-producing strata of the Prudhoe Bay oil fields, occurred while it was a part of present-day northern Canada. Following the joining of the North Slope terrane with ancestral Alaska, a long period of north–south contraction resulted in the uplift of the modern Brooks Range and the shedding of enormous volumes of eroded materials toward the north that eventually covered much of the foothills and coastal plain.

Bedrock of the North Slope

The bedrock of the North Slope terrane is primarily sedimentary in origin. In many places it has been distorted by overthrusting[2] and uplifting. This began with the earliest stirrings of the Brooks Range during the Middle Jurassic (202–146 mya, i.e., prior to the migration of the North Slope terrane away from northern Canada) and continued through the Early Cretaceous (146–100 mya) and the Quaternary (less than 1.8 mya). The bedrock of the present-day Brooks Range is often exposed and readily observed. In the foothills and coastal plain, however, it is usually concealed by sediment layers, or more technically "strata," thousands of meters thick. Although the local bedrock geology of the North Slope can be exceedingly complex due to extreme displacement and distortion, the regional pattern is simple. As one ventures from the Continental Divide toward the Arctic Ocean, the successive exposures of bedrock become younger due to northward dipping of bedrock.[3] To simplify this overview of the geology of the North Slope, we will restrict ourselves to bedrock types observed along the convenient cross section provided by the Dalton Highway. These major bedrock types are presented in order of age, from oldest to youngest, beginning at Atigun Pass.

Fig. 2.1. Hunt Fork Shale (Dalton Highway, MP 248). Note the ice-cored rock glacier and the talus cones. The symmetry of the steep talus cones is maintained by ice, which functions as cement. Both rock glaciers and steep, symmetrical talus cones are typical permafrost features of the Brooks Range (ADH).

Hunt Fork Shale[4] and Kanayut Conglomerate

Two major types of bedrock dominate the landscape from Atigun Pass to Atigun Gorge. The Hunt Fork Shale (Upper Devonian, 385 mya, Figs. 2.1, 2.2) is a thinly foliated, dark brown to black shale averaging more than 1,000 m thick. It was deposited in a shallow marine habitat and now forms many of the interior peaks of the Brooks Range. Its presence is indicated by distinctive steep slopes with symmetrical talus[5] cones that occasionally terminate in ice-cored rock glaciers[6] (Fig. 2.1). Slopes formed by the Hunt Fork Shale have a distinctive shining appearance when viewed from a distance on a sunny day.

Like the Hunt Fork Shale, the Kanayut Conglomerate (Upper Devonian and Lower Mississippian, 385–345 mya, Fig. 2.3) forms many of the interior peaks of the Brooks Range. Conglomerates, or "pudding stones"—so named because they resemble fruitcake—are fine-grained sandstones containing "clasts," or rock particles, of various types and origins. The Kanayut Conglomerate averages 2,600 m in depth and contains clasts of chert (a fine-grained type of rock consisting primarily of tiny quartz crystals) and quartz that may be as large as 23 cm in diameter, indicating that the depositional environment

Fig. 2.2. Road cut showing laminated Hunt Fork Shale. Inset shows detail of shale (Dalton Highway, MP 248.4, ADH).

Fig. 2.3. Southward-dipping bed of Kanayut Conglomerate (Dalton Highway, MP 259, ADH). Dark layers of the erosion-resistant conglomerate are shown in relief against the lighter, readily eroded shale. Inset shows detail of conglomerate with distinctive chert clasts.

Fig. 2.4. *Top:* Cliffs of Lisburne Limestone near Atigun Gorge (Dalton Highway, MP 270, ADH). Two major layers of Lisburne Limestone can be seen. Both layers have identical stratigraphy. The lower layer ("strata normal") is in its original position. The upper layer ("strata inverted") has been overturned due to folding. ***Lower left:*** Detail of Lisburne Limestone cliff showing typical yellowish color when weathered (Guardhouse Rock, ADH). ***Lower right:*** Guardhouse Rock overlooks the Dalton Highway near Atigun Gorge (ADH). This feature is formed from an overturned layer of Lisburne Limestone. Consequently, the fossils of its summit are older than those of its base.

was a broad alluvial plain with numerous braided rivers that transported rock debris from an ancient mountain range. Compared with other regional rock types, it is both readily identifiable and extremely erosion resistant.

Lisburne Limestone

The Lisburne Limestone (Upper Mississippian through Upper Permian, 326–254 mya, Fig. 2.4) is a 600 m or more thick layer of limestone (calcium carbonate–based bedrock), dolomite (magnesium carbonate–based bedrock), and chert that underlies much of the North Slope. It contains abundant fossils of bryozoans, crinoids, corals, brachiopods, foraminiferans, and algae, indicating that it was deposited in a shallow marine environment (Fig. 2.5). In the cold and dry climate of the Brooks Range it is also resistant to erosion and is an important cliff-forming rock. The southern walls of the Atigun Gorge, for example, are formed by towering gray to yellowish-gray cliffs of Lisburne Limestone that reach as high as 700 m (Fig. 2.4). During the overthrusting of the bedrock strata that now comprise the northern front of the Brooks Range, its great tensile strength allowed it to withstand extreme distortion and

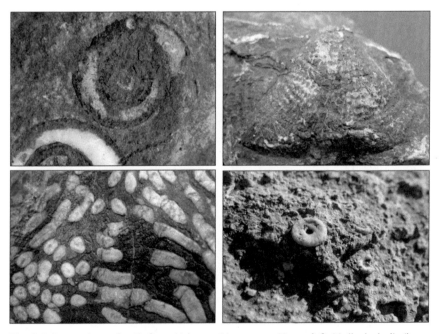

Fig. 2.5. Invertebrate fossils from Lisburne Limestone. *Upper left:* Mollusk shells (base of Guardhouse Rock, H.M. Rantala). *Upper right:* Brachiopod (base of Guardhouse Rock, ADH). *Lower left:* Coral (Kuparuk River, H.M. Rantala). *Lower right:* Crinoid stem (summit of Guardhouse Rock, ADH).

Fig. 2.6. Sandstone and shale of Fortress Mountain Formation near Atigun Gorge (Dalton Highway, MP 273, ADH). Inset shows detail of sandstone.

Imnavait Mountain

Slope Mountain

pull-off (Mile 301)

river-delta sandstone

marine sandstone

Fig. 2.7. Left: Aerial view of Slope Mountain and Imnavait Mountain showing well-defined bedrock strata (ADH). Slope Mountain consists primarily of sandstones of the Nanushuk Group. The upper layers were deposited in a freshwater river environment. The lower layers were deposited in a marine environment. **Upper right:** View of Slope Mountain from Dalton Highway (ADH). **Lower right:** Outcrop of Prince Creek bedrock (Dalton Highway, MP 352, ADH). Exposures of the Prince Creek Formation along the Colville River contain abundant dinosaur fossils.

Fig. 2.8. Franklin Bluffs (Dalton Highway, MP 385, ADH). The Franklin Bluffs consist of soft siltstone that weathers into distinctly rounded, pastel-colored landforms. The sediments forming this siltstone were deposited about 43–56 mya in a protected delta or lake environment.

folding while maintaining structural integrity. In some cases it was folded to such an extent that adjacent layers are, in reality, stratigraphical mirror images[7] (Fig. 2.4).

Fortress Mountain Formation[8]

North of Atigun Gorge, the bedrock geology changes abruptly from Lisburne Limestone to the Fortress Mountain Formation and the related Nanushuk Group (Early Cretaceous, 122–100 mya, Figs. 2.6, 2.7) that form the upper strata of large portions of the major mountains to the north (e.g., Imnavait and Slope Mountains, MP 301). The Fortress Mountain Formation consists of about 3,000 m of dark shale, sandstone, and conglomerate that was deposited in coastal deltas. Unlike the preceding bedrock types, the Fortress Mountain Formation and Nanushuk Group were deposited after the North Slope terrane joined present-day Alaska.

Prince Creek and Sagavanirktok Formations

As one proceeds north of Slope Mountain in the central foothills, out-crops of bedrock are few because they are usually buried by deep Quaternary (less than 1.8 mya) sediments. The porous sandstone and fractured limestone strata that are "reservoir rocks" for the oil reserves of the northern coastal plain, for example, are buried at average depths exceeding 2,500 m. There are a few exceptions, however. The Prince Creek Formation (Late Cretaceous, 86–66 mya, Fig. 2.7) is a 600 m thick layer of nonmarine sandstone, conglomerate, shale, and coal that underlies portions of the central North Slope. Outcrops occur along the Dalton Highway in the Sagwon Uplands (MP 353). Exposures of the Prince Creek Formation along the lower Colville River have revealed dinosaur, fish, turtle, mammal, and plant fossils ranging in age from 66 to 76 mya. The Franklin Bluffs (Fig. 2.8), a spectacular outcrop of the Sagavanirktok Formation (Late Cretaceous to Late Miocene, 84–3 mya), is the youngest significant exposure of bedrock along the Dalton Highway. The Sagavanirktok Formation is as much as 2,600 m thick and consists of sandstone, soft siltstone, conglomerate, and coal deposited in coastal marine and freshwater habitats. The Franklin Bluffs were formed by erosion of outcrops of the Sagavanirktok Formation along the eastern bank of the Sagavanirktok River. They are composed of a soft siltstone that weathers into distinctly rounded pastel-colored landforms. The sediments comprising this siltstone were deposited in a protected delta or lake environment during the Eocene (56–34 mya).

3

Glacial Geology

The North Slope has been subject to at least five to seven episodes of glaciation during the past three million years. The glaciers involved were relatively small because of snow starvation due to the complete freezing of the Arctic Ocean. As a consequence, they were more similar to extra-large alpine glaciers than to the massive ice sheets that affected more southerly regions. In no case did the North Slope glaciers produce ice sheets with their own watershed divides, as required for the formation of continental ice sheets. Present-day glaciers occur in the Brooks Range, where they are limited to mountain cirques (Fig. 3.1).

Pliocene and Early Pleistocene Glaciers

Evidence of the earliest glaciation (Late Pliocene, more than 2.6 mya) on the North Slope consists of outwash[1] and erratics.[2] These ancient glaciers, which were as wide as 330 km and extended north to within 30 km of the modern-day arctic coast,[3] deposited the "Kuparuk gravels" and the "Gunsight Mountain erratics." Erratic boulders of Kanayut Conglomerate (Fig. 2.3) as large as 1.5 m in diameter, deposited 100 km or more into the foothills, provide evidence that the interior cirques[4] of the Brooks Range were the sources of these glaciers. After these earliest episodes, the next major glaciations were the Anaktuvuk (Early Pleistocene, less than 2.5 mya) and Sagavanirktok (Middle Pleistocene, 0.8 mya, Fig. 3.2). The Sagavanirktok- and Anaktuvuk-age glaciers extended as far as 70 km north of the Brooks Range.

Late Pleistocene Glaciers

Evidence of major glacial activity on the North Slope during the Late Pleistocene includes moraines[5] (Figs. 3.3, 3.4), kames[6] (Fig. 3.4), kettle lakes[7] (Fig. 3.5), and U-shaped glacier-scoured valleys (Fig. 3.6), in

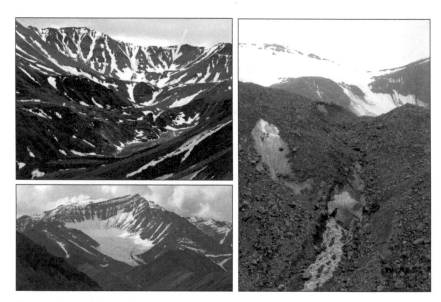

Fig. 3.1. *Upper left:* Grizzly Glacier at Atigun Pass. The glacier (arrow) is buried beneath rock debris (ADH). *Lower left:* Cirque glacier in Brooks Range. This glacier, informally known as the "Gates glacier," is visible from the Galbraith Lake airport road (MP 275, ADH). *Right:* Surface of Gates glacier showing cover of rock debris and a meltwater channel. The reddish color of the meltwater is due to rock flour produced by abrasion between the glacier and underlying bedrock (S.M. Parker).

Fig. 3.2. *Upper:* Southwest view from the divide between the Toolik Lake (top center) drainage and the Kuparuk River drainage showing boulder field deposited by the Itkillik I glacier (about 30,000 years ago, ADH). *Lower:* View northeast showing deposits from the Sagavanirktok River–age glacier (more than 125,000 years ago, ADH).

Fig. 3.3. *Upper:* End moraine of a cirque glacier in the headwaters of the Ribdon River marking the position of the glacier's most recent advance (ADH). The stream has breached the moraine to produce the V-shaped outlet behind the helicopter. *Lower:* Itkillik II–age end moraine of a glacier that advanced through Atigun Gorge (about 11,500 years ago, ADH).

Fig. 3.4. *Left:* Itkillik II moraine showing heath vegetation typical of well-drained tundra soils (Toolik Field Station, ADH). *Upper right:* Heap of gravel deposited after melting of ice below a talus slope (Atigun Gorge, ADH). This is a small-scale version of the process that forms kames, or hill-size heaps of gravel deposited by a melting glacier. *Lower right:* An Itkillik II–age kame near the Toolik Field Station (ADH).

Fig. 3.5. *Upper left:* Kettle lake with slumping banks indicating subsidence, possibly due to melting of buried glacier ice (Toolik Field Station, ADH). *Upper right:* Galbraith Lake from summit of Guardhouse Rock (ADH). The ancestral Galbraith Lake was formed upstream of an end moraine during the final retreat of the Itkillik II glaciation. At this time the lake extended about 18 km south up the Atigun River valley. The draining of the ancestral lake exposed deep accumulations of fine sediment now evident as the dunes along the Atigun River as it enters Atigun Gorge. *Lower left:* Atigun River upstream of the south shore of the ancestral Galbraith Lake (MP 253, ADH) showing coarse sediments. *Lower right:* Atigun River channel downstream of the shoreline of ancestral lake (MP 260) showing abrupt change from coarse to fine sediments (ADH).

addition to outwash and erratics. The Late Pleistocene Itkillik glaciation (less than 125,000 years ago, Figs. 3.2, 3.3, 3.4, 3.5) consisted of three major advances and recessions that were synchronous with those of the familiar Wisconsin glaciation that affected much of the Midwestern United States and Canada. Itkillik II refers to the last advance, which began around 20,000 years ago and ended about 11,500 years ago when the glaciers made their final retreat to mountain cirques. The moraines and kames of the Itkillik glaciation are well preserved as permafrost features and can be identified today as sharp moraine crests, a notably irregular rolling terrain, the occurrence of compound kames kettle lakes with collapsing banks (Fig. 3.5), and clearly defined outwash channels. The Itkillik glaciers left a striking geomorphological footprint over much of the North Slope (Figs. 3.2, 3.3, 3.4, 3.5) that is responsible for the abundant heaths and numerous kettle lakes of the foothills.

Fig. 3.6. Northward view of Atigun River from Atigun Pass showing a classic U-shaped, glacier-carved valley (ADH).

4

Permafrost and Patterned Ground

Permafrost

Because of low annual temperatures, the entire North Slope is underlain by permafrost (Fig. 4.1). Permafrost shapes landscapes, creates dams for ponds and lakes, blocks the downward movement of groundwater, and restricts plant roots to the surface of the soil. It is clearly a major factor defining and controlling the arctic environment. Despite its ubiquity, however, permafrost is difficult to directly demonstrate.

The permafrost layer beneath the North Slope is 90–600 m thick. In the foothills at Toolik Lake it is 200 m thick while on the coastal plain at Prudhoe Bay it is 600 m thick. This corresponds to the distribution of the annual mean air temperatures (lowest in the north). Rising air temperatures and increasing snow cover on the North Slope have in historical times warmed the permafrost. However, here the permafrost is in no danger of thawing for some time. For example, temperatures in a series of boreholes along the Dalton Highway have been measured every year for more than 30 years. At a depth of 20 m, the depth at which seasonal cycles in temperature are dampened, temperatures have risen from −25 to −8°C, from −9 to −7°C, and from −5 to −4°C at three locations from the shore of the Beaufort Sea at Prudhoe Bay to the mountains.

One of the major variables affecting the environmental role of permafrost is the amount of ice it contains (Fig. 4.1). Permafrost may or may not contain inclusions of ice. Alaskans pay attention to the presence of ice in permafrost when building a house, a road, or an airport runway, for if large quantities of permafrost ice melts the soil collapses and structures are destroyed. To avoid melting this type of ice, the 1,289 km Trans-Alaska Pipeline is raised above ground for 50 percent of its length due to the presence of permafrost containing dangerous amounts

Fig. 4.1. Tundra soil exposed by a thermokarst in a tributary of the Toolik River (ADH). The top ~50 cm of soil is the active layer, or the layer of soil that thaws and freezes each year. Below the active layer is permafrost, or permanently frozen soil, rock, and ice. At left is an ice wedge forming the perimeter of a frost polygon. To the right is frozen soil.

Fig. 4.2. *Left:* "Percy pingo" is one of many pingos in the Toolik River pingo field on the coastal plain (Dalton Highway MP 398, JWS). Pingos from this field range from about 1 to 20 m in height. Several can be seen to the west of the Dalton Highway (MPs 375–400). White-fronted geese are in the foreground. *Right:* Percy pingo during summer (ADH).

of ice. This aboveground construction was much more expensive than burial of the pipeline.

Pingos are excellent natural examples of the power of ice within the permafrost layer to affect landscapes (Fig. 4.2). These are conical hills up to several hundred feet high caused by the accumulation of a core of ice. One type of pingo (closed system pingo) begins with the draining of a lake that formerly contained unfrozen water all winter (i.e., more than 2 m deep) with unfrozen, water-saturated sediments. The loss of the insulating lake water allows the top of the sediments to freeze and soon a new permafrost layer forms above the old one. The two layers are separated from each other by a thick layer of water-saturated sediments. A freezing front forms beneath the new permafrost layer, drawing water to it. The expansion of water when it freezes increases the volume of water and sediment beneath the new permafrost layer; the layer is pushed up when the volume of the freezing water increases as ice is formed. Little by little the volume of ice increases over the centuries and the pingo pushes upward. Because of the requirement for water-saturated sediments for their formation, almost all pingos are found on drained lake beds or on the floodplains of major rivers. Conical pingo-like mounds in the foothills are likely kames.

Although the permafrost of the North Slope is not yet beginning to thaw, there is good evidence that a warming climate is increasing the occurrence of thermokarsts (Fig. 4.3). Thermokarsts occur when the

Fig. 4.3. A massive thermokarst in a tributary of the Toolik River caused by thawing of ice-rich permafrost (July 2004, ADH).

thawing of permafrost results in the softening and eventual slumping of soils to produce features such as sinkholes and mudslides. Thermokarsts are so named because of their similarity to features of karst topography, a landscape shaped by dissolution of soluble bedrock, usually limestone or dolomite,[1] resulting in abundant sinkholes. In the case of thermo-karsts, sinkholes and related features are formed by warming of the permafrost and the thawing of ground ice (thus the *thermo* in thermo-karst) rather than the dissolution of bedrock by water. One example of a recent thermokarst is in a small tributary of the upper Toolik River near the Dalton Highway (Fig. 4.3). A stream flowing in the active layer sud-denly began to erode the permafrost and melt extensive accumulations of ice. An erosion channel 3 m deep soon formed and large amounts of nutrients and sediment were transported into the Toolik River (Fig. 4.4).

Patterned Ground

Patterned ground refers to the occurrence of repeated, often geometri-cal patterns on the ground's surface. These are best appreciated when viewed from the air. The processes causing patterned ground are varied but are usually related to cycles of freezing and thawing of the active layer. Perhaps the best-known type of patterned ground is the frost poly-gon network (Figs. 4.5, 4.6). When saturated tundra soils freeze in au-tumn, cracks form that result in a pattern of interlocking polygons like those formed as a mud puddle dries. The frost polygons on the Arctic

Fig. 4.4. Sediment entering the Toolik River from a tributary draining an active thermokarst (August 2003, W.B. Bowden). Sediment-laden water is to the left; clear water is to the right.

Coastal Plain, however, may be tens of meters across. During snowmelt the next spring, water fills the cracks. When this water freezes the following autumn, it forms an ice wedge (Fig. 4.1) that pushes the soil up and away to form a low ridge. Over hundreds of years the ice wedge can become several meters deep as it expands. Shallow ponds often form in frost polygons due to the raised ridges forming their perimeters. The eventual development of drainage channels that breach the polygon perimeters, however, causes the ice wedges to melt and the ground above them to settle, changing low-center polygons to high-center polygons. Stream channels in fields of frost polygons often follow a zigzag pattern with deep, circular pools occurring where the ice wedges of intersecting polygons have melted and collapsed. These are called *beaded streams* due to the occurrence of a series of relatively evenly spaced pools (the beads) connected by shallow channels (Fig. 4.7).

Another type of patterned ground formed by the freeze-thaw cycle is the frost boil and the related sorted circle and stone stripe. Frost boils (Fig. 4.8) are patches of bare soil that occur within the otherwise continuous tundra vegetation. Frost boils form when a pocket of wet clay or silt oozes to the surface due to pressure exerted when the surrounding soil freezes and expands during winter—similar to the squeezing of a tube of toothpaste. Before freezing, the oozing clay or silt forms a

Fig. 4.5. View of Galbraith Lake toward the southwest showing numerous low-center frost polygons with uniform rectangular shapes. The Galbraith Lake airstrip is to the upper right.

Fig. 4.6. *Upper:* High-center frost polygon (Deadhorse, ADH). *Lower left:* Low-center frost polygons (Deadhorse, ADH). *Lower right:* Flooded low-center frost polygons. Only their elevated rims are exposed (Deadhorse, ADH).

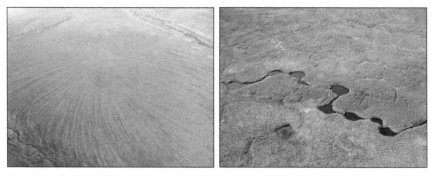

Fig. 4.7. *Left:* Horsetail watertracks (Slope Mountain, ADH). *Right:* Beaded stream (Toolik Field Station, J.P. Benstead). The channel flows along the perimeters of frost polygons.

mound as much as 10 cm or more above the surrounding tundra. During spring, the mound thaws and collapses to form the bare soil patches that indicate the presence of an active frost boil. Frost boils are important to the dynamics of tundra plant communities because they provide rare patches of bare soil, allowing germination and growth of seedlings unable to compete with mature plants.

Sorted circles (Fig. 4.8) are essentially frost boils that form in ground containing stones of various sizes rather than a dense mat of vegetation. When the center of the frost boil rises during winter, the stones roll to its perimeter to eventually form a circle. If a number of such sorted

Fig. 4.8. *Upper left:* Frost boil in ancestral Galbraith Lake sediments (Dalton Highway, MP 266). *Lower left:* An array of frost boils (Dalton Highway, MP 266). *Upper right:* Sorted circle (Ivishak River, ADH). *Lower right:* Stone stripes (Toolik Lake Field Station, ADH).

Fig. 4.9. *Left:* Detail of string bog showing one plant community on the elevated "strings," which is dominated by *Dryas*, and another in the surrounding sedge and grass wetland. *Right:* Aerial view of a string bog (Galbraith Lake, ADH).

circles occur in close proximity, which is often the case, the ground will appear to be covered with interconnected rings of large rocks surrounding discs of gravel and pebbles. Stone stripes (Fig. 4.8) occur when what would otherwise be a sorted circle forms on a slope. Under the influence of gravity, stones are slowly (e.g., a few centimeters a year) displaced downslope, where they eventually produce stripes rather than circles.

String bogs (Fig. 4.9) are relatively flat wetlands with raised string-like features in repeated, roughly parallel lines. The processes producing them are poorly understood. The simplest explanation begins with the accumulation of masses of dead sedge and grass leaves that are rolled into linear "strings" by sheet flow of water during spring thaw. These are formed perpendicular to the direction of flow. Because the strings of string bogs are raised above their immediate surroundings they become colonized by plants requiring microhabitats that are relatively well drained. Once colonized and stabilized by roots, strings become permanent features that support plants such as *Dryas* and dwarf willows in habitats otherwise dominated by sedges. String bogs are common in low-gradient wetlands throughout the North Slope, particularly on the coastal plain.

A final example of patterned ground is the horsetail watertrack (Fig. 4.7). Watertracks are small channels (10 to 20 cm wide) that carry surface water downslope during snowmelt. In summer they are evident as verdant stripes that contrast strongly with the subdued colors of the surrounding tundra. Horsetail watertracks are groups of parallel watertracks that show elegant, synchronized curves, like a horsetail billowing in the wind. These curves are formed by solifluction, which is the downhill slipping of soils as the active layer thaws during summer. This downhill movement is slow (a few centimeters a year), but over long periods of time the once relatively straight watertracks become curved.

5

Habitats and Ecology

Terrestrial Habitats

Reflecting the varied geology, topography, and climate, the Arctic
Coastal Plain, the Arctic Foothills, and the Brooks Range contain distinctly different habitats with characteristic plant and animal communities. At the broadest scale, differences among these habitats are driven
by water availability and elevation and proximity to the Arctic Ocean,
which control patterns of temperature (**Fig. 5.1**). As one moves south
from the coastal plain and across the foothills, there is an increase in
mean July temperature accompanied by an increase in the height and diversity of plants.[1] For example, only dwarf shrubs (less than 15 cm) are
found on the coastal plain adjacent to the arctic coast, where mean July
temperatures are only 5–7°C. In the southern foothills, however, woody
shrubs as high as 40–200 cm are common. Here the mean July temperatures are 12–13°C. The influence of the Arctic Ocean is also shown by
patterns of plant biomass.[2] Although biomass is not particularly high
anywhere on the North Slope due to severe nitrogen limitation, plant
biomass ranges from 160–370 g/m² near the arctic coast to 850–1300
g/m² in the foothills, a difference of four to five times. Of course, plant
biomass again decreases as one proceeds south into the Brooks Range,
where mean temperatures decline approximately 6°C for every 1,000 m
rise in elevation (**Fig. 5.1**).

   At a finer scale, aspect and relief together determine other characteristics of terrestrial habitats on the North Slope. Aspect affects the amount
of available heat, the degree of exposure to prevailing winds, and the
duration and amount of snow cover. Relief affects drainage and soil type.
Knowing this, some generalizations about habitat distribution can be
made depending upon where one happens to be while on the North Slope
(**Fig. 5.2**). Windward slopes and hilltops are both exposed to prevailing
winds and well drained. Consequently, their dry soils support heath communities, or more simply heaths (**Fig. 5.3**). Under the extreme conditions

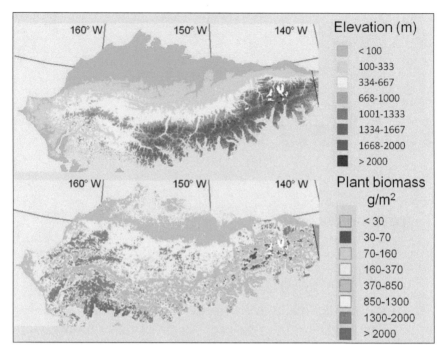

Fig. 5.1. *Upper:* Approximate boundaries of the major physiographic provinces of the North Slope as delineated by elevation: Arctic Coastal Plain (less than 100 m above sea level), Arctic Foothills (101–1,000 m above sea level), Brooks Range (1001–2,000 m or more above sea level). *Lower:* Pattern of plant biomass (grams of dried aboveground plant material per m²) of the North Slope. Adapted with permission from Raynolds, Walker & Maier (2006).

of exposed mountain ridges, soils may form only beneath isolated cushion plants such as purple mountain saxifrage (*Saxifraga oppositifolia*). Lee slopes, protected from wind, accumulate large drifts of snow during winter, which may provide a source of water during spring and early summer (**Fig. 5.4**). Here, snowbed habitats support plant communities that depend on the water from melting snow, such as arctic white heather (*Cassiope tetragona*) and mountain avens (*Dryas integrifolia*). Habitats with less extreme relief, such as the gently rolling tussock tundra of the foothills and the flat terrain of the coastal plain, support both relatively well-drained habitats populated by cotton grass (*Eriophorum vaginatum*) and shrubs (*Salix* spp., *Betula* spp.) and poorly drained habitats populated by sedges (*Carex* spp., **Fig. 5.3**). Extensive tracts of brown soils—with high organic matter content and a loamy texture allowing deep oxygen penetration—are found in moist, moderately well-drained tussock tundra while the soils of poorly drained, wet sedge meadows are usually saturated with water (water-logged), resulting in anoxia (absence of oxygen), low rates of decomposition, and the accumulation of peat. Within this

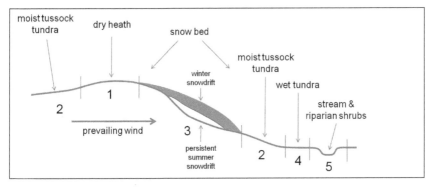

Fig. 5.2. Relationships among major terrestrial habitat types, topography, and direction of prevailing wind. Adapted and redrawn from Raynolds, Walker & Maier (2006).

Fig. 5.3. *Upper left:* Mosaic of major foothills habitats. The gray and blue-green patches in the top half of the photograph are dry heaths; the darker green-brown areas above the snowbanks are snow beds. Moist tussock and shrub tundra is in the foreground (Galbraith Lake, ADH). ***Upper right:*** Detail of a *Dryas*-dominated heath (Toolik Field Station, ADH). ***Lower left:*** Moist cottongrass tundra dominated by *Eriophorum vaginatum* (Slope Mountain, ADH). ***Lower right:*** Wet sedge and grass tundra (Pump Station 4, ADH).

Fig. 5.4. *Left:* The left side of this photograph shows moist tussock tundra. The right side (dark green) at the base of the slope is a snowbed community dominated by arctic white heather (*Cassiope tetragona*, Atigun Gorge, ADH). *Upper right:* High-relief glacial drift showing dry heath on ridge tops (grayish) and snowbed communities and a persistent snow drift near base (dark brown, Toolik Field Station, ADH). *Lower right:* A kame showing a dry heath community on its upwind flank and a snowbed community dominated by *C. tetragona* on its lee flank. Willow shrub habitat is in the foreground.

Fig. 5.5. Shrub habitat with felt-leaf willow (*Salix alaxensis*, tall gray-green riparian shrubs), Richardson's willow (*S. richardsonii*) and arctic dwarf birch (*Betula glandulosa*, short green shrubs), and Siberian alder (*Alnus fruticosa*, dark shrubs at upper right) (Ivishak River, ADH). The inset shows the contrast between Richardson's willows (foreground) and the taller and more sparsely leaved felt-leaf willows along a streambank (background).

Fig. 5.6. *Upper left:* Coastal plain landscape where frost polygons provide the only significant form of topographic relief (Dalton Highway, MP 385, ADH). *Upper right:* "Strings" of string bog showing the importance of subtle differences in topographical relief to habitat structure on the coastal plain. The strings support a plant community dominated by *Dryas*. Between strings, the plant community is dominated by wet sedge and grasses (Dalton Highway, MP 395, ADH). *Lower left:* Shallow thaw pond showing associated sedge-grass wetland habitat (Dalton Highway, MP 384). *Lower right:* Oriented thaw pond with benthic (bottom) habitat visible (Dalton Highway, MP 395, ADH).

general habitat matrix the banks of rivers and streams (riparian habitats) usually support willow thickets dominated by *Salix alaxensis* (**Fig. 5.5**). These generalizations provide a rough guide to the terrestrial habitats of the North Slope. The remainder of this section is devoted to the specifics of its three major ecological regions.

Arctic Coastal Plain

The Arctic Coastal Plain is formed from sediments deposited during the mid- to late Quaternary (less than 1.8 mya). It is roughly defined by the area of the North Slope with elevations of 60 m above sea level or less (**Figs. 5.1, 5.6**). The lowest-lying habitats with water-saturated soils (thaw pond margins, flooded depressions of low-centered polygons) are colonized by wetland plants such as the sedges *Eriophorum angustifolium* and *Carex aquatilis* and grasses such as *Dupontia fisheri* and *Arctophila fulva*. Plant assemblages consisting of dwarf willows (*Salix rotundifolia*), saxifrages (*Saxifraga hieracifolia, S. hirculus*), coltsfoot

(*Petasides frigidus*), buttercups (*Ranunculus nivalis*), and mountain avens (*Dryas ajanensis*) occur in drier habitats such as the perimeters of low-centered polygons (**Figs. 4.5, 4.6**). Finally, in exceptionally well-drained habitats, such as former beach ridges (which may occur as far as 50 km south of the present-day coast) and pingos (**Fig. 4.2**), plant assemblages similar to those of foothills habitats are found (cottongrass *Eriophorum vaginatum*, Labrador tea *Rhododendron tomentosum*, lingonberry *Vaccinium vitis-idaea*).

Because the coastal plain is relatively flat, subtle differences in elevation between the raised ridges and the centers of frost polygons are important in determining the distribution and activity of lemmings and birds. The activity of brown lemmings (*Lemmus trimucronatus*) is concentrated in high-centered polygons that provide a mix of relatively dry (centers) and wet (perimeter troughs) habitats (**Figs. 4.5, 4.6**). Both winter and summer activity is greatest in the troughs that provide cover and food in the form of sedges and grasses. Snowy owls (*Bubo scandiacus*), important predators of lemmings, arrive on the coastal plain in May to nest on high-centered polygons kept snow-free by wind.

Arctic Foothills

Repeated glaciations have shaped much of the rolling terrain of the Arctic Foothills (**Figs. 3.2, 3.4, 5.4**). Here important high-relief habitats include kames and kame-like features, moraines, and mounds of drift. Extensive heath (mountain avens *Dryas ajanensis,* crowberry *Empetrum nigrum,* bearberry *Arctous rubra,* alpine azalea *Kalmia procumbens,* Labrador tea *Rhododendron tomentosum,* net-leaf willow *Salix reticulata*) and fellfield[3] communities are found on upwind slopes. Snowbed communities dominated by arctic white heather (*Cassiope tetragona*) develop on lee slopes (**Figs. 5.3, 5.4**). Vast expanses of low-relief, moist tundra are covered by cottongrass (*Eriophorum vaginatum*) and a rich assemblage of shrubs (diamond-leaf willow *Salix pulchra*) and dwarf shrubs (arctic dwarf birch *Betula nana* and *B. glandulosa,* lingonberry *Vaccinium vitis-idaea*, alpine blueberry *V. uliginosum*, cloudberry *Rubus chamaemorus,* Labrador tea *Rhododendron tomentosum decumbens*). Sedge meadows and willow thickets are found in poorly drained lowland habitats and along watertracks (**Fig. 5.3**). Thickets of felt-leaf willow (*Salix alaxensis*) and Richardson's willow (*S. richardsonii*) are prominent along streams (**Fig. 5.5**).

Brooks Range

The Brooks Range contains peaks as high as 2,700 m. Such high elevations at arctic latitudes result in habitats more similar to the polar deserts of the high Arctic than those found elsewhere on the North Slope. These habitats (more than 1,800 m in elevation) are barren with the exception of sparse patches of crust-forming lichens and isolated vascular plants such as purple mountain saxifrage (*Saxifraga oppositifolia*) and alpine draba (*Draba alpina*) in protected locations (**Fig. 5.7**). At lower elevations, dry meadow and heath communities dominated by mountain avens (*Dryas ajanensis*) are common, and meadows in protected valleys may be surprisingly lush with carpets of moss dotted with buttercups (*Ranunculus nivalis*), coltsfoot (*Petasides frigidus*), bear flower (*Boykinia richardsonii*), and a variety of composites. On dry slopes and fellfields a sparse but diverse assemblage of showy flowers may be found, including blackish oxytrope (*Oxytropis nigrescens*), prickly saxifrage (*Saxifraga tricuspidata*), arctic cinquefoil (*Potentilla hyparctica*), arctic forget-me-not (*Eritrichium aretioides*), and Pallas' wallflower (*Erysimum pallasii*). The floodplains of the larger rivers,

Fig. 5.7. *Upper left:* Steep, well-drained, boulder-strewn mountain slope (Atigun Pass, ADH). ***Upper right:*** Sheltered, moist mountain meadow (Atigun Pass, ADH). ***Lower left:*** Fellfield with sorted circles (Ivishak River, ADH). ***Lower right:*** Exposed mountain ridgetop (Guardhouse Rock, Atigun Gorge, ADH).

such as the Atigun and Canning Rivers, and their headwater valleys contain sedge meadows and willow thickets (Richardson's willow *Salix richardsonii*, diamond-leaf willow *S. pulchra*, felt-leaf willow *S. alaxensis*), dwarf birches (*Betula nana* and *B. glandulosa*), and soapberry (*Shepherdia canadensis*). One important characteristic of mountain habitats in the eastern Brooks Range is the abundance of limestone that provides the raw material for calcium-rich and relatively alkaline soils that support a characteristic community of vascular plants, lichens, and mosses. This effect can be observed as far north as the arctic coast, where the calcium-rich soils of the floodplains and deltas of the large rivers draining the eastern Brooks Range may support twice the plant species found in habitats containing acidic tundra soils.

Freshwater Habitats

Probably the two most critical factors controlling the structure of freshwater communities on the North Slope are winter freezing and low nutrient availability. With few exceptions (see "Spring Streams and Aufeis" below), freshwater habitats on the North Slope less than about 2 m deep freeze solid during winter. By "freeze solid" we mean that the entire water column freezes from top to bottom, which is significantly different from the covering of surface ice on "frozen" lakes and rivers in north-temperate climates. As a rule of thumb, only North Slope lakes and rivers 3 m or more in depth contain sufficient unfrozen water to support significant populations of fish during winter.[4] Lakes with depths exceeding 3 m are relatively numerous here, but only the larger rivers, such as the lower reaches of the Sagavanirktok and Colville Rivers, are deep enough to contain habitats that remain unfrozen during winter.

Freshwater animal species able to tolerate freezing are few. Consequently, total freezing results in freshwater communities with low diversity compared with those of lower latitudes. In addition to having low diversity, freshwater habitats of the North Slope are also relatively unproductive. This is due to low temperatures and low nutrient availability (particularly phosphorous, which is required in relatively large quantities by all organisms to produce ATP—an energy-carrying molecule—nucleic acids, and cell membranes). In fact, most freshwater habitats of the North Slope are ultra-oligotrophic, which means that nutrient concentrations are exceedingly low. This is attributed to two main factors. First, peaty soils with little mineral content and low soil temperatures result in slow rates of weathering and soil microbial activity, and thus the amounts of phosphorous released from terrestrial to aquatic habitats are very small. Second, abundant iron-rich sediments chemically bind phosphorus, which further reduces its availability to freshwater organisms.

Lakes and Ponds

Lakes and ponds are very abundant on the North Slope (**Fig. 5.8**). Despite the desert-like level of annual precipitation, the permafrost forms a barrier to drainage; small ponds and shallow lakes form anywhere there is slight elevation above a delta or coastal plain. In fact, in some areas of the coastal plain, the entire landscape is made up of lakes and shallow ponds lying on top of old drained lakes (**Fig. 5.8**). Ponds are always small and shallow (less than 0.5 m deep) while lakes are large in area and usually deeper than a meter. While there are a handful of relatively deep lakes (more than 20 m) in the foothills and mountain regions of the North Slope, the vast majority of lakes are less than 3 m deep and found on the coastal plain. The uniformity of the depth of the coastal plain lakes appears to be controlled by the volume of ice in the original frozen sediment. When the frozen ground thaws, the ice melts and the soil consolidates to form a lake basin. A calculation shows that thawing a soil with 10 percent of its volume made up of wedge ice (**Fig. 4.1**) will result in a lake with a depth of 1.4 m.

Because the maximum ice thickness that develops on lakes and ponds during the winter is 1.7–2.0 m, all ponds and shallow lakes less than 1.7–2.0 m freeze solid. Fish are usually, but not always, excluded from the shallow lakes. Ikroavik Lake near Barrow, for example, is 2.5 m deep and contains stickleback fish while another Barrow lake, Imikpuk, is approximately 3 m deep and has no fish. By determining the presence of fish, water-column freezing has dramatic effects on the diversity of communities found in lakes (higher diversity, complex food webs, fish are top predators) or ponds (lower diversity, simple food webs, copepod zooplankton are top predators).

There are literally tens of thousands of thaw ponds on the coastal plain of the North Slope (**Fig. 5.8**). These arise when ice wedges form in permanently frozen soil. Over hundreds and thousands of years the soil above the ice wedges is pushed upward by a few centimeters to create a network of polygons, each 10–40 m across and each containing a pond (**Fig. 4.6**). The pond water and dark sediment capture sunlight and the warm water deepens the pond through thawing of the ice-rich soil. These shallow thaw ponds may completely cover large regions or over time the ice wedges may thaw, the pond boundaries break down, and

Fig. 5.8. *Upper left:* Satellite image of Teshekpuk Lake and abundant oriented thaw ponds during late summer. Thaw ponds in various states of the thaw pond cycle are apparent. Some contain water; others have drained and are dry. Teshekpuk Lake is formed by the coalescence of several adjacent thaw ponds. Note the late-season ice remaining on the surface of Teshekpuk Lake. In some years ice is present year-round (L. Moulton, MJM Research, with permission). *Lower left:* Satellite view of the Teshekpuk Lake region during winter. Note that some oriented thaw ponds contain ice while others are dry. The land-fast ice of the Beaufort Sea is visible (L. Moulton, MJM Research, with permission). *Upper right:* Frozen oriented thaw ponds and frost polygons (Deadhorse, October 2007, ADH). Note drifts on western shores of ponds indicating direction of prevailing winds from the east-northeast. *Lower right:* Oriented thaw ponds and lakes with moats of open water surrounding ice in early summer (National Petroleum Reserve, L. Moulton, MJM Research, with permission).

larger thaw lakes form. Thaw lakes are most numerous on the northern coastal plain where they contribute 15–40 percent of the ground cover. They are usually elliptical or cigar-shaped with long axes oriented about 10–20° west of north (**Fig. 5.8**). This pattern has stimulated much study of how groups of essentially round ponds evolve into groups of elliptical and uniformly oriented lakes. The secret is found in the occurrence of relatively continuous, unidirectional winds caused by the combination of a semipermanent cap of high air pressure over the high Arctic ("polar high") and the rotation of the Earth. As these winds sweep across a lake's surface they drive water toward the downwind shore, which tilts the water's surface (higher on the downwind shore), resulting in opposing circulation cells—one that travels northward and then eastward along the shore and another that travels southward and then eastward. These opposing circulation cells erode and elongate the opposite poles of the basin via both thermal processes that thaw sediments and mechanical processes that sweep them away. Over time these basins become elongated in a north–south direction to eventually produce a cigar-shaped, oriented lake. Thaw ponds undergo long development cycles, from patterned ground to lakes and back again. These cycles have been ongoing since the Pleistocene (an age of 12,600 years was reported for the basin of a thaw lake near Barrow). As a consequence, about 50–75 percent of the Arctic Coastal Plain is covered by thaw lakes and their drained basins in various stages of succession (**Fig. 5.8**).

The thaw ponds near Barrow have been the focus of intense ecological study since the 1970s. These ponds are typically less than 1 m in depth. Consequently they freeze solid and do not contain fish. Their relatively simple food webs are actually composed of two semi-independent webs—a water-column web and a benthic (bottom sediment) web. The water-column web is based upon phytoplankton (suspended algae) grazed by zooplankton (up to eight species of water-column-inhabiting crustaceans such as *Daphnia* and fairy shrimp). These in turn are prey for predatory zooplankton such as *Heterocope*, the top predator in fishless ponds (although shorebirds such as phalarope may also be predators of zooplankton). Because phytoplankton production is low due to phosphorus limitation, however, most animal production occurs via the second web, which is based on decaying sedge and grass leaves (detritus), the food of protozoa and larvae of midges[5] living on the bottom.

Although thaw ponds and shallow thaw lakes are most numerous, significant freshwater habitat is also provided by deeper thaw lakes, such as Teshekpuk Lake. Teshekpuk Lake (70°36.613′N, 153°37.660′W)[6] was formed by the coalescence of several adjacent basins[7] and is the largest lake on the North Slope, the third largest lake in Alaska, and an internationally significant molting habitat for waterfowl (**Fig. 5.8**). Because of its large size and high latitude, it is ice-free for only about six weeks each year and winter ice often persists until August. Consequently, Teshekpuk Lake provides poor summer habitat for fish because its relatively low temperature results in low growth rates. Nevertheless, its relatively great depth (maximum about 10 m) provides critical winter habitat for broad whitefish (*Coregonus nasus*), least cisco (*C. sardinella*), and arctic grayling (*Thymallus arcticus*). Teshekpuk Lake is most usefully considered a "lake system" rather than a lake because the low relief of its drainage (a few meters above sea level) results in a maze of interconnected waterways covering 32,600 km² rather than only the 830 km² area of its main basins. Although Teshekpuk Lake receives water from numerous inlets, the Miguakiak River is its only outlet. The flow of this river reverses at times due to its low channel gradient.

Lakes and ponds are much less abundant in foothills habitats than on the coastal plain; nevertheless, they provide significant habitat. The kettle lakes[8] of the glaciated regions of the Arctic Foothills can be relatively large and deep and often occur in clusters or lake districts (**Fig. 5.9**). Toolik Lake (68°37.930′N, 149°36.419′W), for example, is a compound kettle lake with a surface area of 1.5 km^2 and a maximum depth of 25 m (**Fig. 5.9**). The food web of Toolik Lake has been studied since the 1970s. As with tundra thaw ponds, two largely separate food webs have been identified: water column and benthic. The energy source for the water-column food web are tiny algae that swim using flagellae (photosynthetic flagellates) and bacteria that feed on dissolved organic molecules that enter the lake with water draining from the tundra. Other nonphotosynthetic flagellates feed on bacteria. The flagellates and bacteria are prey for zooplankton, including seven species of crustaceans and eight species of rotifers.[9] The low productivity of the flagellates and the bacteria, however, supports such a sparse population of zooplankton that they are unable to effectively fuel the growth of fish (lake trout *Salvelinus namaycush*, arctic grayling *Thymallus arcticus*, round whitefish *Prosopium cylindraceum*, slimy sculpin *Cottus cognatus*, burbot *Lota lota*). Consequently, the fish of Toolik Lake feed primarily on prey from the lake's bottom rather than zooplankton. The benthic (bottom) food web is supported by the primary production of diatoms[10] in the sediment and by organic particles that settle from the water column. These provide food for snails, such as the great pond snail (*Lymnaea stagnalis*), and midge larvae (Chironomidae), which are in turn prey for slimy sculpin, grayling, and young lake trout. Adult lake trout, the top predators in many foothills lakes, feed on smaller fish and snails. Compared with the coastal plain and foothills, lakes are sparse in the Brooks Range, although there are several relatively large and deep lakes formed by the damming action of glacial end moraines. Lake Peters (69°19.334′N, 145°02.717′W) and Lake Schrader (69°22.864′N, 144°59.611′W) are examples of glacier-formed mountain lakes exceeding 50 m in depth.

On the coastal plain, water depth is the main factor determining whether fish are present in a lake. In the foothills and Brooks Range, however, additional factors related to topography are important. Here, deep lakes with gentle outlet gradients may contain up to five fish species (lake trout, arctic grayling, round whitefish, slimy sculpin, and burbot). As the gradient of a lake's outlet becomes steeper, however, the pool of potential colonizers becomes smaller due to differences in swimming ability among species. For example, lakes with moderate outlet

Fig. 5.9. *Upper left:* Toolik Lake is a large, compound kettle lake in the Arctic Foothills (Toolik Field Station, JWS). *Upper right:* A "lake district" with numerous kettle lakes (It-killik River drainage, J.P. Benstead). *Lower left:* Not all lakes formed by glacial processes are kettle lakes. Galbraith Lake has formed upstream of an end moraine that serves as a dam (ADH). *Lower right:* A lake district formed by kettle lakes in the Oksrukuyik Creek drainage in early winter (ADH).

gradients may be colonized by grayling and sculpin but not lake trout, and lakes with steep outlet gradients may be colonized only by grayling or may be fishless.

The presence or absence of fish and the type of fish species can have important consequences for aquatic community structure. Lakes with lake trout, for example, tend to have large populations of nonbiting midges because predation by lake trout reduces the abundance of the small fish (e.g., sculpin) that in turn prey on insect larvae. On the other hand, the great pond snail (*Lymnaea stagnalis*), important prey for lake trout, is rare on open sediments in such lakes. Finally, lake trout indirectly affect the abundance of zooplankton by feeding on smaller, zooplankton-feeding fish or by modifying their behavior, causing them to seek refuge in shallow water and thus reducing their effect on zooplankton abundance in the deep-water habitats.

Rivers and Streams

The running-water habitats of the North Slope range from headwater seeps to large rivers such as the Meade, Colville, and Sagavanirktok

(**Fig. 5.10**). Almost all the major rivers of this region arise on the northern flanks of the Brooks Range and have channels that travel across the foothills and coastal plain before emptying into the sea. Only one major river, the Inaru—which flows only during spring snowmelt—has a drainage that is entirely within the coastal plain.

The Colville River drains an area of 53,000 km^2 and is both the largest and longest river of the North Slope. Its headwaters arise in the Brooks Range and eventually coalesce to form a 600 km long channel that traverses eastward across the foothills before abruptly turning north. As it enters the sea the Colville River divides into as many as 30 distributaries[11] that flow across a 650 km^2 delta (70°25.388′N, 150°36.069′W). Because flow from frozen upstream tributaries effectively ceases during winter, seawater enters the main channel to form a saltwater wedge extending as far as 60 km upstream. Because of its relatively great depth, the lower channel of the Colville River (maximum depth = 12 m) remains unfrozen during winter and provides critical winter habitat for populations of whitefish (*Coregonus*) species.

Fig. 5.10. *Upper left:* View of upper Sagavanirktok River toward north. The Dalton Highway is to the left (west). Pump Station 3 is near the horizon (September 2007, S.M. Parker). *Upper right:* The Sagavanirktok River in winter (January 2008, ADH). The view is northward with the Dalton Highway and Pump Station 3 to the west. The blue ice is overflow ice, or aufeis. *Lower left:* Sagavanirktok River during breakup (May 2010, ADH). *Lower right:* Sagavanirktok River shortly after breakup (May 2010).

The major rivers between the Colville and the Mackenzie include (from east to west) the Aichilik, Hulahula, Sadlerochit, Canning, Saga-vanirktok (**Fig. 5.10**), and Kuparuk (**Fig. 5.11**). These are relatively small compared with the Colville River, however. The Sagavanirktok River, the largest of these, drains only about 5,700 km^2, or only about 11 percent of the area drained by the Colville River. Also unlike the Colville River, the rivers of the eastern North Slope tend to run directly from the Brooks Range to the Arctic Ocean. Because of their relatively short channels and their locations in a geologically active portion of the eastern Brooks Range, these rivers contain immense amounts of eroding gravels, cobbles, and boulders. The volume of sediment, in fact, is so large that these eastern rivers lack the power to move it effectively and have become braided[12] (**Fig. 5.12**). Braided channels are relatively shallow and provide poor overwintering habitat for fish.

Headwater Streams

Although less conspicuous than large rivers, headwater streams are more numerous. The topographical position of a headwater stream has important effects on the gradient and size of the rocks forming its channel, on the temperature of its water, and on the amount and variability

Fig. 5.11. Left: View of Kuparuk River west of the Dalton Highway during summer (July 2007, J.P. Benstead). The Kuparuk River, a large tundra stream, has been the focus of research by scientists from the Toolik Field Station since the mid-1970s. **Upper center:** Kuparuk River during summer (July 2003, J.P. Benstead). **Lower center:** Kuparuk River during winter when the completely frozen river channel is often obscured by drifting snow (March 2007, Dalton Highway, ADH). **Right:** View of Kuparuk River west of the Dalton Highway during winter (April 2009, ADH).

of its discharge.[13] Factors such as these control the type of habitat the stream provides. For example, is a stream's channel steep and bouldery or relatively flat and peaty? Is its flow relatively constant or will there be periods of very high and very low flow? Will it freeze solid during winter or flow year-round? All these factors have important effects on the diversity and types of organisms one might find in a given stream.

Four types of headwater streams occur on the North Slope—mountain, glacier, tundra, and spring streams. Mountain and glacier streams are found in the Brooks Range, where their steep channels arise in high-elevation valleys (**Fig. 5.13**). Mountain streams gain their water as run-off from rain and snowmelt. Glacier streams receive most of their water from melting cirque glaciers. The bouldery channels of mountain and glacier streams consist of alternating cascades and pools. The channels of glacier streams differ from mountain streams, however, by having angular stones rather than the rounded stones commonly found in stream channels (**Figs. 3.1, 5.13**). This difference in shape is due to the fact that the stones in the channels of glacier streams are relatively close to their bedrock sources and so have not been significantly tumbled and eroded

Fig. 5.12. Braided channel of the Ivishak River (ADH). Numerous parallel channels, or distributaries, are visible. Roots of willow thickets provide patches of stability to the otherwise-shifting floodplain gravels. These gravels may contain large volumes of sub-surface flow, which contribute to downstream aufeis formation during winter.

by flowing water. Glacier streams also carry suspended rock flour,[14] causing their water to be tinged with colors ranging from blue-white to rusty red (**Figs. 3.1, 5.13**). The tundra streams of the foothills and coastal plain are the most abundant stream type; they contribute more than 30,000 km or 82 percent of the total stream length on the North Slope (**Figs. 5.11, 5.13**). Like mountain streams, their flow originates primarily as rain and snowmelt. Unlike mountain streams, however, their basins are covered by deep layers of peat underlain by permafrost. Tundra streams often have beaded channels consisting of a series of pools connected by short channels (**Figs. 4.7, 5.13**).

Food webs of mountain, glacier, and tundra streams are well known. Those of glacier streams are the simplest and are based on biofilms[15] on stone surfaces, biofilms that serve as food for midge larvae (Chironomidae). Mountain streams and foothills tundra streams have more complex food webs containing numerous species of midge, black fly, stonefly, mayfly, and caddisfly larvae that feed on biofilms, organic particles suspended in the current, or one another. These insects, in turn, are food for arctic grayling (*Thymallus arcticus*), slimy sculpin (*Cottus cognatus*), and

Fig. 5.13. *Upper left:* Mountain stream (Holden Creek, Dalton Highway, MP 267.6, ADH). *Upper right:* Frozen channel of Trevor Creek, a mountain stream (Dalton Highway, MP 258.5, October 2007, ADH). *Lower left:* Tundra stream (Toolik River, Dalton Highway, MP 292, ADH). *Lower right:* Glacier stream draining the informally named "Gates glacier" west of the Dalton Highway, MP 275.

round whitefish (*Prosopium cylindraceum*). Food webs of tundra streams of the Arctic Coastal Plain are less well known. The peat bottoms of their low-gradient channels provide habitat for larvae of midges and caddisflies and amphipods, snails, and fingernail clams (Sphaeriidae), some of which are prey for arctic grayling, least cisco (*Coregonus sardinella*), and nine spine sticklebacks (*Pungitius pungitius*).

Spring Streams and Aufeis

Although spring streams are correctly considered headwater streams, they are different enough to warrant a separate discussion. This is based on the fact that many spring streams of the North Slope flow year-round, whereas most mountain, glacier, and tundra streams freeze solid during winter (**Figs. 5.14, 5.15**). With the exception of a few truly hot springs, such as Red Hill Spring (69°37'35.98"N, 146°01'37.57"W, water temperature = 33°C) and Okpilak Spring (69°19'49.45"N, 144°02'41.06"W, water temperature = 49°C), there are two types of springs on the North Slope: mountain and tundra. Mountain springs have winter temperatures ranging from 4–11°C (remember that air temperatures range below –30°C during winter, which makes water temperatures of 10°C or even 4°C seem pretty warm by comparison). Mountain springs are found where the Lisburne Limestone contacts layers of sandstone along the lower slopes of the northern Brooks Range (**Fig. 5.16**). The source of the water discharged by these springs is poorly understood. Tundra springs have winter water temperatures of 1°C or so and are in the foothills. Tundra springs are fed by water from upstream lakes and the deep gravel beds of large rivers (**Fig. 5.16**). Although many tundra springs flow year-round, some will freeze when their groundwater sources become depleted during winter.

Although spring streams provide a negligible amount of habitat (less than 1 percent of total stream length) on the North Slope, they have important consequences for biodiversity because they provide 100 percent of flowing stream habitat during winter. This is critical for organisms unable to tolerate freezing, such as some stoneflies (e.g., *Isoperla petersoni*), caddisflies (e.g., *Glossosoma nigrior*), and Dolly Varden char (*Salvelinus malma*). The American dipper (*Cinclus mexicanus*) and the northern river otter (*Lontra canadensis*) also require warm springs as overwintering habitat on the North Slope. Unlike most other North Slope streams, the food webs of warm springs include abundant large predacious stoneflies that are important prey for Dolly Varden char (*Salvelinus malma*) and the American dipper (*Cinclus mexicanus*), a semiaquatic songbird.

Fig. 5.14. Kuparuk River during snowmelt (May 2007, J. P. Benstead). During spring, completely frozen river channels gradually thaw from the surface down.

Fig. 5.15. *Left:* Main channel of the Atigun River (Atigun River 2 Bridge, ADH) during late winter showing exposed bottom sediments across the entire channel beneath the pipeline crossing. The complete freezing of upstream sources of water results in the cessation of flow during winter. *Right:* First flow of water in the main channel of the Atigun River during 2011 (May 15, 2011, Atigun Gorge, ADH). At the time this picture was taken surface water had been flowing on the surface of the river channel for less than 24 hours. The water is flowing over the deep layer of ice remaining frozen to the bottom.

Fig. 5.16. *Upper left:* A warm spring near the Ivishak River during July 2009 (ADH). *Upper right:* Ivishak Hot Spring during January 2008. When this picture was taken the air temperature was −40°C and the water temperature was about 5°C (ADH). *Lower left:* Aerial view of Ivishak River during February 2009 (ADH). Extensive warm spring activity in the eastern tributaries of the Sagavanirktok River (e.g., Echooka River, Ivishak River, Ribdon River) results in long river reaches that remain unfrozen during winter. *Lower right:* Tundra-spring tributary of the Kuparuk River (ADH). The aufeis formed by this spring is visible through the willow scrub at the center of the photograph. This spring's source is the deep gravels of the braided Kuparuk River channel upstream.

A good question concerning the fate of the water flowing from springs during winter is "How far from the spring's source will water flow before freezing?" The answer can be found in the form of river icings or aufeis.[16] An aufeis is a mass of ice formed by the successive freezing of overlying sheets of water that flow from a spring (**Fig. 5.17**). In the case of warm springs, the water in a spring stream's channel will flow downstream, cooling along the way until it reaches a point in a river channel that has become frozen solid or is otherwise dammed. Here water must flow over the river ice, where it eventually freezes and forms an aufeis. Since this process continues throughout the winter, the volume of an aufeis can be enormous, ranging up to 5 m or more thick and many square kilometers in area. Depending on its volume and the conditions of a given summer, an aufeis may persist well into August or even later. Aufeis are abundant in the eastern Brooks Range, where they

Fig. 5.17. *Upper left:* Melting aufeis formed by a tundra spring west of Galbraith Lake (June 27, 2009, ADH). This aufeis is visible from the Dalton Highway during much of the summer. *Upper right:* New overflow ice forming on the surface of the Galbraith Lake aufeis (March 2008, ADH). *Lower left:* Aerial view of Ribdon River aufeis (July 2004, S.M. Parker). *Lower right:* Calcium carbonate slush ($CaCO_3$) released from aufeis. Freezing results in the precipitation of calcium carbonate that was dissolved by stream water passing over limestone. This white, chalky powder is deposited on the floodplain as the aufeis melts (Galbraith Lake aufeis, June 27, 2009, ADH).

are usually associated with warm springs. The aufeis on the Echooka River (about 21 km² in early summer, 69°18.097′N, 147°36.383′W) is the largest and most spectacular and can be seen from outer space (take a moment to search for this aufeis—and others—using Google Earth). In some years residual ice from the Echooka aufeis may persist through the summer to freezeup. The presence of an aufeis on a river can have a large effect on seasonal flow patterns since the water that accumulates as ice during winter is slowly released during summer. Aufeis are often used by caribou seeking relief from mosquitoes.

So, back to the original question—how far from a spring's source will water flow before freezing? The answer depends on the water's temperature and volume. Sadlerochit Spring, a large and relatively warm mountain spring (about 11°C, 69°39.367′N, 144°23.706′W), flows about 5 km before forming a persistent aufeis (i.e., large enough to last through August). Echooka Spring, another large but relatively cool mountain spring (about 4°C, 69°16.069'N, 147°21.341'W), flows for about 6 km before forming an aufeis, as does Ivishak Hot Spring, a small but moderately warm mountain spring (about 7°C, 69°01.852'N, 147°43.003'W).

Although the presence of open streams flowing over relatively long distances during the North Slope winter may be hard to believe, this is indeed the case. One of us (ADH) actually measured the flow dynamics of a small, spring-fed tributary of the Ivishak River during January 2008 (Fig. 5.16). On a day when air temperatures hovered around −40°C (about −40°F), the temperature of the stream's water decreased from 5.4°C to 4.5°C over 200 m of channel length. Given this observed decrease in temperature, the water of this shallow stream (average depth = 13 cm, or about 5 inches) would have to travel 800 to 1,200 m before its temperature decreased to 0°C. Since a relatively large amount of heat must be lost before water at 0°C is converted to ice, the water in this stream would travel several more kilometers before actually freezing.[17] One must be mindful that these statistics are based on a very shallow stream; the channels of larger rivers such as the Ivishak, Echooka, and Sadlerochit are much deeper and will thus be less directly affected by air temperature. Given these facts, the occurrence of rivers on the North Slope that flow distances of 5–6 km before freezing during winter loses much of its mystery.

6

Mushroom Madness

Mushrooms, the fruiting bodies of certain fungi, are common on the North Slope tundra, where they are a favorite food of caribou and arctic ground squirrels. In addition to being important food, mushrooms are also the visible sign that a vast underground network of tiny threadlike hyphae are working with bacteria to break down soil organic matter. Without this process there would be no recycling of nutrients, and all the nutrients in the ecosystem would soon be tied up in dead organic matter in the soil; the whole ecological system would come to a stop.

The underground network of fungi can best be seen with a high-powered microscope because hyphae are threads only a few microns (thousandths of a millimeter) in diameter. But there are many of these small threads: a cubic centimeter of tundra soil contains about 100 cm of hyphae, or 10 km in a liter. Bacteria are also small and numerous, around 500 million per cubic centimeter.

There are two major types of fungi on the North Slope. One, the saprotrophic fungi, is relatively uncommon on the North Slope. These fungi obtain carbon and nutrients from dead organic material. The commercial mushroom (*Agaricus bisporus*) sold in supermarkets is one example, as are North Slope species of *Microcollybia* (**Fig. 6.1**), puffballs, slime molds, and bracket fungi (**Fig. 6.2**). The second is a very common type that also attacks dead organic matter but is symbiotic and attaches by hyphae to the roots of plants. These fungi, symbiotic with most of the flowering plants, trees, and shrubs of the tundra, are called mycorrhizal fungi from *myco* meaning fungi and *rhizae* meaning roots (**Figs. 6.1, 6.3**). As symbionts they obtain sugars from their photosynthetic hosts while providing nutrients in return.

Mycorrhizal fungi encompass several distinct groups. One group, the ectomycorrhizal fungi, ensheath the fine roots of host plants and produce hyphae that penetrate spaces between root cells; other

Fig. 6.1. ***Upper left:*** *Lichenomphalia,* an ectomycorrhizal fungus (Toolik Field Station, J. Deslippe). ***Lower left:*** *Microcollybia,* a saprotrophic fungus that grows on other decomposing fungi (Toolik Field Station, J. Deslippe). ***Upper right:*** *Cortinarius favrei,* an ectomycorrhizal fungus (Toolik Field Station, J. Deslippe). ***Lower right:*** *Russula,* an ectomycorrhizal fungus (Toolik Field Station, J. Deslippe).

hyphae-like structures extend outward into the soil. They are common in the Arctic where they produce large mushrooms of different types. One type produces spores on gills, such as *Russula, Cortinarius,* and *Amanita.* These are symbiotic with trees and shrubs (*Salix, Betula*). Another type releases spores from pores on the bottom of their caps (e.g., the birch bolete *Leccinum scabrum*). Still other types have small fruiting bodies that remain hidden belowground and are symbiotic with ericaceous plants, such as *Vaccinium, Empetrum,* and *Rhododendron tomentosum.*

One ecological function of all fungi is recycling phosphorus and nitrogen from organic forms to chemical forms that plants use for growth. On the tundra surrounding Toolik Lake, where nitrogen limits plant growth, the mycorrhizal fungi provide 70–90 percent of the nitrogen needed by all the trees and shrubs. The sugars the plants provide in return are 17 percent of their total photosynthetic production. Another important ecological function of fungi is food for animals. The consumption of mushrooms by animals can be traced because a process

Fig. 6.2. *Upper left:* Slime molds (Mycetozoa) have complex life cycles including a feed-ing stage (usually a single-celled, motile amoeba-like organism that feeds on organic particles and bacteria) and a nonmotile spore-producing stage (fruiting body). Shown is the fruiting body of the white crust slime mold (*Mucilago crustacea*, Toolik Field Sta-tion, ADH). The fruiting body of this slime mold occurs near the ground on living plants. This species is covered by a powdery layer of calcium carbonate crystals and is common in foothills habitats in some years. *Upper right:* The fruiting body of a morel (*Morchella*, Galbraith Lake, ADH). The strategies used by morel mycelia for obtaining energy and nutrients range from saprotrophy to mycorrhizal relationships with living vascular plants. *Lower left:* Puffballs (Gasteromycetes, Atigun Gorge, ADH) are essentially round sacs filled with powdery spores. Spores are dispersed as a "puff" through an opening in the "ball" when disturbed. Puffballs are common saprotrophs in tussock tundra. *Lower right:* Bracket fungi (polyporoid fungi) are fruiting bodies usually found on fallen logs. They are produced by extensive networks of hyphae that permeate and decompose dead wood. Shown are bracket fungi on a dead poplar log (Echooka Spring, ADH).

Fig. 6.3. *Left:* A mushroom of the family Boletaceae (Kuparuk River, ADH). Many Boletaceae are ectomycorrhizal on roots of *Betula*. *Upper right:* Underside of the cap of a
boletinoid (pore-bearing) mushroom showing distinctive pores (Kuparuk River, ADH).
Lower right: Underside of the cap of an ectomycorrhizal agaricoid (gilled) mushroom
(*Russula*) showing "gills" (Kuparuk River, ADH). The tiny dark organisms visible on the
gills are springtails (Collembola).

in the hyphae changes the abundance of a rare nonradioactive isotope
of nitrogen (^{15}N) before it is transferred to host plants. The result of
this wholly natural process is an increase in ^{15}N in mushrooms and
a decrease in their host plants. The ^{15}N concentration in hair from
ground squirrels from the tundra surrounding Toolik Lake shows that
mushrooms are important to their diet. Twenty kilometers to the south,
however, in a sandy area north of the Atigun River 2 Bridge, there are
few mushrooms as shown by the low ^{15}N content in hair of the ground
squirrels there. Caribou also love mushrooms and can smell them from
9 m away. They will consume many kilos of mushrooms during their
migration in the early fall through the tundra and boreal forest. As
a result, the ^{15}N concentration of their body increases. In Siberia and
Lapland, where reindeer (which are closely related to caribou) have been
domesticated, herders lose control of their animals in the fall as they
forage for mushrooms. They call this behavior "mushroom madness."

7

Lichens

Lichens are conspicuous and extraordinary members of the North Slope biota (**Figs. 7.1–7.4**). In many habitats their diversity and biomass exceed those of vascular plants. At Anaktuvuk Pass (about 90 km west of Atigun Pass), for example, almost 300 species and 70 genera of lichens have been recorded. Reasons for the dominance of lichens here are several, but primary among these is their simple structure based on a symbiosis between an exceptionally hardy fungus, which forms the thallus,[1] and an algae or cyanobacterium held internally within clusters of fungal hyphae. The fungal component determines the species of lichen. The algal component is less specific. A single algal species may be symbiotic with many lichen species.

The simple nonvascularized structure of lichens contributes to their ability to withstand freezing and drying, allowing them to persist through long periods of inactivity—several years, in some cases. Because of their algal symbionts, lichens are guaranteed a dependable source of energy in the absence of the organic carbon supply required by typical fungi. These two characteristics underlie the critical role of lichens as the first colonizers of barren habitats. In such habitats lichens speed up the release of inorganic nutrients from rocks, contribute organic matter to nascent soils, and generally prepare the environment for further colonization by vascular plants. Like many other pioneers, lichens are poor competitors and are thus usually dominant only in habitats where vascular plants are disadvantaged. Such habitats are typically subject to long dry periods and have either shallow or perennially frozen soils that impede root development. In habitats where the root systems of vascular plants are able to access soil mineral layers, and thus a dependable nutrient and water supply, lichens are quickly overgrown and displaced.

Oldest Living Organisms on the North Slope

Given the harsh environment and the short window of opportunity for growth, it is not surprising that most arctic lichens grow very slowly, often only a fraction of a millimeter per year. The fact that their growth rates are both slow and predictable has lead to the development of *lichenometry*, the use of lichens to estimate the age of landscape features such as glacial moraines and rock slides. Since the age of colonies of the common crust-forming lichen *Rhizocarpon geographicum* (**Fig. 7.1**) may exceed an astonishing 9,000 years, this technique can be a very powerful tool. Measurements of the diameter of circular colonies of *R. geographicum* indicate that the most recent retreat of cirque glaciers at Atigun Pass was four to five millennia ago. In this case lichens with a diameter of 145 mm on boulders in end moraines were about 4,500 years old. Although the precision of such distant dates should be suspect, lichens clearly are

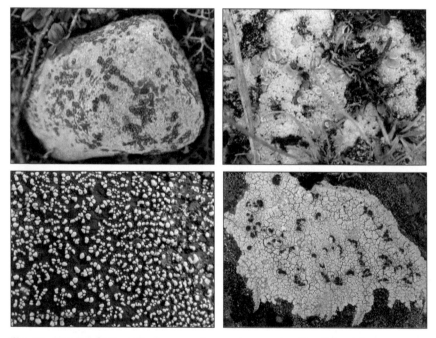

Fig. 7.1. *Upper left: Porpidia flavocaerulescens* (orange boulder lichen) forms orange crusts with black apothecia (spore-bearing structures) on noncarbonate rocks (Atigun Pass, ADH). *Lower left: Rhizocarpon geographicum* (map lichen) forms uniformly speckled, black-and-yellow crusts on noncarbonate rocks (Atigun Pass, ADH). *Upper right: Icmadophila ericetorum* (candy lichen) often overgrows mounds of humus and mosses (Toolik Field Station, ADH). *Lower right: Ophioparma lapponicum* (alpine bloodspot), a pale crust-forming lichen with conspicuous blood-red fruiting bodies. *O. lapponicum* often grows on cliffs formed from noncarbonate rocks (Atigun Pass, ADH).

the oldest living organisms on the North Slope and are comparable in age to the celebrated bristlecone pines (*Pinus longaeva*) of the Sierra Nevada.

Ecology of Lichen Grazing

Lichens compose about 90 percent of the winter diet of caribou on the North Slope, when as much as 5 kg of lichens (dry weight) may be consumed per individual per day. The primary species consumed are the reindeer lichens of the genus *Cladina* (**Fig. 7.2**), although a number of others are also eaten. During winter, caribou withstand exposure to long periods of subzero temperatures by assimilating the high concentrations of high-energy carbohydrates contained in lichens. The energy from this diet is released by the highly efficient fermentation-based digestive system of these ruminants.

Fig. 7.2. *Upper left: Cladina stellaris* (star-tipped reindeer lichen) showing the characteristic "cauliflower head" growth form (Atigun Pass, ADH). *Upper right: C. mitis* (green reindeer lichen), a branching lichen that forms lush turfs on heaths (Toolik Field Station, ADH). *C. stellaris, C. mitis,* and *C. rangiferina* are the principal winter food of caribou on the North Slope. *Lower left: Flavocetraria nivalis* (crinkled snow lichen) is a pale, lacy lichen of tundra snowbank habitats (Toolik Field Station, ADH). *Lower right: Vulpicida tilesii* (goldtwist, limestone sunshine lichen) forms conspicuous lemon-yellow cushions on calcium-rich soils (Ivishak Hot Spring, ADH). The white object in the lower right is a ptarmigan scat.

Fig. 7.3. *Upper left: Masonhalea richardsonii* (arctic tumbleweed), a robust branching lichen that resembles tiny caribou antlers. It is a "tumbleweed lichen" that grows unattached, often rolling freely over windswept tundra, where it eventually becomes concentrated in sheltered depressions (Atigun Gorge, ADH). *Upper right: Cladonia* is a large genus of "pixie-cup lichens," common on shallow, humic tundra soils (Galbraith Lake, ADH). *Lower left: Dactylina arctica* (arctic finger lichen) forms conspicuous yellow-brown, hollow, finger-like thalli that protrude from turfs of mosses and other lichen species. It is common in snowbank habitats (Galbraith Lake, ADH). *Lower right: Thamnolia vermicularis* (whiteworm lichen) has eerie white, hollow, usually unbranched and pointed strands that occur singly or in tangled, worm-like tufts. It usually protrudes from turfs of other lichen species on shallow soils on exposed ridges (Galbraith Lake, ADH).

The dynamics of the caribou–lichen grazing system on the North Slope are unlike those of the familiar grassland systems because of the extraordinarily slow growth rates of lichens. Growth rates for the branching (fruticose) reindeer lichens *Cladina stellaris* and *C. rangifera* are only about 4 mm per year. As a consequence, heavily grazed habitats may not recover for 30 to 50 years or, in some cases, as many as 200 years. In general, caribou avoid lichen turfs younger than about 50 years. Grazing by caribou also has long-lasting effects on lichen community structure. Grazed tundra may have as little as 12–16 percent of the biomass of branching and foliose (leaf-like) lichens as found in ungrazed tundra. On the other hand, crustose (crust-forming or scale-like) lichens, which are less easily cropped compared to branching and

Fig. 7.4. *Upper left:* *Xanthoria* species (sunburst lichens) form conspicuous orange splashes on carbonate (limestone, dolomite) rock in mountain and foothills habitats. Colonies are common on boulders and outcrops used as perches by birds and ground squirrels that deposit high amounts of nitrogen as urine (Galbraith Lake, ADH). *Upper right:* Stone wall on summit of Hunter's Hill showing colonies of *Xanthoria*. This wall, which is often used as a perch by raptors, was probably built by Nunamiut in the early to mid-1900s (ADH). *Lower left:* *Asahinea chrysantha* (arctic rag lichen), a pale, foliose lichen that is found on noncarbonate rock in exposed habitats. It often overgrows other species of lichens and mosses and rapidly colonizes newly exposed rock surfaces (Toolik Field Station, ADH). *Lower right:* *Nephroma arcticum* (arctic kidney lichen) is a light-green, foliose lichen found in mossy heath habitats (Toolik Field Station, ADH).

foliose species, are essentially absent in grazed tundra but may cover up to 20 percent of the ground in ungrazed tundra.

Mosses and Liverworts

Mosses and liverworts are bryophytes—plants that lack well-developed water-transport (vascular) systems. Consequently, they must supply their tissues with water, gases, and nutrients by diffusion directly through the surface of their leaves. This is possible because the leaves are constructed of thin, usually single layers of cells. Given this requirement, it is not surprising that bryophytes are usually found in wet, protected habitats (e.g., streambanks, dripping cliff faces). A number of mosses, however, are able to persist in a dormant dry state when water is scarce. These are ecological analogues of lichens, with which they often share harsh, exposed habitats.

Arctic Alaska hosts more than 500 species of mosses and liverworts (**Figs. 8.1, 8.2**). Like lichens, mosses achieve enormous biomass in some habitats, where they are essential in ecosystem functions through their ability to regulate soil moisture, temperature, and pH; the depth of the active layer; and nutrient availability. The *Sphagnum* mosses (**Fig. 8.1**) are of primary importance in such roles. They are conspicuous on tussock tundra, where they form mats among sedge tussocks and the edges of ponds that may be more than 20 cm thick. *Sphagnum* mosses are critical to the water balance of tundra communities due to the enormous water-holding capacity of their tissues and their high biomass. A thick layer of water-saturated moss also affects soil temperatures. By providing insulation, for example, moss layers reduce daily temperature fluctuations. Evaporative cooling due to water-saturated tissues during summer also decreases soil temperatures, reduces the depth of the active layer, and slows rates of decomposition and nutrient cycling.

The presence of mosses can also play a more direct role in nutrient cycling because of their ability to absorb and retain scarce nutrients dissolved in rainwater. Once these are incorporated into their tissues, they are released slowly over relatively long periods as the mosses themselves die and slowly decompose. *Sphagnum*, in particular, selectively absorbs

Fig. 8.1. *Upper left:* Sphagnum warnstorfii (red buds) and *S. aongstroemii* (yellow buds, Atigun Gorge, ADH). *Sphagnum* mosses are conspicuous in tundra habitats where their living and dead tissues form mats that may be more than 20 cm thick. *Upper right:* S. linbergii (large bud upper-center) with *S. squarrosum* (Kuparuk River, ADH). *Lower left:* Hylocomium splendens is an abundant species that carpets large areas of tundra, where it can persist in a dormant dry state during periods of water stress (Atigun Gorge, ADH). The feathery fronds of *H. splendens* efficiently overgrow other moss and lichen species. *Lower right:* Bryum wrightii is an alpine moss found in small mountain streams and springs and patches of recently exposed mineral soils. It is identified by its brilliant scarlet color (Atigun Pass, ADH).

nutrient ions from rainwater while releasing hydrogen ions, a process that can reduce pH levels to as low as 3 (lemon juice has a pH of 2 to 3). This results in further slowing of decomposition rates and has other effects on the availability of nutrients to other plant species. Finally, mosses can have important effects on soil formation in barren habitats. *Racomitrium lanuginosum* (**Fig. 8.2**), for example, is a common arctic moss that forms mats up to 10 cm thick over bedrock and mineral soils, where it is an important pioneer plant that forms nascent soil layers, providing the basis for colonization by other plant species.

Fig. 8.2. *Upper left: Tetraplodon angustatus* (note abundant stalked sporophytes) is a "dung moss" that grows on the nitrogen-rich scats and decomposing carcasses of large mammals (Atigun Gorge, ADH). Because of this nutrient-rich substrate, *T. angustatus* grows quickly, usually overgrowing a dung patch in one or two summer seasons. Its sticky spores are dispersed to new dung patches by flies. *Upper right: Pohlia nutans* (note abundant stalked sporophytes) occurs in habitats subject to frequent drying in both the Arctic and Antarctic (Atigun Gorge, ADH). *Lower left: Racomitrium lanuginosum* is an "ectohydric" moss (i.e., virtually all its nutrients and water are obtained directly from the atmosphere rather than absorbed from soils). It forms mats up to 10 cm thick over bedrock and mineral soils (Atigun Gorge, ADH). *Lower right: Marchantia polymorpha* is a large and distinctive liverwort distinguished by broad, leaf-like thalli anchored by root-like rhizoids (Ivishak River, ADH). It grows in moist habitats such as banks of streams and pools and rapidly colonizes burnt ground following tundra fires.

9

Vascular Plants

Compared with temperate regions, the plant communities of the North Slope have a low level of species richness (about 340 spp.) dominated by sedges and grasses (graminoids, about 20 percent). In comparison, Nebraska, with approximately the same area as the North Slope, hosts more than 1,900 vascular plant species. Arctic plant communities differ from their temperate counterparts in other ways as well. Perhaps the most important are: 1) a near absence of trees; 2) the dominance of long-lived plants (often approaching a century or more) that reproduce primarily by vegetative propagation;[1] 3) competition among flowers for pollinators rather than vice versa; and 4) an abundance of root parasites.

Why No Trees?

When entering the North Slope through Atigun Pass, one of the most striking changes to the landscape is the absence of trees.[2] Although trees are rare, the North Slope does host a diversity of shrubs. Shrubs differ from trees by their short stature (usually much less than 2 m or so) and by the presence of multiple woody stems rather than a single, dominant trunk. Dwarf shrubs are another important growth form with woody, usually prostrate stems only a few centimeters tall.

Alaska's northern tree line generally follows the 10°C limit of mean July temperature. In other words, the mean July temperature is less than 10°C north of the tree line and vice versa. A specific mechanism that determines the tree line has not yet been conclusively identified and current explanations remain controversial. Several likely factors have been implicated, including exposure above the snowpack during winter, failure of seedlings, poor root development due to permafrost (i.e., depth of the active layer), the energetic cost of producing compounds required to withstand winter temperatures (cryoprotectants), and slow growth due to relatively low temperatures during the short summer growing season. Although there is evidence that all of these factors contribute to some degree, the effect of slow growth due to low summer temperatures is currently thought to be most significant. Photosynthetic rates are less sensitive to low temperatures than are processes such as cell division and growth. This imbalance results in low growth rates even when reasonable high rates of photosynthesis are possible—it's not a material *supply* problem but rather a material *use* problem. Given the thermal conditions provided by most habitats of the North Slope, the expected annual growth rate of trees may simply be zero.

Although the physiology of trees and shrubs is essentially identical, shrubs are able to extend well beyond the tree line because they are, by definition, near the ground. This is important because the near-ground climate, especially in habitats with insulating thickets, can be 5–10°C warmer than the air above. In the Arctic, where temperatures are often near the threshold for production of plant tissues anyway, there is a strong thermal advantage to being short and shrubby.

Why Are Flowers So Colorful and Abundant?

First-time summer visitors to the North Slope are often amazed by the spectacular display of colorful flowers. Given the dominance of vegetative reproduction by structures such as rhizomes and bulbils[3] and the presence of numerous species capable of self-pollination, a good question is: why should arctic flowers be so showy? Perhaps the most compelling explanation is competition for pollinators by flowers requiring cross-pollination, such as the willows (*Salix* spp.), the purple mountain saxifrage (*Saxifraga oppositifolia,* **Fig. 9.1**), and the moss campion (*Silene acaulis*). Due to the unpredictable climate—remember, it may snow any day of the year—the abundance of pollinating insects varies markedly from year to year; their pollinating services are unreliable. Unreliability, combined with the short summer season, results in a relatively low probability of a flower being visited by a pollen-laden insect.

Although infrequent in tundra habitats where most plants reproduce primarily by vegetative propagation, some level of sexual reproduction must occur to maintain long-term population viability. Otherwise, why would so many plant species invest scarce resources into such dazzling flowers? Answers to this question clearly relate to understanding the evolutionary ecology of arctic plant communities, particularly when compared with temperate and tropical ecosystems, where the pollinators

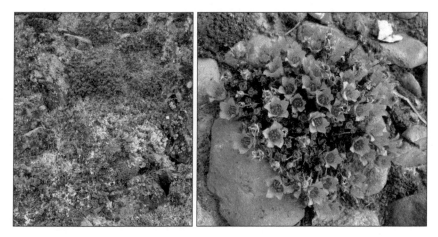

Fig. 9.1. *Left:* Purple mountain saxifrage (*Saxifraga oppositifolia*, Ivishak River, ADH). *Right:* Detail of flower (Atigun Pass, ADH).

themselves are more likely to compete for floral resources in the form of pollen and nectar.

The most abundant pollinating insects in the Arctic are the true flies (Diptera—mostly Muscidae, Anthomyiidae, Syrphidae, and Empididae), which make up more than 70 percent of flower visitors (**Fig. 9.2**). Bumblebees are also significant pollinators here. Compared with flies, bumblebees are more efficient pollinators because of their constancy to specific flower species and their wide-ranging flights. Diptera are more effective pollinators, however, by virtue of their sheer abundance. This differs markedly from temperate regions, where pollinating insects are primarily bees and wasps (Hymenoptera) and moths and butterflies (Lepidoptera). Pollinators are attracted to flowers due to factors such as their color, size, shape, and scent. In the Arctic, however, an additional factor—heat—is important. The methods used by flowers to do this are diverse. The dense "fuzz" of the flowers of louseworts and willows traps heat in a fashion similar to greenhouses; this trap causes them to be as much as 7°C warmer than ambient (surrounding) air (**Fig. 9.3**). Flowers shaped as hanging bells, such as heather (*Cassiope*), trap warm air rising from the heated ground, resulting in interior temperatures as much as 4°C above ambient. The reflective discs of other flowers (*Dryas* and *Papaver*) focus heat onto the flower's center, resulting in interior temperatures more than 10°C above ambient (**Fig. 9.4**). These warm microhabitats attract heat-seeking insects such as mosquitoes and dance flies (Empididae), which achieve body temperatures as high as 4–14°C above ambient while basking within flowers (**Fig. 9.2**). Because the ability to retain heat also

Fig. 9.2. Flies (Diptera) feeding or basking in flowers. *Upper left:* Muscoid fly in glacier avens (*Geum glaciale*). *Upper center:* Flower fly (*Syrphidae*) in small-flower anemone (*Anenome parviflora*). *Upper right:* Dance fly (*Empididae*) resting on Eriophorum flower. The larvae of dance flies are common predators in North Slope streams (Atigun Gorge, ADH). *Lower left:* Muscid fly (*Muscidae*) in *Dryas* flower (Atigun Gorge, ADH). *Lower center:* Corpse of muscoid fly in Saxifraga hirculus flower (Atigun Gorge, ADH). *Lower right:* Anthomyiid fly (*Anthomyiidae*) in grass-of-parnassus flower (*Parnassia palustris*).

Fig. 9.3. *Left:* Woolly lousewort (*Pedicularis lanata*, Toolik Field Station, ADH). *Right:* Sprout of *P. lanata* showing "woolly greenhouse" that appears shortly after snowmelt (Galbraith Lake, ADH).

Fig. 9.4. Lapland poppy (Papaveraceae, *Papaver hultenii*, Toolik Field Station, ADH).

increases the rate of seed production, it is not possible to determine whether heat-trapping mechanisms evolved to attract pollinators, enhance seed development, or both. Some of the best examples of heat focusing and retention mechanisms by arctic flowers, for example, are the poppies (*Papaver*), which show high rates of self-pollination and appear to be unattractive to insects.

Given the surplus of flowers available to pollinators on the North Slope, it is not surprising that few specific pollinator–flower relationships have evolved. An important example of one such relationship, however, involves louseworts (Scrophulareacae, **Figs. 9.3, 9.5**) and bumblebees (*Bombus*). Lousewort flowers are pollinated almost exclusively by bumblebees. These flowers have a specialized platform from which bumblebees force themselves into the interior of the flower to gain access to its deep nectar pot. This activity results in the dusting of the bee's thorax with pollen, which is then transferred to the stigma of the next flower visited.

Strange Behavior of Arctic Flowers Under the Midnight Sun

Several North Slope plants have flowers that move in such a way that they are continuously turned toward the sun. This behavior (heliotropism) is caused by changes in the fluid pressure of cells within their stems, which controls the orientation of the flower. The arctic poppies (*Papaver*) are well known for their heliotropic behavior (**Fig. 9.4**). During the arctic summer, poppy flowers face the sun for 24 hours a day! This behavior, combined with the parabolic shape of a poppy flower's

Fig. 9.5. *Upper left:* Labrador lousewort (*Pedicularis labradorica*, Kuparuk River, ADH). ***Lower left:*** Roots of *P. labradorica*. Location where parasitic root (haustorium) is attached to root of *Betula* sp. is indicated by arrow (Toolik Field Station, J.R. Deslippe). ***Right:*** Few-flowered lousewort (*P. capitata*, Toolik Field Station, ADH).

corolla, allows the continuous focusing of maximum solar radiation on its central seed capsule. Heliotropic poppy flowers receive two to three times more radiation than those that have their movements experimentally arrested. Heliotropism results in an increase in the internal temperature of the seed capsule of the flowers by as much as 3–6°C compared with ambient air and translates into a virtual 25 percent increase in the growing season compared with nonheliotropic plants, a clear advantage for the successful production of seeds in the short, cool arctic summer. The dryads (*Dryas*) and some species of arctic buttercups (*Ranunculus*) also show heliotropic behavior. Unlike the poppies, these species track the sun only during midday.

A Plethora of Parasites

One remarkable feature of the plant communities of the North Slope is the abundance of root parasites (hemiparasites) such as the louseworts (*Pedicularis*). Root parasites highjack the root systems of other plants and use them to gather water and nutrients for their own use. This strategy is important in tundra ecosystems, where low nutrient availability is an important limiting factor. Root parasites use a specialized root-like organ (haustorium) to penetrate and divert water and nutrients from the root of a host plant (**Fig. 9.5**). The diversion of fluids from host to parasite is accelerated by high transpiration (water loss) rates on the part of the parasite due to poor control of their stomata.[4] Because their root systems are connected, the rapid rates of water loss from the parasite results in the diversion of high volumes of fluids from the host. As a consequence, nutrients once carried in the host's fluids become increasingly concentrated in the foliage of the parasite as the water is lost via transpiration. The parasitic species of *Pedicularis* generally show little host specificity. Hosts used by *P. lapponica*, for example, include species from the families Betulaceae, Cyperaceae, Empetraceae, Equisetaceae, Ericaceae, Fabaceae, Poaceae, Lenibulariceae, Liliaceae, Polygonaceae, and Salicaceae.

9a: Ferns, Clubmosses, and Horsetails

On the North Slope, ferns (Athyriaceae, Fig. 9a.1) are found in moist, protected habitats, often in association with limestone outcrops. Clubmosses (Lycopodiaceae, Fig. 9a.1) are common in tussock tundra and mountain meadows. Horsetails (Equisetaceae, Fig. 9a.2) are common on gravel floodplains, roadsides, and other recently disturbed habitats.

Fig. 9a.1. *Upper left:* Smooth woodsia fern (*Woodsia glabella*, Ivishak River, ADH). *Lower left:* Fragile bladder fern (*Cystopteris fragilis*, Ivishak River, S.M. Parker). *Right:* Clubmoss (*Huperzia selago*, formerly *Lycopodium selago*, Atigun Gorge, ADH).

Fig. 9a.2. Left: Horsetail *Equisetum fluviatile* (Imnavait Creek, ADH). ***Center left:*** Horsetail *E. arvense*, vegetative summer phase (Oksrukuyik Creek, ADH). ***Center right:*** Brown cone-bearing spring phase of *E. arvense*. **Right:** Horsetail *E. scirpoides* (Atigun Gorge, ADH).

9b: Grasses and Sedges

Sedges and grasses dominate most plant communities of the North Slope. The most common sedges (Cyperaceae) are the true sedges *Carex* (about 35 or more species) and the cottongrasses *Eriophorum* (four species, **Fig. 9b.1**). Species of *Carex* are difficult to identify, even by specialists (**Fig. 9b.2**). The common species of cottongrasses, however, can be easily identified when flowering. *Eriophorum vaginatum* produces stems with single flowers on compact tussocks and is the dominant tussock-forming plant in foothills habitats. *E. scheuchzeri* forms dense monocultures in wetland habitats and has stems with large, persistent single flowers. Unlike the previous species, *E. angustifolia* has several flower heads on a single stem. Like E. *scheuchzeri*, E. *angustifolium* is a wetland specialist and is common in coastal plain habitats.

The true grasses (Poaceae) are the most species-rich family of arctic vascular plants, with approximately 17 genera and 58 species reported from the North Slope. As with the true sedges, the identification of grasses is difficult and differences among species are often vague due to frequent hybridization. Common and widespread taxa include *Arctagrostis latifolia* (polar grass), *Calamagrostis* (blue joint), *Arctophila fulva* (arctic marsh grass), *Dupontia fisheri* (tundra grass), *Hierchloe alpina* (holy grass), and *Poa* and *Festuca* (**Fig. 9b.3**). *Hordeum jubatum* (foxtail barley) is a common, attractive roadside invader along the Dalton Highway (**Fig. 9b.3**). The arctic grasses and sedges reach their greatest abundance

Fig. 9b.1. *Upper left:* Early spring flowers of tussock cottongrass (*Eriophorum vaginatum*, Toolik Field Station, ADH). *Lower left:* Mature seed-bearing blooms of *E. vaginatum* (Toolik Field Station, ADH). *Upper right:* Tall cottongrass (*E. angustifolium*, upper Atigun River valley, ADH). *Lower right:* White cottongrass (*E. scheuchzeri*, Kuparuk River, ADH).

Fig. 9b.2. *Left:* Flowering *Carex bigelowii* (Toolik Field Station, ADH). *Right: C. bigelowii* wetland (Toolik Field Station, ADH).

Fig. 9b.3. *Left:* Foxtail barley (*Hordeum jubatum*, Ice Cut, ADH) is a recent invader of the North Slope. *Right:* Natural *Poa* lawn grazed by Dall sheep (Atigun Gorge, ADH).

in coastal-plain wetland habitats where *Dupontia fisheri*, *Carex*, and *E. angustifolium* may account for 80 percent or more of plant productivity.

At the risk of oversimplification, the arctic sedges and grasses can be divided into two distinctly different growth forms: *creeping*, of which the widespread sedge *C. bigelowii* provides an example (**Fig. 9b.2**), and *tussock*, of which *E. vaginatum* provides an example (**Fig. 9b.1**). Knowledge of the biology of creeping sedges and tussock sedges is central to understanding their ecology. Before further discussion, it is important to become familiar with the concept of "modular" growth. Sedges and grasses share a similar growth pattern. Each individual plant is composed of repeated modules ("shoots" or "tillers"), each of which consists of the roots, a stem, and leaves. These modules are then interconnected by horizontal rhizomes. Vegetative reproduction, which is the dominant form of reproduction by tundra sedges and grasses, occurs when rhizomes elongate and produce new modules. This modular growth form (a repeated series of shoots connected by rhizomes) may result in a single individual covering a large area. After many "generations" of shoot production (7–28 generations in *C. bigelowii*) older rhizomes die, resulting in populations of clones of independent (unconnected) individuals.

Guerrilla Tactics and the Forward March of Sedges Across the Tundra

In the case of *C. bigelowii* and other creeping species, rhizome extension and shoot production is really a type of exploration for favorable habitats. In a sense, clones of *C. bigelowii* "march" across the tundra

Fig. 9b.4. *Left: Eriophorum vaginatum* tussock. Arrows indicate early spring flowerbuds (Galbraith Lake, ADH). *Right:* Cross section of tussock showing: a) leaves, b) densely compacted culms (stems) enveloped by bases of leaf sheaths, and c) roots and dead organic matter (Galbraith Lake, ADH).

continuously searching for and exploiting favorable habitats. To accomplish this, two types of shoot-rhizome combinations are produced. The first are the "guerrilla" or spreading shoots produced from long rhizomes that rapidly expand the area occupied by the plant, allowing it to quickly sample new habitat patches. Once a favorable patch (appropriate moisture and nutrient supply) is located, closely spaced phalanx or clumping shoots are produced from short rhizomes. Phalanx shoots enable the efficient use of local resources. At least five interconnected generations of shoots are required to ensure a plant's ability to thrive. This is because younger, rapidly growing shoots depend on nutrients stored in older shoots. Incidentally, the eventual fragmentation of rhizomes results in a population of independent clones that makes it impossible to estimate their age since germination from the original seed. In theory, a clone may remain active for thousands of years while marching over vast areas of tundra.

Unlike the creeping sedges, tussock sedges—such as *E. vaginatum*—produce compact groups of shoots that may be more than about 20 cm tall and 20–25 cm in diameter (**Fig. 9b.4**). These tussocks are produced by the same modular growth process used by creeping sedges. Daughter shoots, however, are produced directly adjacent to parent shoots, resulting in radial compression that forces those at the center of the clone upward and those at the edge of the clone outward. Rather than a widely spreading clone, as occurs with creeping sedges, the shoots of tussock sedges are forced upward and away from the tundra! This results in dome-shaped tussocks containing 300–600 or more tightly

Fig. 9b.5. Mineral soil exposed by frost boils provides patches of "early successional" habitat where *E. vaginatum* may propagate by seed, a relatively rare event (Toolik Field Station, ADH).

compressed shoots. *E. vaginatum* is a long-lived plant with average size tussocks ranging in age from 122 to 187 years (average 158 years). Since the generation time for individual shoots is only about five years, older tussocks contain live shoots as well as large quantities of organic matter contributed by dead shoots and roots.

The tussock growth form is particularly advantageous in tundra habitats. Because of their height, tussocks become snow-free sooner than inter-tussock areas. They also absorb low-angle solar radiation more efficiently. Consequently, tussock-forming plants experience a longer growing season than those growing between them. Furthermore, nutrients released by decomposing organic matter within tussocks are recycled as much as 10 times more rapidly than those within inter-tussock soils. The dominance of *E. vaginatum* and related tussock-forming species in tundra habitats should be understandable given the thermal and nutritional advantages of the tussock growth form.

Carex bigelowii, E. vaginatum, and essentially all other tundra sedge species are long-lived and reproduce almost exclusively by vegetative propagation. Reproduction by seedlings is infrequent at best. Seedlings appear to be successful only where mineral soils have been exposed, such as frost boils and cracks caused by soil contraction during dry periods (**Fig. 9b.5**). Even in such habitats, however, seedling survival is low due to desiccation and frost heaving. Although seedling establishment is infrequent, the chance of a seed being in the right place at the right time is improved by the existence of abundant seed banks. Seed banks are assemblages of buried seeds that become available as colonists when a habitat is disturbed. Seed banks may contain seeds that remain viable for a few years to centuries and are critical to the dynamics of plant succession. Viable seeds of *C. bigelowii* as old as 197 years, for example, have been recovered from tundra soils.

9c: Forbs

Bur-Reed (Sparganiaceae)

Narrow-leaved bur-reed (*Sparganium angustifolium*, **Fig. 9c.1**) is abundant in shallow-water habitats, particularly slow-moving streams. With the exception of the sedges and grasses, S. *angustifolium* is one of a very few species of aquatic vascular plants found on the North Slope.

Lilies (Liliaceae)

The most common lily on the North Slope is the mountain death camus (*Anticlea elegans*, formerly *Zygadenus elegans*, **Fig. 9c.2**). It is found primarily in mountain habitats and can be identified by narrow

Fig. 9c.1. *Upper left:* Narrow-leaved bur-reed (*Sparganium angustifolium*, Toolik Field Station, ADH) is abundant in shallow water habitats, particularly slow-moving streams. *Lower left:* Detail of fruit of *S. angustifolium*. *Right:* Mare's tail (*Hippuris vulgaris*, Ice Cut, ADH).

blue-green leaves and conspicuous cream-colored flowers with green nectaries near the bases of their petals. These flowers are pollinated by flies. Most species of *Anticlea* are poisonous due to toxic alkaloids. Ingestion will likely cause nausea, vomiting, tingling sensations, headache, and profuse sweating and salivation. At this point one may rightly be wondering, "Why the heck would anyone eat a death camus anyway?" Apparently *Anticlea* has been mistaken for wild onions. A sure sign that a bulb of *Anticlea* is not an onion, however, is the lack of an onion-like odor.

Bistorts and Docks (Polygonaceae)

The Polygonaceae have unusual flowers. Rather than petals, it is their sepals[5] that provide the color of their showy spikes. Three species are common on the North Slope (**Fig. 9c.3**): the bistort (*Bistorta plumosa*, senior synonym[6] of *Polygonum bistorta*), the alpine bistort (*B. vivipara*, formerly *P. viviparum*), and the arctic dock (*Rumex arcticus*). *R. arcticus* is a large plant with long red-tinged leaves with a tall spike of bright red flowers sometimes approaching 80 cm in height. *B. plumosa* is ubiquitous in tundra foothills habitats and its striking pink spike is unmistakable. Despite its common name, *B. vivipara* is most abundant on the coastal plain. It has a white spike that usually shows a series of bulblets or bulbils near its base. Although producing abundant flowers, all North American populations of *B. vivipara* apparently reproduce asexually by dispersing bulblets. As with many arctic flowers, production of the flower buds of *Bistorta* begins several years in advance with as many as five "generations" of buds born simultaneously on a single flower spike.

Moss Campion and Chickweeds (Caryophyllaceae)

The most conspicuous member of the North Slope Caryophyllaceae (**Fig. 9c.4**) is the moss campion (*Silene acaulis*). It is abundant in the mountains where it forms cushions and carpets of densely matted, needle-like evergreen leaves and striking pink flowers. The roughly circular cushions are anchored by a long, central taproot. The combination of needle-like leaves and taproot allow *S. acaulis* to grow in dry, exposed environments. The moss campion reproduces by seed production. Insect pollination (primarily by flies and bumblebees) is required to produce abundant seeds. The diameters of their slow-growing cushions have been used to estimate the age of *S. acaulis* plants and their associated landscape features (e.g., river terraces, moraines). Cushions

Fig. 9c.2. *Left:* Mountain death camus (*Anticlea elegans*, Ivishak River, S.M. Parker). ***Right:*** Detail of flower with visiting fly (Ivishak River, ADH).

Fig. 9c.3. *Left:* Arctic dock (*Rumex arcticus*, Toolik River, J.P. Benstead). ***Center:*** Alpine bistort (*Bistorta vivipara*) with bulblets, Toolik Field Station, ADH). ***Right:*** Bistort (*B. plumosa*, Toolik Field Station, ADH).

Fig. 9c.4. *Left:* Moss campion (*Silene acaulis*, Ivishak River, ADH). ***Center:*** Mouse-ear chickweed (*Cerastium beeringianum*, Toolik Field Station, ADH). ***Right:*** Merckia (*Wilhelmsia physodes*, Kuparuk River, ADH).

Fig. 9c.5. *Upper left:* Small-flower anemone (*Anemone parviflora*, Atigun Gorge, ADH). *Lower left:* Snow buttercup (*Ranunculus nivalis*, Atigun Gorge, ADH). *Right:* Marsh marigold (*Caltha palustris*, Kuparuk River, ADH).

about 30 cm or more in diameter in southern Alaska may exceed 300 years in age.

Buttercups, Anemones, Monkshood, and Larkspurs (Ranunculaceae)

To the botanically challenged, the Ranunculaceae present a bewildering array of species with both regular (with radial symmetry) and irregular (without radial symmetry) flowers that seem to defy their inclusion in the same family (**Figs. 9c.5, 9c.6**). Nevertheless, the presence of more than 12 stamens (pollen-producing organs) per flower indicates a close relationship. All Ranunculaceae are poisonous to some degree due to alkaloids in their tissues. Root extracts of some taxa (e.g., *Anenome*) were apparently an ingredient of Iñupiat arrow poisons. Five genera occur on the North Slope: buttercups (*Ranunculus*), marsh marigolds (*Caltha*), monkshoods (*Aconitum*), larkspurs (*Delphinium*), and anemones (*Anemone*). Buttercups and marsh marigolds (**Fig. 9c.5**) are identified by glossy yellow flowers formed from either true petals (buttercups) or sepals (marsh marigolds). Buttercups (about 12 North Slope species) are abundant in habitats ranging from tundra pools to alpine snowbanks. Reproduction occurs by seed (flies are major pollinators) or rhizome production. The marsh marigold (*Caltha palustris*) is found in shallow peat-bottom pools and streams. The monkshoods and larkspurs, with irregular deep purple flowers, are probably the most specialized

Fig. 9c.6. *Left:* Monkshood (*Aconitum delfiniifolium*, Toolik Field Station, ADH). *Center:* Tall larkspur (*Delphinium glaucum*, Ivishak River, S.M. Parker). *Right:* Few-flowered co-rydalus (Fumariaceae, *Corydalis arctica*, Kuparuk River, ADH). *C. arctica* is the food plant for larvae of Eversmann's parnassian (*Parnassius eversmanni*), an unusual and primitive arctic butterfly.

members of the family. Both *Aconitum delfiniifolium* and *Delphinium glaucum* are common in the mountains and foothills (**Fig. 9c.6**). Their complex flowers with stout trap doors are entered only by bumblebees.

Poppies (Papaveraceae)

Both *Papaver hultenii* (**Fig. 9.4**) and *P. keelei* are common on the North Slope. In stable habitats plants may live 20 years or more. See "Why Are Flowers So Colorful and Abundant?" and "Strange Behavior of Arctic Flowers Under the Midnight Sun" (above) for more information about arctic poppies.

Mustards (Brassicaceae)

Like the Ranunculaceae, the flowers of the Brassicaceae are exceedingly variable in structure (**Figs. 9c.7, 9c.8**). They all, however, have flowers with four petals arranged as a cross and six stamens. At least 13 genera occur on the North Slope, with the bittercresses (*Cardamine*, **Fig. 9c.7**) and wallflowers (*Erysimum*, **Fig. 9c.8**) being most conspicuous, and *Draba* (**Fig. 9c.7**) being the most diverse (12 or more species recorded from alpine and tundra habitats). Species of *Draba* are usually long-lived, low-growing, cushion-forming herbs with unremarkable yellow or white flowers. Although species of *Draba* are inconspicuous, to say the least, they should be treated with respect. *D. depressa* has been

Fig. 9c.7. Left: *Draba* (probably *Draba corymbosa*, Atigun Pass, ADH). **Upper right:** *Parrya* (*Parrya nudicaulis*, Kuparuk River, ADH). **Lower right:** Alpine bittercress (*Cardamine bellidifolia*, Atigun Gorge, ADH).

Fig. 9c.8. Left: Pallas' wallflower (*Erysimum pallasii*, Atigun Gorge, ADH). **Right:** Small-flower wallflower (*Erysimum coarctatum*, senior synonym of *E. inconspicuum*, Atigun Gorge, ADH).

recorded at 5,600 m on Mt. Chimborazo in Ecuador. This is the highest elevation known for a flowering plant.

Saxifrages (Saxifragaceae)

Like the Brassicaceae and Ranunculaceae, the Saxifragaceae includes a bewildering diversity of form. Nevertheless, the consistent occurrence of paired styles (divided seed capsule) reveals their close relationship. Of the four arctic genera, the saxifrages (*Saxifraga*) are by far the most diverse in both form and number of species (15 or more species reported

Fig. 9c.9. *Upper left:* Matted saxifrage (*Saxifraga bronchialis*, Atigun Pass, ADH). *Upper center:* Prickly saxifrage (*S. tricuspidata*, Atigun Pass, ADH). *Upper right:* Alpine brook saxifrage (*S. hyperborea*, Kuparuk River, ADH). *Lower left:* Golden carpet (*Chrysosplenium tetrandrum*, Cobblestone Spring, S.M. Parker). *Lower right:* Heart-leaved saxifrage (*Micranthes nelsoniana*, formerly *Saxifraga nelsoniana*, Kuparuk River, ADH).

from the North Slope, **Figs. 9.1, 9c.9, 9c.10**). Perhaps the most familiar species is *S. oppositifolia*, the purple mountain saxifrage (**Fig. 9.1**). *S. oppositifolia* is an evergreen that produces showy purple flowers. It occurs in two distinct growth forms depending upon habitat. A prostrate, mat-like form is found in protected habitats and a low, cushion-like form is found on dry, exposed mountain ridges. Cushions grow slowly, with individuals 16 cm in diameter estimated to be about 65 years old. *S. oppositifolia* is one of the earliest flowering species on the North Slope. It flowers almost as soon as it is exposed by melting snow, usually within a day or so of the first willow catkins, and is pollinated primarily by queen bumblebees. *S. oppositifolia* is a member of an elite group of plants found in mountain habitats exceeding 4,000 m in elevation and is one of a very few species of plants known from the northernmost angiosperm habitat on Earth (Lockwood Island, 83°N off Greenland's north coast).

Prickly saxifrage (*S. tricuspidata*, **Fig. 9c.9**) is a cushion-forming plant of dry, rocky foothills and mountains. It is identified by stiff three-spine leaves and creamy flowers with scattered orange dots. The yellow

Fig. 9c.10. *Upper left:* Yellow marsh saxifrage, bog saxifrage (*Saxifraga hirculus*, Cobblestone Spring, S.M. Parker). *Lower left:* Thyme-leaved saxifrage (*Saxifraga serpyllifolia*, Atigun Pass, ADH). *Right:* Bear flower (*Boykinia richardsonii*, Atigun Pass, ADH).

marsh saxifrage or bog saxifrage (*S. hirculus*, **Fig. 9c.10**) is found in wetland habitats. Its flowers are single bright-yellow cups with petals marked by distinctive rows of orange dots. They may be mistaken for buttercups (*Ranunculus*), from which they differ by having conspicuously divided seed capsules and petals that lack a glossy sheen. *S. hirculus* usually propagates by producing shoots from short, slender rhizomes. These tend to separate after one season or so, leading to populations of independent clones. A final example of arctic Saxifragaceae is golden carpet or water carpet (*Chrysosplenium tetrandrum*, **Fig. 9c.9**). This species may be the strangest member of the family. It is a small, delicate, greenish-golden plant that forms mats of slender, creeping horizontal stems in protected seeps and wet rock crevices. Its weird, inconspicuous flowers are tiny green bowls filled with clusters of shiny seeds that are dispersed by splashing raindrops!

Lupines, Vetches, and Oxytropes (Leguminosae)

Legumes are identified by their distinctive pea-like bumblebee-pollinated flowers. Their ability to "fix" nitrogen[7] allows them to rapidly colonize recently disturbed, nutrient-poor habitats. Common legumes of the

Fig. 9c.11. *Upper left:* Locoweed (*Oxytropis campestris,* Kuparuk River, ADH). *Upper right:* Blackish crazyweed (*Oxytropis bryophila,* Atigun Gorge, ADH). *Lower left:* Seed pod of oxytrope (Dalton Highway, MP 395). *Lower center:* Uprooted oxytrope plant showing relatively simple root structure (Galbraith Lake, ADH). *Lower right:* Arctic lupine (*Lupinus arcticus,* Happy Valley, ADH).

North Slope are contained in the genera *Astragalus, Hedysarum, Lupinus,* and *Oxytropis.*

The arctic lupine (*Lupinus arcticus,* **Fig. 9c.11**) is a miniature version of the familiar garden lupine with striking blue flower spikes. Its tissues contain a neurotoxin that may deter herbivory. The seeds of legumes are known to remain viable for long periods and are often abundant in soil seed banks. Even among legumes, however, the seeds of *L. arcticus* are legendary. Viable seeds at least 10,000 years old have been discovered in "fossil" lemming burrows frozen at depths of 3–6 m in Pleistocene-age sediments in Yukon Territory.

Licorice root or bear root (*Hedysarum alpinum,* **Fig. 9c.12**) and alpine sweetvetch (*H. mackenziei,* **Fig. 9c.12**) are common in recently disturbed habitats, such as sand and gravel floodplains. Species of *Hedysarum* can be distinguished from other look-alike genera (e.g., *Astragalus* and *Oxytropis*) by their distinctive seed pods that are flattened and have conspicuous constrictions. *H. alpinum* has long, scraggly spikes of pale purple-to-pink flowers, compound leaves with numerous leaflets, and multiple stems arising from shoots supported by branching rhizomes. Its leaves and stems are critical to the diet of a number of North Slope mammals, including moose, Dall sheep, and caribou. Grizzly bears

Fig. 9c.12. *Upper left:* Licorice root, bear root (*Hedysarum alpinum*, China Valley Creek, ADH). *Upper right:* Uprooted plant showing the large taproots that are eagerly consumed by grizzly bears in spring and autumn (China Valley Creek, ADH). *Lower left:* Northern sweetvetch (*Hedysarum mackenziei*, Ice Cut, ADH). *Lower right:* Seed pod of *Hedysarum* (MP 395, Dalton Highway).

feed on its long, carrot-like taproots (**Fig. 9c.12**) and rhizomes during early spring and late summer when they are both most palatable and nutrient-rich. Sure signs of grizzly bear foraging are the deep pits produced by the bears' raking away of soil to expose taproots. The roots of *H. alpinum* were an important traditional food used by the Nunamiut.[8] The consumption of *H. alpinum* roots by casual visitors to the North Slope is not recommended, as those of the similar species *H. borealis* are poisonous.

The remaining common genera are the milk vetches (*Astragalus*) and oxytropes (*Oxytropis*, **Fig. 9c.11**). Due to their recent diversification, the Alaskan species of these genera are difficult to identify. Even specialists are uncertain of the validity of some species. As a rule, milk vetches have leafy flower stems while those of the oxytropes are leafless. Oxytropes are relatively small (less than 10 cm high and 30 cm wide), long-lived (20–40 years) plants of well-drained habitats. Unlike most other arctic plants, they reproduce by seeds rather than rhizomes, which results in relatively simple root systems. In early spring, oxytropes are an important food source for lactating muskoxen and their rapidly growing calves.

Fireweed and River Beauty (Onagraceae)

Fireweed (*Chamerion angustifolium*, formerly *Epilobium angustifolium*, **Fig. 9c.13**) is easily distinguished by its height, usually exceeding 1 m or more, and by its showy spikes with up to 100 dark-pink flowers about 2–3 cm in diameter. River beauty (*C. latifolium*, **Fig. 9c.13**) is similar but forms low bushes less than 0.5 m high and has waxy, blue-green leaves. Its showy flowers are larger than those of fireweed and are formed in loose clusters rather than tall spikes. Both fireweed and river beauty are abundant in disturbed habitats, particularly gravel floodplains. Fireweed occurs in dense stands of shoots connected by horizontal root systems that may exceed 35 years in age. The flowers are hermaphroditic (reproductive structures from both sexes present in each flower) and the flowering of a spike is sequential with flowers lowest on the spike opening first. Since the male flower structures mature and senesce before the female structures, the flowers toward the top of the spike are usually functional males while those toward the base of the spike are functional females. This pattern ensures cross-pollination by bumblebees, which tend to forage from the bottom to the top of a spike. Consequently, pollen-laden bumblebees leave functionally male flowers at the top of a flower spike and fly directly to functionally female flowers at the bottom of the next spike. The sudden appearance of fireweed in recently disturbed habitats is due to the effective and widespread dispersal of seeds. The small, fluffy, windblown seeds have been collected more than 100 m above the ground and are likely transported hundreds of kilometers during gales.

Fig. 9c.13. *Left:* Fireweed (*Chamerion angustifolium*, Oksrukuyik Creek, ADH). *Right:* River beauty (*C. latifolium*, Atigun Pass, ADH).

Fig. 9c.14. *Left:* Buckbean (*Menyanthes trifoliata*, Ice Cut, ADH). *Right:* Detail of buckbean flower (Ice Cut, ADH).

Buckbean (Menyanthaceae)

Buckbean (*Menyanthes trifoliata*, **Fig. 9c.14**) may be abundant in shallow thaw ponds along the Dalton Highway. Plants can be identified by leaves with three leaflets when flowers are not present.

Primroses (Primulaceae)

Northern shooting star (*Dodecatheon frigidum*) is common in protected mountain and foothills habitats where its nodding flowers can be confused with no other species (**Fig. 9c.15**). The flowers of *Dodecatheon* are fertilized by buzz pollination during which pollen is dislodged from anthers by vibrations of a bumblebee's flight muscles. Rock jasmine (*Androsace chamaejasme*, **Fig. 9c.15**) is found in well-drained fellfields and talus slopes in mountain habitats.

Mare's Tail (Hippuridaceae)

Mare's tail (*Hippuris vulgaris*) can be extremely abundant in tundra thaw ponds and the pools of beaded streams (**Fig. 9c.1**).

Forget-Me-Nots (Boraginaceae)

Two species of the distinctive forget-me-nots are found on the North Slope. The alpine forget-me-not (*Myosotis asiatica*) is found in sheltered riparian habitats along mountain streams. The more common arctic forget-me-not (*Eritrichium aretioides*, **Fig. 9c.15**) occurs on dry, well-drained mountain slopes.

Fig. 9c.15. *Left:* Northern shooting star (Primulaceae: *Dodecatheon frigidum*, ADH). *Upper right:* Rock jasmine (Primulaceae: *Androsace chamaejasme*, Atigun Gorge, ADH). *Lower right:* Arctic forget-me-not (Boraginaceae, *Eritrichium aretioides*, Atigun Gorge, ADH).

Wintergreens (Pyrolaceae) and Gentians (Gentianaceae)

Arctic wintergreen (*Pyrola grandiflora*, **Fig. 9c.16**) is readily identified by its basal rosette of fleshy green leaves. It is common in sheltered tundra habitats where plants are often clustered around the bases of shrubs. Several species of gentians may be found in foothills and mountain habitats. Their unusual tubular and missile-like blue flowers are diagnostic (**Fig. 9c.16**). Although never abundant, gentians usually can be found in appropriate habitats if one searches carefully, particularly in late summer.

Phlox and Jacob's Ladder (Polemoniaceae)

Alaskan phlox (*Phlox alaskensis*, **Fig. 9c.17**) is a striking mat-forming plant found in foothills and mountain habitats, particularly those with abundant limestone. Two species of Jacob's ladder are common on the North Slope. Northern Jacob's ladder (*Polemonium boreale*, **Fig. 9c.17**) occurs in the mountains while tall Jacob's ladder (*P. acutiflorum*, **Fig. 9c.17**) is found in both the foothills and mountains in moist, riparian habitats.

Fig. 9c.16. Left: Arctic wintergreen (Pyrolaceae, *Pyrola grandiflora*, Toolik Field Station, ADH). **Center:** Glaucous gentian (Gentianaceae, *Gentiana glauca*, Kuparuk River, ADH). **Right:** Four-petaled gentian (Gentianaceae, *Gentianella propinqua*, Atigun Gorge, ADH).

Louseworts (Scrophulariaceae)

Three genera of the Scrophulariaceae occur on the North Slope: the paintbrushes (*Castilleja*, **Fig. 9c.18**), the weasel snout (*Lagotis glauca*, **Fig. 9c.18**), and the louseworts (*Pedicularis*, **Figs. 9.3, 9.5, 9c.19**). The louseworts are species-rich, abundant, and unmistakable due to spikes of brightly colored (yellow, pink, or red) flowers and fern-like leaves. Common species include *Pedicularis arctica*, *P. labradorica*, *P. lapponica*, and *P. lanata*. *P. labradorica* and *P. lapponica* have yellow flowers, but *P. labradorica* has branched stems while *P. lapponica* has a single stem. *P. arctica* and *P. lanata* have pink flowers, but the flower spike of *P. lanata* has a thick, cottony pile (tomentum) through which the flowers emerge. The paintbrushes are similarly unmistakable (**Fig. 9c.18**). They have strange, raggedy "flowers" that are really enlarged bracts[9] that enclose the inconspicuous flower within. Although variable in color, the paintbrushes of the North Slope are probably all members of *Castilleja caudata*. See "Why Are Flowers So Colorful and Abundant?" and "A Plethora of Parasites" (above) for more information.

Butterworts and Bladderworts (Lentibulariaceae)

The butterwort (*Pinguicula vulgaris*, **Fig. 9c.20**) is widespread in wet coastal plain and foothills habitats. These insectivorous plants are

9c.17. *Left:* Alaskan phlox (Polemoniaceae, *Phlox alaskensis*, Toolik Field Station, ADH). *Center:* Northern Jacob's ladder (Polemoniaceae, *Polemonium boreale*, Atigun Pass, ADH). *Right:* Tall Jacob's ladder (*Polemonium acutiflorum*, Ivishak River, S.M. Parker).

9c.18. *Left:* Little weasel snout (*Lagotis glauca*, Toolik Field Station, ADH). *Center:* Paintbrush (*Castilleja pallida*, Ice Cut, ADH). *Right:* Detail of *C. pallida* flower (Ice Cut, ADH).

identified by a conspicuous basal rosette of leaves with upturned edges and a sticky coating of mucopolysaccharides. This coating contains digestive enzymes and is used to both entrap and digest small invertebrates (usually adult midges and springtails). As much as 85 percent of the nitrogen assimilated by butterworts may be derived from insect prey, although the usual amount is much less. The uncommon bladderworts (Lentibulariaceae: *Utricularia*, **Fig. 9c.21**) are inconspicuous rootless plants that may be found in shallow tundra ponds. They are identified by the presence of small bladders attached to narrow filamentous leaves. The bladders trap and digest zooplankton to obtain nutrients. Each bladder has a trap door surrounded by a tuft of fine "trigger" hairs. Water is pumped from the bladder by an osmotic mechanism that results in a negative pressure gradient. When the trigger hairs are disturbed by a swimming invertebrate, the trap door opens and water—along with prey—rushes into the bladder

Fig. 9c.19. *Left:* Sudeten lousewort (*Pedicularis albolabiata*, Kuparuk River, ADH). *Center:* Langsdorf's lousewort (*P. langsdorfii*, Toolik Field Station, ADH). *Right:* Oeder's lousewort (*P. oederi*, Toolik Field Station, ADH).

Fig. 9c.20. *Left:* Common butterwort (*Pinguicula vulgaris*, Ivishak River, ADH). *Right:* Detail of leaves with adult midges adhering to sticky surface (Dalton Highway, MP 384).

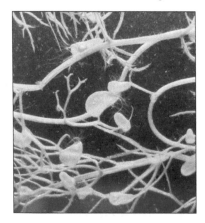

Fig. 9c.21. *Left:* Bladderwort (*Utricularia* sp., floodplain pond, Kuparuk River, ADH). Note the trigger hairs on the bladders. *Right:* Fairy shrimp (*Polyartemiella hazeni*) captured by bladderwort. Its eye is distorted by the suction produced when the trap was activated. The orange objects in the bladders are captured copepods.

(**Fig. 9c.21**). The bladderwort species of the North Slope is presumably *Utricularia vulgaris.*

Twinflowers (Caprifoliaceae) and Heliotropes (Valerianaceae)

The diminutive twinflower (*Linnaea borealis*, **Fig. 9c.22**) seems to be everyone's favorite. Although relatively uncommon on the North Slope, it can be found in protected foothills habitats if one looks carefully. Twinflowers are identified by their long runners with tiny pairs of tiny oval leaves held perpendicular to the stem. The equally tiny pinkish, tubular flowers, which appear in early August, hang in pairs from short, forked stems at regular intervals along the runners. Mountain heliotrope (*Valeriana capitata,* **Fig. 9c.22**) can be identified by its dense, snowball-like pinkish to white flower spikes. Prior to flowering, the buds appear as compact, reddish structures that may be mistaken for mature flowers, leading to confusion about their identity. Mountain helitrope is common in sheltered mountain and foothills habitats.

Composites (Compositae or Asteraceae)

The Compositae includes the familiar daisies, dandelions, sunflowers, and asters and contains some of the most conspicuous and abundant flowering plants on the North Slope (**Figs. 9c.22, 9c.23, 9c.24**). The flowers of this exceedingly large and diverse family tend to be white, yellow, or purple. Their structure is also relatively uniform among species, consisting of a central button composed of a composite of hundreds of tiny, closely packed disk flowers, surrounded by a corona

Fig. 9c.22. *Left:* Twinflower (Caprifoliaceae: *Linnaea borealis*, Kuparuk, ADH). *Center:* Fully opened flower of mountain heliotrope (Valerianaceae: *Valeriana capitata*, Ivishak River, S.M. Parker). *Right:* Arctic sweet coltsfoot (Asteraceae: *Petasites frigidus*, Atigun Gorge, ADH).

Fig. 9c.23. *Upper left:* Lessing's arnica (*Arnica lessingii*, Toolik Field Station, ADH) showing the diagnostic "drooping" or "nodding" flowers. *Upper right:* Northern goldenrod (*Solidago multiradiata*, Toolik Field Station, ADH). *Lower left:* Dwarf hawk's beard (*Askellia nana*, formerly *Crepis nana*, Galbraith Lake, ADH). *Lower right:* Mountain fleabane (*Erigeron humilis*, Imnavait Creek, ADH).

Fig. 9c.24. *Left:* Black-tipped groundsel (*Senecio lugens*, Oksrukuyik Creek, ADH). *Center:* Siberian aster (*Eurybia sibiricus*, formerly *Aster sibiricus*, Oksrukuyik Creek, ADH). *Right:* Fireworks flower (*Saussurea angustifolia*, Oksrukuyik Creek, ADH).

of "petals" formed by ray flowers that make up the perimeter of the central button.

9d: Trees and Shrubs

Spruces (Pinaceae)

Although the climate of the North Slope has likely been warm enough to support spruce seedlings for many centuries, the presence of mature spruce trees approaching 500 years in age just south of the Continental Divide, combined with the virtual absence of spruce on the North Slope, indicates that conifers have been unable to cross the Brooks Range. In 2008, however, a white spruce (*Picea glauca*) seedling was reported from the margin of the Dalton Highway near Atigun Gorge. Presumably this seedling originated from a seed transported by a passing vehicle. This record is apparently the first documentation of a spruce tree on the North Slope that was not intentionally planted (spruces were experimentally planted at the Toolik Field Station and elsewhere on the North Slope as early as 1980).

Willows (Salicaceae)

The willows (*Salix*) are the most diverse and ecologically significant genus of shrubs on the North Slope. Their leaves and twigs provide critical habitat and food for many animals (ptarmigan, songbirds, voles, lemmings, ground squirrels, snowshoe hare, muskoxen, moose), particularly during winter and spring. The nectar of pussy willows (*Salix* flowers) is critical food for bumblebees that begin foraging shortly after spring snowmelt. Willows were also essential for the survival of the Nunamiut. The felt-leaf willow (*S. alaxensis*, **Fig. 9d.1**) was the only effective source of fuel wood and tall poles on the inland North Slope, and the young leaves and inner bark of both *S. alaxensis* and the diamond-leaf willow (*S. pulchra*, **Fig. 9d.2**) served as food. The quote "no caribou, no humans" with regard to the habitability of the inland North Slope by humans could as accurately be "no willows, no humans."

Willows are often described more or less as shrubs with multiple stems, about 1–2 m or more high, and often forming thickets in riparian habitats. This definition may be true for temperate and boreal regions, but when considering tundra habitats it must be broadened to embrace the abundant dwarf species that form creeping mats only a few centimeters high (**Figs. 9d.3, 9d.4**). These have branches slightly below the

Fig. 9d.1. *Upper left: Salix alaxensis,* male catkin (Ivishak River, ADH). *Upper center:* Seeds (Ivishak River, ADH). *Upper right:* Early female catkin (Ivishak River, ADH). *Lower left:* Mature female catkin (Ivishak River, ADH). *Lower center:* Foliage (Ivishak River, ADH). *Lower right:* Cross section of a 6.5 cm diameter stem showing slow growth as 43 annual growth rings (Atigun Gorge, ADH).

Fig. 9d.2. *Upper left: Salix pulchra,* twig-stripping by moose browsing (Oksrukuyik Creek, ADH). *Upper center:* Summer foliage (Oksrukuyik Creek, ADH). *Upper right:* Autumn foliage with view of shiny, reddish stems (Oksrukuyik Creek, ADH). *Lower left:* Catkins and persistent leaves in May (Oksrukuyik Creek, ADH). *Lower right:* Thicket showing uniform browse line caused by moose browsing (Oksrukuyik Creek, ADH).

soil's surface so that only their tips are exposed. This is an excellent adaptation because it allows the entire plant to be buried by snow during winter, which protects the plant from extreme cold temperatures, low humidity, and wind.

Unlike the dwarf willows, the exposed stems of tall willows and similar tundra shrubs (e.g., birches, poplars) are subject to temperatures below −60°C. Their cell contents are protected by supercooling (i.e., staying liquid below the freezing point due to factors such as high solute concentrations) or by conversion to a glass state, a condition of extreme viscosity that appears to be a solid. The freezing of extracellular fluids is less of a danger because the wood of willows is unusually soft and flexible and allows them to accommodate ice crystals in their vascular tissues without damage. As winter approaches, willows undergo a physiological cold hardening process when compounds (cryoprotectants) required for supercooling and glass formation are produced. This process is energetically demanding and is yet another factor explaining the slow growth of woody plants in the Arctic.

Willows are dioecious, meaning that male and female flowers occur on separate plants. Willow flowers (pussy willows, e.g., **Fig. 9d.1**) are both insect- and wind-pollinated. The female flowers produce minute seeds attached to long, downy fibers that facilitate wind transport. These seeds contain little energy and few nutrients and are viable for only a few weeks under the best conditions. Consequently, willow seedlings are poor competitors, requiring full sunlight and the freshly disturbed soils of habitats such as frost boils and exposed river sediments. Willows often reproduce vegetatively as suckers that grow from roots and stems as well as fragments of plants eroded from banks and then transported to new habitats. This latter process is an important source of colonizers following flooding.

About 18 species of willow occur on the North Slope. The felt-leaf willow (*Salix alaxensis,* **Fig. 9d.1**) is the most conspicuous and is identified by large gray-green leaves with pale and densely felted undersides. It is found along the banks and on floodplains of almost all mountain and foothill streams and rivers. In protected habitats with abundant groundwater it may attain heights approaching 3 m and stem widths approaching 10 cm. Like other shrubs of the North Slope, felt-leaf willows grow slowly due to the short summer growing season. A stem with a diameter of 5 cm or so is probably at least 20 years old. The diamond-leaf willow (*S. pulchra,* **Fig. 9d.2**) and Richardson's willow (*S. richardsonii,* **Fig. 9d.5**) are also common thicket-forming willows in riparian habitats. Unlike many other willow species, however, both diamond-leaf willow and Richardson's willow are easily identified in both summer and winter by their twigs. Twigs of diamond-leaf willow are shiny and reddish

Fig. 9d.3. *Left: Salix reticulata* with catkins (Ivishak River, ADH). *Center:* Autumn foliage with mature female catkins (Ivishak River, ADH). *Right:* Female catkin (Ivishak River, ADH).

Fig. 9d.4. *Left: Salix polaris* with catkins. The abundant red catkins are female; a single male catkin is visible on the far center right. The mushroom and cup lichens provide a sense of scale (Toolik Field Station, ADH). *Right: S. rotundifolia* with catkins and diagnostic persistent dead leaves. The familiar blue-bottle blow fly (Diptera: Calliphoridae) provides a sense of scale (Atigun Gorge, ADH).

while those of Richardson's willow have leaf stipules[10] that persist as dried, recurved spikes on the stems. This gives them a distinctive scraggly appearance (**Fig. 9d.5**).

Perhaps the most unusual willows of the North Slope are the dwarf willows, the most common of which are the net-vein (*S. reticulata*, **Fig. 9d.3**), least (*S. rotundifolia*, **Fig. 9d.4**), and polar (*S. polaris*, **Fig. 9d.4**) willows. The net-vein willow is one of the most widespread and abundant shrubs of the North Slope. It has relatively large, round leaves (2–4 cm in length) with an obvious reticulated pattern and a long reddish petiole (leaf stem). The least and polar willows—the smallest willow species in the world—have prostrate, creeping stems that reach only a few centimeters above the ground. These are usually embedded in the ground or woven into dense mats when growing over stones or hard, rocky ground.

Fig. 9d.5. *Left: Salix richardsonii* with female catkins (Ivishak River, ADH). *Center: S. richardsonii* during winter showing the persistent leaf stipules that give it a scraggly appearance. The debris on the snow is due to ptarmigan foraging (Ivishak River, ADH). *Upper right:* Male catkin. *Lower right:* Mature female catkins.

Their tiny leaves may appear un-willow-like to the nonbotanist and are dwarfed by surrounding mosses and sedges.

Poplars (Salicaceae)

On the North Slope, scattered groves of balsam poplar (*Populus balsamifera,* **Fig. 9d.6**) are found along perennial spring streams and similar groundwater-rich habitats. Balsam poplars require large amounts of water and their root systems can be enormous, extending 30 m or more from their trunks. Such root systems are unable to develop in the shallow active layers of most tundra soils, and significant groves develop only in habitats providing abundant groundwater and shelter from wind. Consequently, successful colonization of new habitats by poplars on the North Slope is a rare event because the unlikely intersection of viable wind-borne seeds and a groundwater-rich habitat is required. Because the probability of colonization of suitable habitat by multiple seeds is low, groves are usually clones of one or a few individuals that reproduce asexually by the propagation of stems or suckers along extensive root systems. These groves may contain several hundred slow-growing trees that may eventually reach heights of 6–10 m and 250 or more years in age.

Balsam poplar groves provide the only "forest" habitat on the North Slope and are essential for breeding by the gray-headed chickadee (*Poecile cincta*),[11] which requires tree-size poplars for nesting cavities. Gray-headed chickadees may not be the only bird species using tree-size

Fig. 9d.6. *Upper left:* Grove of *Populus balsamifera* (Dalton Highway, MP 307, ADH). *Lower left:* Grove of large *P. balsamifera* at Echooka Spring (S.M. Parker). Many of these trees are well over 100 years old. *Right:* Autumn foliage of *P. balsamifera* (Ivishak Hot Spring, ADH).

poplars as nesting habitat on the North Slope. A cavity inhabited by a pair of northern flickers (*Colaptes auratus*) was reported from an 8 m tall poplar near the Canning River, and a cavity that was apparently formed by a small woodpecker species was observed in a standing-dead poplar trunk near the Ivishak River.

Birches and Alders (Betulaceae)

The dwarf arctic birch (*Betula nana*) and the resin birch (*B. glandulosa*) are common tundra shrubs (**Fig. 9d.7**). Although they are themselves difficult to separate, *B. nana* and *B. glandulosa* are easily distinguished from other arctic shrubs by their small (0.5–2 cm) oval leaves with bluntly toothed margins. By late August, the leaves of *Betula* spp. change from green to brilliant red, which further distinguishes them. In protected habitats *Betula* form dense, tangled thickets about 0.5–1.0 m high and in exposed habitats they form prostrate mats. Unlike willows and poplars, the dwarf birches are monoecious, that is, both male and female catkins are produced on the same plant (males at the twig tips, females along the branches). Fragmentation of woody rhizomes and vegetative

Fig. 9d.7. *Upper left:* *Betula glandulosa* shrub (Atigun Gorge, ADH). *Upper right:* Twig showing abundant resin droplets (Atigun Gorge, ADH). The resin droplets have been shown to deter herbivory. *Lower left:* Leaves. Ladybird beetle provides a sense of scale (Ivishak River, ADH). *Lower center:* Female catkins (Atigun Gorge, ADH). *Lower right:* September foliage with frost (Ivishak River, ADH).

layering[12] are the most common modes of propagation, although numerous tiny seeds are shed during winter. Leaves and buds of birches are grazed by voles, lemmings, arctic ground squirrels, moose, and ptarmigan. Various species of songbirds feed on their catkins, buds, and seeds.

The Siberian alder (*Alnus fruticosa,* **Fig. 9d.8**) grows on well-drained soils with abundant moisture, usually as isolated shrubs about 0.5–2.0 m high. It is identified by leaves with distinctive double-toothed margins and the presence of woody cones that persist year-round on reproducing plants. The cones are female catkins that are produced along the branches while the drooping male catkins are produced at the tips of twigs and drop from the plant once pollen is produced in spring. Alder shrubs have multiple stems that sprout from a central rootstock. These stems often become bent toward the ground by snow cover, enabling the production of adventitious roots[13] and the eventual formation of dense clonal stands. Alder twigs and buds provide food for ptarmigan during winter, and their flowers and seeds are eaten by many other bird species during spring, summer, and autumn. The alders are one of only a few North Slope shrubs able to fix elemental nitrogen into organic forms by means of a symbiotic relationship with bacteria that colonize specialized root nodules.

Fig. 9d.8. *Upper left:* Siberian alder (*Alnus fruticosa*) foliage (Ivishak River, ADH). *Upper center:* Male catkin buds (twig tips) and persistent female "cones" (Ivishak River, ADH). *Right:* A. fruticosa shrubs (vicinity of Happy Valley, ADH). *Lower left:* Male catkin buds (Ivishak River, ADH). *Lower center:* Mature female catkins (Ivishak River, ADH).

Roses (Rosaceae)[14]

The dryads or mountain avens (*Dryas*, **Fig. 9d.9**), "true" avens (*Geum*, **Fig. 9d.9**), cloudberries (*Rubus chamaemorus*, **Fig. 9d.10**), and cinquefoils (*Potentilla*, **Fig. 9d.11**) are the most common and conspicuous members of the Rosaceae on the North Slope. The flowers of the Rosaceae often superficially resemble buttercups (*Ranunculus*) but have shallower bowls and lack a waxy sheen.

The white dryas (*Dryas integrifolia*, **Fig. 9d.9**) and the eight-petaled dryas (*D. ajanensis*, senior synonym of *D. octopetala*, **Fig. 9d.9**) are long-lived (100-plus years) dwarf shrubs that form low, mat-like carpets in snowbed and heath habitats. *D. integrifolia* and *D. ajanensis* are identified by their leaves. The leathery leaves of *D. integrifolia* have smooth margins while those of *D. ajanensis* have toothed margins. Each plant has a single taproot, which may reach 2 m or more in depth. Vegetative reproduction occurs through the lateral extension and branching of stems. The eventual fragmentation of individuals results in a population of independent clones. Cross-pollination is required for effective seed production, although self-pollination also occurs. *Dryas* seeds are wind-dispersed by the aid of distinctive feathery styles (**Fig. 9d.9**). Like many arctic angiosperms, they produce mature flower buds during autumn, allowing flowering shortly after snowmelt.

The cloudberry (*Rubus chamaemorus*) is a common herbaceous berry-producing plant of foothills tundra (**Fig. 9d.10**). Prolific berry production in some years provides evidence that significant resources are devoted

Fig. 9d.9. *Upper left:* Glacier avens (*Geum glaciale*, Toolik Field Station, ADH). *Upper right:* White dryas, mountain avens (*Dryas integrifolia*, tributary of Ivishak River, ADH). *Lower left:* Eight-petaled dryas, mountain avens (*Dryas ajanensis*, Atigun Pass, ADH). *Lower center:* Maturing flower head of *D. integrifolia* showing twist of maturing seed styles. *Lower right:* Flower head of *D. integrifolia* showing detail of elegant styles used to aid wind dispersal of seeds.

Fig. 9d.10. *Left:* Cloudberry flower (*Rubus chamaemorus*, Toolik Field Station, ADH). *Center:* Ripe cloudberry fruit (Toolik Field Station, ADH). *Right:* Prickly rose (*Rosa acicularis*, Oksrukuyik Creek, ADH).

Fig. 9d.11. *Left:* Shrubby cinquefoil (*Potentilla fruticosa*, Toolik Field Station, ADH). *Right:* Cinquefoil (*Potentilla* sp., Atigun Gorge, ADH).

to sexual reproduction. Nevetheless, cloudberries usually reproduce by the propagation of shoots from underground rhizomes up to 10 m long. Due to extensive rhizome systems a single plant may occupy many square meters, and what appears to be a large population of cloudberries may consist of a single individual. The conspicuous creamy flowers are produced from overwintering buds containing flowers that are nearly fully formed. Pollination (usually by flies and bumblebees) is required for fruit formation. The soft yellow cloudberries (**Fig. 9d.10**) ripen in August and are consumed by many birds and mammals. The Iñupiat traditionally mixed berries with fat and sugar to produce a tasty dessert that also provided protection against scurvy due to high concentrations of vitamin C.

Soapberry (Elaeagnaceae)

Soapberry (*Shepherdia canadensis*, **Fig. 9d.12**) is a woody, nitrogen-fixing shrub recognized in late summer by its red berries and at other times by its distinctive leathery leaves with silvery, orange-dotted undersides. It is common in mountain habitats, where grizzly bears feed on berries in late summer.

Crowberry (Empetraceae)

Crowberry (*Empetrum nigrum*, **Fig. 9d.13**) is a prostrate dwarf shrub with stiff, needle-like leaves and long, woody stems anchored at intervals

Fig. 9d.12. *Left:* The tiny flowers of soapberry (*Shepherdia canadensis*, Atigun Gorge, ADH). *Right:* Ripe fruit of soapberry (Atigun Gorge, ADH).

by adventitious roots. Crowberry propagates primarily by creeping vegetative growth, which results in single plants that cover relatively large areas. The wind-pollinated flowers of crowberry are tiny (about 1–2 mm), inconspicuous, and red. Look for them in early spring. The fruit— black, fleshy berries about 4–8 mm in diameter—may be the best diagnostic character for the casual observer. Crowberries are eaten by caribou, foxes, ground squirrels, ptarmigan, and other birds. Crowberry is long-lived, with some individuals attaining 140 years.

Heaths (Ericaceae)

The Ericaceae is one of the dominant families of vascular plants in foothills habitats. Common species of ericoid shrubs are alpine blueberry (*Vaccinium uliginosum*, **Fig. 9d.14**), lingonberry (*V. vitis-idaea*, **Fig. 9d.14**), arctic white heather (*Cassiope tetragona*, **Fig. 9d.15**), bog rosemary (*Andromeda polifolia*, **Fig. 9d.16**), northern Labrador tea (*Rhododendron tomentosum*, senior synonym of *Ledum palustre*, **Fig. 9d.15**), Lapland rosebay (*Rhododendron lapponicum*, **Fig. 9d.17**), alpine azalea (*Kalmia procumbens*, formerly *Loiseleuria procumbens*, **Fig. 9d.17**), and alpine (*Arctous alpina*, formerly *Arctostaphylos alpine*, **Fig. 9d.16**) and red bearberry (*Arctous rubra*, formerly *Arctostaphylos rubra*, **Fig. 9d.16**).

The alpine blueberry (*Vaccinium uliginosum*, **Fig. 9d.14**) is a low shrub with small deciduous leaves and inconspicuous, drooping, bell-like

Fig. 9d.13. *Left:* The tiny flowers of crowberry (Toolik Field Station, ADH). *Right:* Ripe fruit of crowberry (*Empetrum nigrum*, Toolik Field Station, ADH).

Fig. 9d.14. *Upper left:* Flowers of lingonberry (*Vaccinium vitis-idaea*, Toolik Field Station, ADH). *Upper right:* Ripe fruit of lingonberry (Toolik Field Station, ADH). *Lower left:* Flowers of alpine blueberry (*Vaccinium uliginosum*, Ivishak River, S.M. Parker). *Lower right:* Ripe fruit of alpine blueberry.

flowers that produce the familiar blueberries. Although closely related, the lingonberry (*V. vitis-idaea*, **Fig. 9d.14**) is a prostrate dwarf shrub with glossy evergreen leaves and shiny, fire-engine-red berries. The alpine blueberry and lingonberry form dense thickets of shoots connected by extensive networks of underground rhizomes. As a consequence of creeping vegetative propagation, a single individual of *V. uliginosum* may cover tens of square meters. While the actual age of a genetically distinct individual cannot be determined due to the eventual separation of shoots, the shoots themselves may live as long as 60 years or more. The flowers of *Vaccinium* are cross-pollinated by bumblebees, butterflies, and flies. Self-pollination by wind and gravity also occurs but results in poor seed production. Although seedlings are seldom found on the tundra, berries are abundant in most years. Seeds are dispersed by birds and mammals.

Arctic white heather (*Cassiope tetragona*, **Fig. 9d.15**) is an evergreen dwarf shrub that is abundant on dry heaths. It has white, drooping, bell-shaped flowers and tiny, scale-like leaves that form four distinctive rows, giving its stem a decidedly square cross section. Individual leaves live for about four to five years but remain attached to the plant for many years. This is significant because the seasonal pattern of stem elongation and leaf production (smaller leaves are produced in spring and late summer; larger leaves are produced in midsummer) results in a record of annual growth. In essence, the number of "wavelengths" of annual leaf-size variation provides an estimate of a stem's minimum age. This method has shown that individuals of *C. tetragona* regularly attain 60 years, with exceptional individuals attaining ages of 100–135 years. Since the

Fig. 9d.15. *Left:* Northern Labrador tea (*Rhododendron tomentosum*, Toolik Field Station, ADH). *Right:* Arctic white heather (*Cassiope tetragona*, Atigun Gorge, ADH).

Fig. 9d.16. *Upper left:* Flowers of red bearberry (Toolik Field Station, ADH). *Upper right:* Overwintered fruit of red bearberry (*Arctous rubra,* Toolik Field Station, ADH). *Lower left:* Alpine bearberry, black bearberry (*Arctous alpina,* Toolik Field Station, ADH). *Lower right:* Bog rosemary flower (*Andromeda polifolia,* Kuparuk River, ADH).

numbers of leaves per wavelength has been shown to be closely correlated with mean July temperature, the information recorded by the stems of *C. tetragona* has been used to reconstruct historical patterns of summer temperatures from as much as 4,000 years ago using subfossils[15] preserved in peat.

Labrador tea (*Rhododendron tomentosum,* **Fig. 9d.15**) and Lapland rosebay (*R. lapponicum,* **Fig. 9d.17**) are arguably the two most beautiful flowering shrubs of the North Slope. These long-lived (30 or more years) dwarf shrubs are essentially miniature versions of the familiar boreal and temperate species. Labrador tea has distinctive, aromatic evergreen leaves with rolled edges and undersides covered with reddish-brown fuzz. The high concentrations of phenolics that deter both herbivory and root growth of potential competitors are responsible for their aroma. The distinctive white flowers are held upright in compact clusters. Lapland rosebay is readily identified as a rhododendron, even though individual plants are usually less than 10 cm high. Its deep-pink to magenta flowers are formed in upright clusters and its leathery evergreen leaves with slightly rolled edges are clustered at the tips of sparsely branched stems.

Fig. 9d.17. *Left:* Lapland rosebay (*Rhododendron lapponicum*, Atigun Gorge, ADH). *Right:* Alpine azalea (*Kalmia procumbens*, Toolik Field Station, ADH).

Fig. 9d.18. Lapland diapensia (*Diapensia lapponica*, Atigun Pass, ADH).

As with many arctic angiosperms, the production of the flower buds of *R. lapponicum* begins at least one year prior to blooming.

The bearberries (*Arctous*) are common in heath communities, particularly on well-drained river terraces, glacial moraines, and kames. Two species are easily distinguished by their fruit: red bearberry (*A. rubra*, Fig. 9d.16) has bright-red berries while those of alpine bearberry (*A. alpine*, Fig. 9d.16) are black. Further, the leaves of the alpine bearberry are relatively thick and after senescing they persist on the plant for several years, but the thinner leaves of the red bearberry fall off each winter. Both species are dwarf shrubs that form long, trailing mats of stems and rhizomes. Their fruits provide food for numerous mammals and birds.

Lapland Diapensia (Diapensiaceae)

Diapensia lapponica (**Fig. 9d.18**) is an evergreen, cushion-forming dwarf shrub of windswept slopes and exposed ridges, where it forms low (about 1–5 cm high) cushions anchored by a taproot containing annuli that allow scientists to estimate the plant's age. Cushions of *D. lapponica* reach ages of 50 years or more, with plants almost 400 years old being reported.

10

Invertebrates

Compared with temperate regions of North America, the invertebrate diversity of the North Slope is low. This is attributed to the effects of harsh winters and short, cool summers; low precipitation; and low plant diversity and productivity. The invertebrates of the North Slope provide numerous examples of adaptations that overcome these environmental challenges. The North Slope, as part of Beringia,[1] is particularly notable because it provided a refuge for arctic invertebrate species that were extirpated elsewhere during the widespread continental glaciations of the Pleistocene.

The invertebrates of the North Slope are dominated by insects, arachnids, and crustaceans. By far, the most abundant groups are the mites (Arachnida: Acari) and springtails (Insecta: Collembola). These tiny organisms comprise the soil microfauna and are unlikely to be observed by nonspecialists (**Fig. 10.1**). Nevertheless, they are critical agents of organic matter decomposition, soil production, and nutrient cycling. The numerous species of parasitic lice (Phthiraptera) and fleas (Siphonaptera) that are sheltered by the feathers and fur of arctic birds and mammals are similarly not likely to be encountered (**Fig. 13.10**). The large invertebrate macrofauna, however, is quite conspicuous and provides the focus of this chapter. The major groups of invertebrate macrofauna are mollusks, crustaceans, spiders (Arachnida: Araneae), and insects.

Freeze Tolerance and Freeze Avoidance

The concepts of freeze tolerance and freeze avoidance are central to understanding how all terrestrial and many aquatic invertebrates survive the harsh North Slope winter. Freeze-tolerant invertebrates survive the actual freezing of their tissues. Freeze-avoiding invertebrates survive subzero temperatures only by allowing their body fluids to supercool (i.e.,

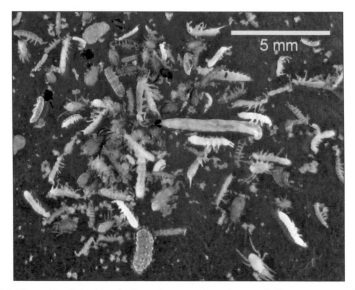

Fig. 10.1. The soils of the North Slope host an abundant and diverse microarthropod community. Mites (Acarina), springtails (Collembola), and fly larvae (Diptera) collected from heath soils (Kuparuk River, ADH) are all shown. Soil microarthropods play important ecological roles by building soil, facilitating the release of nutrients from dead organic matter, and presenting prey for larger arthropods.

body fluid temperatures drop below 0°C without freezing).[2] Although often presented as either-or strategies, many species combine attributes of both. For example, some species tolerate freezing of their haemolymph (invertebrate blood) and gut contents while avoiding freezing of their cell contents via the production of special protective compounds (cryoprotectants). It is important to realize that an organism's ability to attain a state of freeze tolerance or avoidance requires a period of "cold hardening" for the production of cryoprotectants. The timing of the cold hardening is a critical part of the annual cycle that usually begins when a specific seasonal temperature threshold is reached.

The most important mechanism imparting freeze tolerance to invertebrates is the controlled dehydration of their cells. This reduces the risk of formation of damaging ice crystals. The process of dehydration is initiated by ice-nucleating agents. These small proteins accumulate in the haemolymph (insect blood), where they catalyze the formation of ice crystals in extracellular spaces during freezing temperatures. Controlled dehydration of cells results as water diffuses from their cytoplasm to join the rapidly forming extracellular ice crystals.

Invertebrates that are freeze avoiders produce cryoprotectants that reduce the freezing point of their tissues. Although hard to imagine, some arctic freeze-avoiding insects can supercool to temperatures exceeding −60°C.[3] The most common cryoprotectant used by freeze-avoiding invertebrates is glycerol, although a number of other compounds have been identified, including alcohols, sugars, proteins, and lipids. The synthesis of glycerol during cold hardening may be related to the breakdown of mitochondria (energy-producing cell structures), enhancing anaerobic respiration and thus the production of glycogen, a precursor of glycerol. The process of cold hardening may thus require a period of anaerobic metabolism during summer involving a period of apparent aestivation (inactivity). In any event, once an individual is in a supercooled state it is in danger of flash freezing if it contacts ice crystals, which function as ice nuclei.[4] This danger is reduced by preparing cocoons and other protective hibernacula. Prior to overwintering, queens of yellowjacket wasps (*Vespula vulgaris*) in the Fairbanks region, for example, clear spaces within the forest litter layer where they suspend themselves by their mandibles, thus reducing the risk of contact with ice nuclei. The ability to supercool is further enhanced by the evacuation of gut contents to rid the body of potential ice nuclei, such as dust, food particles, and bacteria.

Regardless of the physiological strategy used for overwintering, the selection of an appropriate habitat is critical to survival. This selection process usually requires a trade-off between exposure to different levels of temperature and the length of the summer season. By overwintering in an exposed habitat where little snow accumulates, such as ridges or the tops of kames, an organism can begin summer activity earlier than those that overwinter beneath the deep snow accumulating in valleys or the lee side of ridges. On the other hand, the insulating effect of snow moderates the effect of winter cold snaps. The insulation provided by 25 cm of snow, for example, will allow the temperature of the soil's surface to be maintained at a cozy 0°C when air temperatures hover at −20°C. Consequently, soil temperatures in protected North Slope habitats where snow accumulates rarely drop below −5 to −10°C. This is well within the range of supercooling capabilities of many freeze-avoiding invertebrates. Finally, many freshwater invertebrates are able to avoid freezing by living in habitats that contain water year-round, such as deep lakes and perennial spring-fed streams.

Insects

Mayflies (Ephemeroptera) and Dragonflies (Odonata)

The aquatic larvae of mayflies and dragonflies and damselflies are important members of freshwater communities worldwide. Nineteen mayfly species occur on the North Slope. Their larvae (**Fig. 10.2**) are abundant in both ponds and streams, where they feed on algae and decomposing organic matter (detritus); they reach their highest level of species richness in streams. The short-lived terrestrial adults (**Fig. 10.2**) of most arctic species emerge in late July or August. Dragonflies and damselflies are relatively uncommon on the North Slope, where six species have been recorded (**Fig. 10.3**). Both terrestrial adults and their aquatic larvae are predators. On the North Slope their larvae are found in lakes and ponds that do not freeze completely during winter.

Stoneflies (Plecoptera) and Grasshoppers (Orthoptera)

Sixteen species of stoneflies (Plecoptera) and two species of grasshoppers (Orthoptera: Acrididae) are found on the North Slope. Although larvae of most species of stoneflies are stream-dwelling, those of some species occur in lakes. Larvae of some species of stonefly feed on detritus and algae, whereas others specialize on invertebrate prey (**Fig. 10.4**). The terrestrial adults feed on algal films and lichens, although adults of some taxa may not feed at all. Many arctic species are brachypterous, meaning that their wings are short and nonfunctional (**Fig. 10.4**). Brachyptery is particularly common among arctic insect species (e.g., grasshoppers, crane flies, moths) and is an adaptation to the short growing season that allows energy and nutrients that would otherwise be used to produce flight muscles to be diverted to other structures, particularly

Fig. 10.2. Mayflies (Ephemeroptera). *Left:* Subimago of *Baetis bicaudatus* (Baetidae: Ephemeroptera, Ivishak River, ADH). Unlike all other insects, most mayfly species molt once during the terrestrial winged stage, resulting in two winged life-cycle stages. The first winged stage is the subimago. The subimago then molts to produce the imago, which is the sexually mature form. *Right:* Larvae of *Acentrella* (Baetidae, Kuparuk River, M.R. Kendrick). The spongy yellow-green mass in the center of the picture is a colony of stalked diatoms.

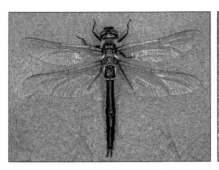
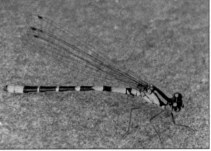

Fig. 10.3. Dragonflies and damselflies (Odonata). *Left:* Treeline emerald (*Somatochlora sahlbergi*, Corduliidae, Toolik Field Station, ADH). *Right:* Northern bluet (*Enallagma cyathigerum*, Coenagrionidae, Oksrukuyik Creek, ADH).

Fig. 10.4. Stoneflies (Plecoptera). *Left:* Larva of *Alaskaperla* (Chloroperlidae, Kuparuk River, ADH). The predacious chloroperlids are widespread in North Slope streams. Adults are recognized by their green color. *Left center:* Adult male of *Arcynopteryx compacta* (Perlodidae, Toolik Lake, ADH). The relatively large predacious larvae of the Perlodidae are found in deep lakes and spring streams that do not freeze. The specimen shown is brachypterous. *Right center:* Larva of *Nemoura arctica* (Nemouridae, Kuparuk River, ADH). *N. arctica* is the most abundant and widespread stonefly on the North Slope. Larvae occur in essentially all mountain and foothills streams, where they feed on decaying organic matter and biofilms. *Right:* Adult of *Zapada haysi* (Nemouridae, Ivishak Hot Spring, ADH). On the North Slope larvae of *Zapada* are found primarily in spring streams.

the ovaries. In essence, it is hypothesized that a brachypterous insect trades the ability to fly in exchange for a higher probability of successful reproduction. The brachypterous spur-throated grasshopper *Melanoplus frigida* (**Fig. 10.5**) is widespread in mountain and foothills habitats. As a relatively large insect that presumably completes growth and development over the short arctic summer, *M. frigida* is unusual among arctic insects, which often require more than one year to complete growth and development.

Fig. 10.5. Grasshoppers (Orthoptera). *Left:* Young specimen of the spur-throated grass-hopper (*Melanoplus frigida*) resting on a *Dryas* flower in late May (Atigun Gorge, ADH). *Right:* The brachypterous adult form of *M. frigida* in early August (Ivishak River, ADH).

A Fly's World

Unlike temperate and tropical regions, where insect communities are dominated by beetles (Coleoptera), true flies (Diptera), butterflies and moths (Lepidoptera), and bees, wasps, and ants (Hymenoptera), the insect communities of the Arctic are dominated by the Diptera. In fact, true flies make up only about 15 percent of the global insect fauna but contribute a whopping 50 percent to that of the North American low Arctic! Similarly, the Earth's beetle fauna outnumbers fly species by about two to one, but the tables are turned in the North American Arctic, where there are about four fly species for every beetle species.

As adults, the true flies are distinguished from other insects by having a single pair of wings. Their hind wings are reduced to a pair of stubs (halteres) that have a stabilizing function similar to the gyroscopes of jet airplanes. Their larvae are also easily recognized because they lack the thoracic legs typical of the larvae of other insect orders. Flies perform a number of important ecological roles in the Arctic. Midges (Chironomidae) and crane flies (Tipulidae), for example, are abundant prey for fish, birds, and shrews, and the adults of numerous species of flies are important pollinators of tundra flowers. Flies are relatively inefficient pollinators, due to their lack of flower constancy (i.e., a tendency to visit flowers of a single species) and a small body size that limits the amount of pollen they can carry. Nevertheless, they are the primary pollinators of arctic plants due to their sheer abundance and behaviors that include feeding and basking within flowers. A summer visitor to the tundra who takes a moment to search is likely to be surprised at the number of flowers that have flies basking within (**Fig. 9.2**).

Finally, no summer trip to the tundra would be complete without contributing a yarn or two to the rich store of tales about the legendary swarms of biting flies, including mosquitoes (Culicidae), black flies

(Simuliidae), and horseflies (Tabanidae). Although adding little to overall species richness, the mosquitoes and the parasitic bot flies (Oestridae) have had a major effect on the evolution of both annual and day-to-day movement behaviors of caribou with important consequences for the dynamics of the North Slope ecosystem.

Mosquitoes (Culicidae)

The poorly drained landscape and relatively warm summers of the interior North Slope result in excellent mosquito habitat. Two genera of mosquitoes are found here. The most notorious is *Aedes* (also referred to as *Ochlerotatus* in recent publications, **Fig. 10.6**). Species of *Aedes* are responsible for the intense, sometimes suffocating swarms that occur from late June through mid-July. Common North Slope species include *A. communis, A. hexodontus, A. impiger, A. nigripes,* and *A. punctor.* Of these, *A. hexodontus* is arguably the most troublesome. The second genus of mosquitoes occurring on the North Slope is *Culiseta.* Biting females of *C. alaskensis* (**Fig. 10.6**) are active only for a short period following snowmelt in May.

Mosquito Life Cycle

Adult *Aedes* emerge from tundra pools during late June and early July, when males congregate in swarms (leks) to attract females. Following mating, females show considerable variation in reproductive strategy. Some feed only on nectar and produce small clutches of eggs; others seek blood meals from vertebrate hosts located using cues such as temperature, CO_2 concentration, and color. The payback for the time and risk required to secure a blood meal is enormous. Successful blood-seeking females produce a large egg clutch. Unsuccessful blood-seeking females may still produce egg clutches, but these will be small. Females of *A. impiger*, for example, produce an average of three to six eggs after meals of nectar alone while those feeding on blood produce clutches of about 50 eggs. This is a "bet hedging" strategy. Because of short summers and low host abundance, the probability that a female will be unable to obtain a blood meal is high. In the absence of a blood meal, all is not lost—she can still produce a small clutch of eggs. Birds (particularly nesting females, which must remain immobile to avoid detection), caribou, moose, muskoxen, and, of course, humans are all significant hosts for mosquitoes on the North Slope.

During mid- to late summer, female *Aedes* lay clutches of eggs in habitats likely to receive water during spring snowmelt. These eggs

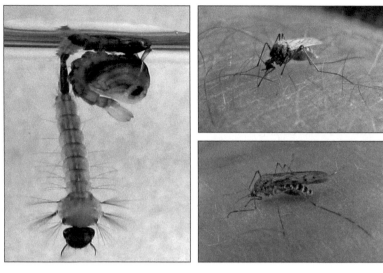

Fig. 10.6. Mosquitoes (Diptera: Culicidae). *Left: Aedes* larva and pupa. The larva is on the left and is suspended from the water film by the spiracles of its posterior breathing tube. The pupa is on the right, suspended from the water's surface by its thoracic "gills" (Toolik Field Station, ADH). *Upper right:* Female *Aedes* taking a blood meal from host (Ivishak River, ADH). *Lower right:* Female *Culiseta alaskensis* taking a blood meal (Toolik Field Station, ADH).

remain dormant through winter and hatch shortly after becoming submerged in spring, even at water temperatures near 0°C. If not flooded, the eggs may remain viable for several years. Following hatching, larvae feed on suspended organic particles, algae, and protozoa. Arctic *Aedes* larvae grow at relatively low water temperatures, with "developmental zero" (temperature below which no growth occurs) ranging from 1 to 3°C depending upon species. By seeking warm microhabitats (e.g., shallow pool margins), larvae are able to select the temperature of their surroundings to some degree. Even at mean temperatures as low as 9°C, larvae of some arctic *Aedes* will mature in less than a month. The peak emergence of mosquitoes on the North Slope usually occurs within five to six weeks following snowmelt. Females of most arctic mosquito species are able to pursue hosts at temperatures as low as 5°C. Optimum activity, however, occurs at about 18°C. As temperatures climb toward 25°C mosquito activity decreases significantly, especially in direct sunlight.

Culiseta has a life cycle that differs greatly from *Aedes*. Overwintered females of *C. alaskensis* seek blood meals shortly after snowmelt in early spring. Rafts of eggs are produced on the surface of tundra pools by early summer and the resulting larvae pupate as early as mid-July. Adults emerge shortly thereafter and mate. Mated females seek sheltered habitats, where they hibernate until the following spring when they emerge as "snow mosquitoes." Although *Culiseta* species can be important pests in the Alaskan interior, *C. alaskensis* is relatively scarce on the North Slope, where it is restricted to sheltered habitats in the mountains and northern foothills.

The abundance of mosquitoes in any given summer is determined to a large degree by precipitation during the preceding winter and summer. For example, the abundance of mosquitoes during the summer of 2010 was strongly affected by precipitation during the winter of 2008–2009 and the summer of 2009. This is because the pattern of precipitation during this period controlled the number of adults emerging to successfully deposit eggs during the summer of 2009, and thus the number of larvae hatching in 2010. In a nutshell, a winter with heavy snow followed by a wet summer will likely produce a bumper crop of mosquitoes the next summer.

Although there are reports of the death of caribou calves due to exsanguination (blood loss) from mosquito attacks on the North Slope, these appear to be mostly anecdotal. Nevertheless, there is little doubt that harassment by mosquitoes has strong negative effects on their hosts. At the broadest scale, mosquito harassment underlies the evolution of the migratory behavior of caribou such that females move to the windy coastal plain to escape mosquitoes while calving. At a narrower scale, mosquito harassment causes potential hosts to seek local refuges. Caribou, for example, attempt to escape mosquitoes by congregating on aufeis or exposed, windy hilltops while marmots retreat to their burrows and moose submerge themselves in ponds. During years when mosquitoes are exceedingly abundant, the behavior of some animals can be downright weird. During the summer of 1995, harassment by mosquitoes was so intense that one adult moose apparently lost all fear of humans and stood for days in the breeze of an exhaust fan at the Sag River DOT Camp of the Alaska Department of Transportation near the Dalton Highway. During the same summer another adult male immersed himself up to his neck in Toolik Lake for several days. Such behaviors may provide respite from mosquitoes, but they are not optimal behaviors for obtaining food during the short summer season that is used to accumulate fat reserves required for successful overwintering. Arctic mosquitoes are clearly annoying to the point where they interfere with otherwise more optimal behaviors, but can they really present a direct a threat to life?

Mosquitoes and Humans

Scientists at the Toolik Field Station have been involved in an informal but macabre contest for many years—the "mosquito squish." The rules of the contest are simple: during years of great mosquito abundance, an area of skin or clothing is gently slapped, and the squished mosquitoes are counted. The 1994 record of 278 mosquitoes is held by Robert Golder, who was a research assistant working with the Marine Biological Laboratory (Woods Hole, Massachusetts) at that time. Assuming that the area of Bob's hand was 100 cm^2 and that it takes 1.5 minutes for a mosquito to fill its crop, about 110 bites/cm^2/hr were possible under the extraordinary conditions of 1994. To put this in perspective, consider that a 64 kg person will experience symptoms of mild anemia after losing about 675 mL (200,000 to 700,000 bites, assuming mosquito crop volume is 1–3 µL) of blood and severe anemia after losing about 1,350 mL (400,000 to 1.5 million bites) of blood. Given a completely exposed skin surface (body surface of a 64 kg, 1.7 m tall individual is about 1.7 m^2) and a more moderate rate of mosquito activity—let's say 10 rather than 110 bites/cm^2/hr—blood loss to the point of severe anemia would occur in about 11 hours and death in about 22 hours. The example used is extreme (a naked person stranded on the tundra no less!), and additional effects, such as immune responses, have been ignored. Even with these caveats, the threat of mosquitoes to unprotected hosts on the tundra should be clear.

On the North Slope, one often hears remarks such as "at least the mosquitoes around here don't carry diseases." Unfortunately, this is not true. Fortunately, however, the risk of contracting a mosquito-borne disease is low. Encephalitis-causing arboviruses (viruses transmitted to hosts through the bites of arthropods) of the genus *Bunyavirus* have been isolated from *Aedes* mosquitoes on the North Slope. These include both the Jamestown Canyon and snowshoe hare viruses. The primary reservoir host for the Jamestown Canyon virus is likely moose. Despite its name, the primary host for the snowshoe hare virus is unknown because a diverse group of mammals and birds can be infected. These viruses cause flu-like symptoms in humans and may also be responsible for central nervous system diseases such as meningitis and encephalitis. Actual cases directly attributed to these viruses are few, however, and symptoms are usually mild or unrecognized. Long-term residents of the North Slope are obviously at greatest risk of infection. A 1999 study of the residents of Anaktuvuk Pass (a village in the Brooks Range west of Atigun Pass) showed that 21 percent of individuals tested had been exposed to the Jamestown Canyon virus and 2 percent had been exposed to the snowshoe hare virus. In comparison, only 5 percent of the residents of Kaktovik (a village located on Barter Island) showed evidence of exposure to the Jamestown Canyon virus, and no individuals showed evidence of exposure to the snowshoe hare virus.

Midges (Chironomidae, Chaoboridae) and Crane Flies (Tipulidae)

The nonbiting or chironomid midges (Chironomidae) are critical to aquatic and terrestrial food webs on the North Slope. Adults, which resemble mosquitoes but do not feed, are consumed by spiders, fish, and birds (**Fig. 10.7**). Larvae, which may be aquatic or terrestrial depending upon species, feed on decomposing organic matter (detritus), biofilms, or invertebrate prey (**Fig. 10.7**). They are themselves prey for numerous predators. Arctic midges may also be relatively long-lived. The larvae of those dwelling in coastal plain ponds may take as long as seven years to complete growth and development. Adults of the phantom midges (Chaoboridae: *Chaoborus*) are similar to those of the chironomids. Their bizarre zooplanktivorous larvae, however, feed by capturing prey with grasping antennae while suspended in the water column of lakes and ponds. The position of larvae in the water column is controlled by

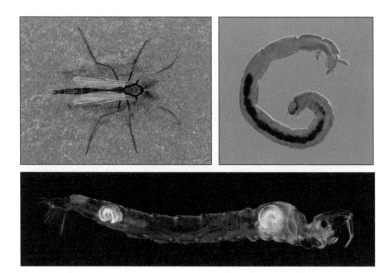

Fig. 10.7 Midges (Diptera: Chironomidae, Chaoboridae). ***Upper left:*** Adult male nonbiting midge (Chironomidae, Toolik Field Station, ADH). Note the bushy antennae used to detect vibrations made by flying females. ***Upper right:*** Nonbiting midge larva (*Chironomus*). The red color is due to hemoglobin (Toolik Field Station, ADH). ***Lower:*** Larva of a phantom midge (Chaoboridae, *Chaoborus americanus*). Larvae of Chaoborus capture passing prey with grasping antennae while suspended motionless in the water column of lakes and ponds. The silvery bubbles, both anterior and posterior, are gas-filled "hydrostatic" organs that are used to maintain the position of the larva in the water column (Toolik Field Station, ADH).

gas-filled organs appearing as silvery internal bubbles (**Fig. 10.7**). Crane fly larvae (Tipulidae) are abundant in terrestrial and aquatic habitats where most feed on decaying organic matter; some species are predators (**Fig. 10.8**). The terrestrial adults do not feed (**Fig. 10.8**). Like midges, crane flies are important prey in both terrestrial and aquatic habitats.

Black Flies (Simuliidae)

Black flies (**Fig. 10.9**) are the second most numerous blood-seeking insect on the North Slope. As with mosquitoes, only females feed on blood. Although black flees are closely related to mosquitoes, the nonspecialist will see little obvious resemblance. Adult black flies are short, stout, and humpbacked while mosquitoes are long and skinny. There is even less of a resemblance between larvae. Mosquito larvae inhabit still pools, where they feed on particles suspended just beneath the surface film (**Fig. 10.6**). Larvae of most black flies anchor themselves in the most rapid flow of streams, where they use specialized, fan-like filtering devices formed from modified mouthparts to capture drifting organic particles on which they feed (**Fig. 10.9**). Larvae of the genus *Gymnopais*, however, feed directly on films of algae and bacteria and have lost the ability to filter feed.

At least seven genera of black flies occur on the North Slope (*Cnephia, Gymnopais, Helodon, Metacnephia, Prosimulium, Simulium, Stegopterna*). They are abundant in mountain and foothill streams,

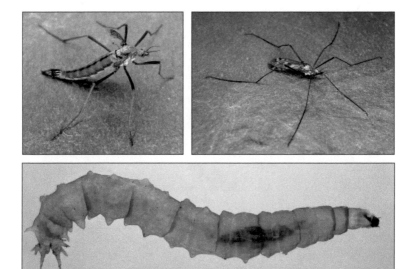

Fig. 10.8. Crane flies (Diptera: Tipulidae). *Upper left:* A brachypterous female crane fly (Toolik Field Station, ADH). *Upper right:* A fully winged male crane fly (*Tipula*, Toolik Field Station, ADH). *Lower:* Stream-dwelling crane fly larva (*Tipula*, Kuparuk River, ADH).

where they are among the most productive insects. The typical black fly life cycle begins with overwintering eggs that hatch shortly after snow-melt. Larvae then grow and develop over a period of about six weeks, and adults emerge in late July or early August. Eggs laid in late summer may remain dormant for as long as 8–10 months. Variations of this cycle include possible overwintering of larvae for some species of *Simulium*.

Not all species of black flies require blood meals to produce eggs. Females of all North Slope species of *Cnephia*, *Prosimulium*, and *Gymnopais*, and some species of *Helodon*, *Stegopterna*, *Metacnephia*, and *Simulium*, do not feed as adults. Such non-blood-feeding species are more common in the Arctic than in temperate and tropical regions. This is attributed to the long developmental times for larvae that—in theory—allow them to accumulate sufficient fat stores for the successful production of eggs by nonfeeding adults. This appears to be an adaptation to the low probability of locating a vertebrate host in the short arctic summer.

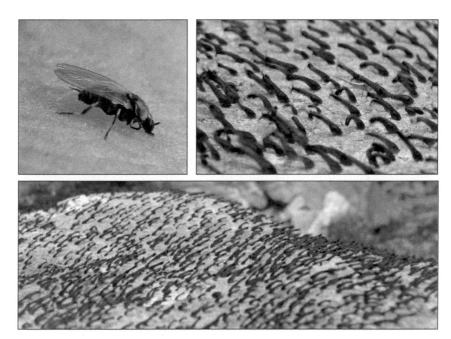

Fig. 10.9. Black flies. ***Upper left:*** Adult female black fly (*Simulium*) taking a blood meal (Simuliidae, Ivishak River, ADH). ***Lower:*** Black fly larvae in their stream habitat (Ivishak River, ADH). ***Upper right:*** Detail of a group of black fly larvae in their stream habitat. The posterior of each larva is anchored to the rock by microscopic hooks engaged with a pad of silk that it has cemented to the rock's surface. Once anchored, larvae are free to extend their heads into the current, allowing them to filter food particles with specially modified mouthparts ("labial fans"; Ivishak River, ADH).

Horse Flies (Tabanidae)

Although only three species of horse flies (Tabanidae) occur on the North Slope, they can be abundant at times with as many as a dozen or so adult females pestering a single host. The most abundant species, *Hybomitra frontalis* (**Fig. 10.10**), has the widest range of all North American horseflies. Adults are about 15 mm in length and gray in color. Their predacious larvae require two to three years to mature and live in the sediments of wet meadows. Both adult males and females depend on a diet of nectar for energy required for flight. Females use the protein acquired from blood meals to produce eggs. In some cases, however, nutrients accumulated during the larval stage may be adequate to mature a small clutch of eggs.

Bot Flies (Oestridae)

Two species of bot flies (Oestridae) are found on the North Slope: the caribou warble fly (*Hypoderma tarandi,* **Fig. 10.10**) and the caribou nasopharyngeal bot fly (*Cephenemyia trompe,* **Fig. 10.10**). Their larvae are endoparasites (internal parasites) of caribou. The free-living adults do not feed but devote this stage of their life cycle to mating and locating hosts. The main cues that bot flies use to locate caribou are movement and CO_2 concentration. The life cycle of *H. tarandi* begins when females attach their eggs to the hair of the legs and lower body of a caribou. Following hatching, larvae penetrate the host's skin and migrate to the spine and rump, where they cut an airhole and begin to feed. The lump that is caused by the growing larva is called a *warble*. After about one year, the mature larvae exit the warble through the airhole and drop to the ground, where they pupate. Larvae of warble flies taken from the hides of freshly slaughtered caribou were considered a tasty food by the Nunamiut. The life cycle of *C. trompe* begins when a female deposits larvae (rather than eggs) near the nostrils of a caribou. The larvae move into the host's nasal sinuses or throat, where they attach and begin to feed. Mature larvae detach and make their way out through the nostrils the following spring, whereupon they fall to the ground and pupate.

Of the two species of bot flies, *C. trompe* most seriously affects its host. Relatively severe infestations (e.g., 50 or more larvae) can result in suffocation or pneumonia. In comparison, the pathological effects of the *H. tarandi* are relatively mild except in cases of exceptionally high infestations. Adult females of both species cause significant stress to caribou when they attempt to lay eggs or deposit larvae. Caribou react by running and jumping, and mass attacks can result in debilitation.

Fig. 10.10. Bot flies, warble flies (Diptera: Oestridae), and horse flies (Diptera: Tabanidae). *Upper left:* Caribou nasopharyngeal bot fly (*Cephenemyia trompe*, Toolik Field Station, ADH). *Upper right:* Caribou warble fly (*Hypoderma tarandi*, Toolik Field Station, JWS). *Lower left:* The bumblebee *Bombus flavifrons*. The North Slope bot flies are apparent mimics of this common bumblebee. The banding pattern of *B. flavifrons* and *H. tarandi* are both yellow-black-yellow-red. The banding pattern of *C. trompe*, however, is black-black-yellow-red (Toolik Field Station, ADH). *Lower right:* Horse fly (*Hybomitra frontalis*, Toolik Field Station, ADH).

Caribou respond to the presence of abundant bot flies by assembling into compact herds. Individuals at the edge of the herd remain susceptible to bot fly attacks. Those in the center, however, are protected. Such aggregative behavior, which has been called the "selfish herd response," reduces the per capita infestation rate.

The adults of *H. tarandi* and *C. trompe* are impressive flies. They are quite large with strongly contrasting bands of black, orange, and red fuzz. Given their size and visibility, and the fat-rich eggs of the females, one might expect that they might be prime targets for insectivorous birds. Apparently, however, they are protected by Batesian mimicry, which occurs when an unprotected species (one that has no defensive mechanism such as a sting or disagreeable odor) gains protection by resembling a species with a defensive mechanism. In this case, *H. tarandi* shows a banding pattern identical to that of the bumblebee *Bombus flavifrons* (yellow-black-yellow-red), not to mention similar body size and proportions (**Fig. 10.10**). *C. trompe* varies from the banding pattern of *B. flavifrons* only by having the anterior portion of its thorax black rather than yellow (e.g., black-black-yellow-red). Mimicry of bumblebees presumably deters would-be vertebrate predators from attacking these otherwise defenseless flies. This mimicry was noticed by the Swedish scientist Modeer, who in 1786 first named this bot fly—he called it *trompe* after the French *tromper*, which means to deceive.

Hot-Blooded Bumblebees

The Hymenoptera is the second most diverse insect order of the North Slope. Most of this diversity is contributed by the primitive sawflies (Tenthredinidae, **Fig. 10.11**) and the tiny parasitic wasps (e.g., Ichneumonidae, Braconidae); the diversity of the social Hymenoptera—the ants and social bees and wasps (**Fig. 10.12**)—is much lower. What the social Hymenoptera of the North Slope lack in diversity, however, is made up in conspicuousness.

Bumblebees (**Fig. 10.13**) are the only social insects occurring in the high Arctic (e.g., Ellesmere Island, Canada), where two species are found (*Bombus polaris* and *B. hyperboreus*). In the less extreme environment of the North Slope at least nine different species have been recorded. Here it is not unusual to find queens foraging for nectar and pollen on willow blossoms during snowstorms in early May when air temperatures are a few degrees below 0°C. In fact, they have

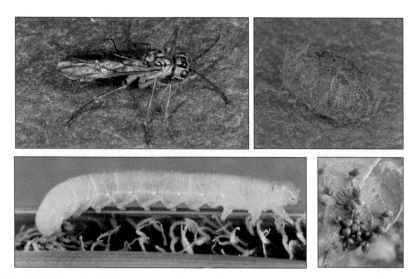

Fig. 10.11. Sawflies (Hymenoptera: Tenthredinidae) are primitive wasps with herbivorous, cocoon-forming, caterpillar-like larvae. Most arctic species feed on or within (in the case of gall-forming species) *Salix* leaves. Nesting warblers often provision their young with sawfly larvae. *Upper left:* Sawfly (*Rhogogaster virescens*, Kuparuk River, ADH). *Lower left:* Sawfly larva (Toolik Field Station, ADH). *Upper right:* Sawfly cocoon (Toolik Field Station, ADH). *Lower right:* Leaf-bean galls containing larvae of the sawfly *Pontania* on felt-leaf willow leaf (Oksrukuyik Creek, ADH).

Fig. 10.12. Yellowjackets (Hymenoptera: Vespidae) and ants (Hymenoptera: Formicidae). *Left:* Paper nest of *Vespula vulgaris* colony (Ivishak River, ADH). North Slope yellowjacket colonies are small (usually fewer than 100 individuals) and are usually in riparian shrubs, although some are constructed in underground cavities. Both *V. vulgaris* (yellow-and-black species) and *Dolichovespula norvegicoides* (black-and-white species) are common in the mountains and foothills. Yellowjackets are primarily predators of other insects. *Right:* Colony of the ant *Leptothorax acervorum* (Toolik Field Station, ADH). Adult workers (w), pupae (p), larvae (l), and eggs (e) are all visible. Ants are rare but widespread on the North Slope, with colonies reported from Anaktuvuk Pass, Toolik Lake, Slope Mountain, and Happy Valley.

been observed actively foraging at air temperatures as low as –3.7°C. Bumblebees are able to function under such conditions because they are truly hot-blooded.

While flying, the internal temperature of a bumblebee's thorax can reach or exceed 39°C, even when air temperatures are below 5°C. Such high body temperatures—the human body temperature is maintained at 37°C—are the result of heat produced by the contraction of flight muscles fueled by a diet of high-energy sugar combined with an effective insulating pile (fuzz) that may be more than 1 mm deep for some species. By selectively shunting heated haemolymph (insect blood) from thorax to abdomen, bumblebees can regulate their abdominal temperatures at about 30°C over a range of air temperatures from 0°C to 22–24°C. Even when resting, they are able to maintain high internal temperatures by continually shivering their flight muscles.

Bumblebee Life Cycle

The environment of the North Slope presents a rigorous challenge to bumblebees and other social insects. During a brief 9–10-week growing

Fig. 10.13. Bumblebees (Hymenoptera: Bombidae) are abundant in the mountains and foothills, where five species are common. ***Left:*** *Bombus moderatus* queen taking nectar from felt-leaf willow catkin (Ivishak River, ADH). *B. moderatus* is probably the easiest North Slope bumblebee to identify. Its abdomen shows consecutive black, yellow, black, and white bands (anterior to posterior). Some authorities consider *B. moderatus* to be a synonym of *B. lucorum*, a common north Eurasian species with an essentially identical color pattern. In contrast to *B. moderatus*, *B. flavifrons*, *B. silvicola,* and *B. frigidus* all show red, orange, and black bands (e.g., Fig. 10.10). ***Upper right:*** *B. fernaldae* queen foraging on *Arnica* blossom (Ivishak River, ADH). *B. fernaldae* is a yellow-and-black bumblebee that differs from the other common bumblebees of the North Slope by having no white or red bands. ***Lower right:*** Adult solitary bee (Megachilidae, *Osmia*) foraging on an *Anemone* blossom. At least three species of solitary bees occur on the North Slope. Unlike bumblebees, all females are fertile and they nest independently.

season they must found colonies capable of producing the next generation of drones and queens. Consequently, a successful queen produces not one but a minimum of two generations of offspring—one generation of female workers who then assist in the production of a second generation of males and queens. In comparison, almost all other arctic insects (with the exception of a few species of aphids and yellowjackets) require at least one year to complete a generation and many species require several years.

The ability of bumblebees to grow and develop so rapidly is related to their ability to heat their nests using physiological mechanisms, a common strategy of social insects worldwide. Yet even among the social insects, the queens of arctic bumblebees are exceptional because they can produce a generation of workers in less than three weeks after emerging from winter dormancy, a rate much faster than bumblebees from other regions. This unusual ability is attributed to three factors: 1) the ovaries of arctic queens mature at an unusually rapid rate because of high abdominal temperatures compared with temperate queens; 2) they initiate nests very early in spring; and 3) they are able to forage for pollen and nectar for relatively long periods each day due to continuous sunlight, thus increasing the daily rate of food delivery to a developing brood.

The life cycle of bumblebees in the foothills and mountains of the North Slope begins when queens emerge from winter dormancy during May (*B. fernaldae* provides an exception; see below). Queens of the more common species of bumblebees (*B. frigidus*, *B. silvicola*, *B. moderatus*, or *B. flavifrons*) begin foraging within 24 hours of the first willow blooms in mid- to late May. Within a few days, they start searching for a nest site. Good nest sites provide shelter from wind and ample supplies of fur, feathers, mosses, or dried leaves. These materials are fashioned into a tightly packed sphere about 5 cm in diameter with a central chamber and a single entrance. Abandoned vole or lemming nests or the feather-lined nests of birds such as snow buntings are sometimes chosen.

Once her insulated nesting chamber is prepared, the queen provisions it with a thick pad of pollen upon which she lays about 8 to 16 eggs that are covered with a wax canopy. The queen also forms a wax nectar pot (about 2–3 cm high and 1–2 cm in diameter) in which she stores food reserves that enable her to produce physiological heat when the weather is too cold for foraging. After sufficient provisions are collected, the queen incubates her eggs by pressing her heated abdomen against them. Except when foraging for pollen and nectar supplies, the queen continuously incubates her eggs and developing brood. By shivering her flight muscles, a queen is able to maintain the temperature of her nest at about 25–30°C. During the queen's foraging trips of 30 minutes or so, however, the nest temperature may decline to 20°C.

The first generation of offspring may be produced in as little as two to three weeks and are invariably female workers that soon take over the duties of nest construction, brood tending, heat generation, and foraging while the queen does little else but lay eggs. Once a sufficient number of workers is produced, nest temperatures can be maintained at 30–35°C with little variation. When the colony reaches a size threshold (probably fewer than 150 bees in the Arctic) worker production ends and queen and drone (male bumblebee) production begins. The new queens mate during late summer and begin accumulating fat reserves and producing cryoprotectants such as glycerols, allowing them to supercool without freezing during the upcoming winter. As summer wanes queens prepare overwintering chambers in shallow soils and organic debris. These chambers are usually 5–10 cm deep and on south-facing slopes that tend to lose their snow cover early in spring.

Unlike the other bumblebees likely to be encountered on the North Slope, *B. fernaldae* is a cuckoo bumblebee (**Fig. 10.13**). The queens of cuckoo bumblebees emerge from dormancy relatively late in the season, enter established colonies of other bumblebee species, kill the resident queen, and begin laying eggs. The workers of the host colony then proceed to raise the queens and males of the cuckoo bumblebee. Cuckoo bumblebees produce only queens and males; there is no worker caste. Queens even lack the pollen-gathering structure (corbicula) found on the hind leg of females of other bumblebees. The degree of host specificity varies among species of cuckoo bumblebees. Some parasitize one host species and others parasitize several species. The host for *B. fernaldae* is unknown but is probably *B. frigidus, B. silvicola,* or *B. flavifrons.*

Butterflies and Moths (Lepidoptera)

At least 50 species of butterflies and 74 species of moths have been reported from the North Slope, making them the fourth largest contributor to insect richness of the region, following the Diptera, Hymenoptera, and Coleoptera. The life cycles of most North Slope butterfly species require two years or more with most time spent as dormant larvae. The adult phase of the life cycle is characterized by short periods of mass activity from late June through mid-July. There is great year-to-year variability in abundance, with some years having numerous butterflies and others very few. Less is known about the life cycles of arctic moths, but these can be long, approaching or exceeding a decade for some species.

Butterflies

The major families of truly arctic butterflies include the sulphurs and whites (Pieridae *Pieris, Colias*), the lesser fritillaries (Nymphalidae *Boloria*), and the alpines and arctics (Nymphalidae *Erebia, Oeneis*). Together these taxa contribute more than 60 percent to the regional species richness. The swallowtails (Papilionidae) and the blues (Lycaenidae) may also be common in some habitats but are not major contributors to regional species richness.

The color of the upper wing surface of the adult arctic whites and sulphurs (*Pieris, Colias,* **Figs. 10.14, 10.15**) ranges from white to olive green to yellow or orange, typically with dark wing margins. The underside of the hind wing is often a dingy green. Their larvae feed on foliage of the Fabaceae, Ericaceae, and Salicaceae. The adults are usually

Fig. 10.14. Butterflies (Lepidoptera). *Upper left: Pieris angelika* (Toolik Field Station, ADH). *Upper right:* Same (Toolik Field Station, ADH). The white arctic is a common tundra butterfly and a member of a widespread and poorly understood species complex. It is believed that *P. angelika* is distinct from other species of North American whites and survived the Pleistocene in a Beringian refuge. Its larvae feed on species of Cruciferaceae. *Lower left: Colias hecla* (Toolik Field Station, ADH). *Lower right:* Same (Oil Spill Hill, ADH). The hecla sulphur is distinguished from other common sulphurs by its deep orange coloration. Its larvae feed on legumes and possibly *Salix*.

Fig. 10.15. Butterflies (Lepidoptera). *Upper left: Colias nastes* (Toolik Field Station, ADH). *Upper right:* Same (Toolik Field Station, ADH). Compared with other North Slope *Colias*, the Labrador sulphur is small and dark. Its larvae feed on legumes. *Lower left: Colias palaeno* (Toolik Field Station, ADH). *Lower right:* Same (Toolik Field Station, ADH). The common yellow sulphur seen on the tundra is likely the palaeno sulphur. Its larvae feed on *Vaccinium*.

observed flying rapidly over the tundra, usually within a meter of the ground. Such ground-hugging flight, typical for arctic butterflies, keeps them in the warm boundary layer. The flight paths of sulphurs, particularly males, are often relatively straight with only occasional stops for basking or nectaring. At least eight species of *Colias* have been reported from the North Slope. Although some species are relatively easy to recognize, others can only be reliably identified by experts.

The lesser fritillaries (*Boloria*, **Fig. 10.16**) are common in mountain and foothill habitats. The wings of the adults of the eight *Boloria* species reported from the North Slope are marked with complex patterns of dark spots against a ginger background. They are rapid, erratic fliers that remain close to the ground and stop frequently to bask. Like the sulphurs, the taxonomy of *Boloria* can be difficult, but most species are identified using color patterns of the underside of the hind wing. Their larvae feed on *Salix*, *Vaccinium*, *Arctous*, and *Bistorta*.

Fig. 10.16. Butterflies (Lepidoptera). *Upper left: Oeneis bore,* male tilting its wings and body to maximize absorption of solar radiation (Toolik Field Station, ADH). *O. bore* is the most abundant "arctic" (the common name for species of *Oeneis*) on the North Slope and can be identified by the white veins on the underside of its hind wing. *Lower left: O. chryxus,* basking male (Toolik Field Station, ADH). *Upper right: Erebia disa* (Toolik Field Station, ADH). *E. disa* is an abundant North Slope "alpine" with an arctic distribution. *Lower right: Boloria freija* using wings to reduce convective cooling (Atigun Gorge, ADH). *B. freija* is a common and widespread arctic and boreal fritillary and the earliest *Boloria* to to emerge in spring. Several other North Slope species of *Boloria* are truly arctic butterflies occurring as far north as the Canadian Arctic Archipelago and Greenland.

The alpines (*Erebia,* **Fig. 10.16**) are dark-brown butterflies, with a low, fluttering flight. They can be extremely abundant in some years, particularly near wet sedge meadows. Most of the nine North Slope species are identified by their wing patterns, which include various combinations of reddish patches and "eye spots." The identification of a few species, however, is difficult, requiring the examination of genitalia. Larvae of all species feed on grasses, sedges, or rushes and pupate on the ground, sometimes in loose, silken cocoons.

The arctics (*Oeneis,* **Fig. 10.16**) are light-brown butterflies, usually without obvious wing patterns. The pigmented scales coating their wings are quickly lost, giving them a slightly gossamer appearance. Unlike the slow, fluttering flight of the alpines, that of the arctics is rapid. They also tend to follow erratic paths with frequent stops for basking. Given their exposed habitat, they are often carried away by wind when disturbed. Males provide an excellent example of hilltopping behavior. Hilltopping occurs when males congregate on the summits of kames and other topographical high points to await females that search for males by flying uphill. Males aggressively defend hilltops by aerial sparring with other encroaching males. Their larvae feed on grasses and sedges. Pupae, which are concealed in silk-lined cells beneath stones, are formed in spring.

Two species of swallowtails are likely to be encountered on the North Slope. First-time visitors to the tundra are often surprised to find these large and striking butterflies in a treeless habitat. The old world swallowtail (*Papilio machaon,* **Fig. 10.17**) is a typical swallowtail of the subfamily Papilioninae. It is the largest butterfly of the North Slope and is immediately recognizable by its bold yellow and black colors. Like *Oeneis,* males of *P. machaon* show hilltopping behavior, so are most likely to be encountered near isolated kames and ridges. Their larvae feed on the leaves and flowers of *Artemesia.*

The second North Slope swallowtail is Eversmann's parnassian (*Parnassius eversmanni,* **Fig. 10.17**), a primitive swallowtail of the subfamily Parnassiinae. Although perhaps usually underappreciated as "just another butterfly," the opportunity to see *P. eversmanni* in the wild ranks with spotting a wolf or wolverine. It is a true tundra butterfly, and a member of an unusual and primitive group of spectacular insects usually restricted to isolated alpine habitats. Adults lack the tails typical of true swallowtails (Papilioninae) but can be identified by their relatively large size, yellow color (males only), and the presence of conspicuous red spots on the hind wings (males and females). The relationship of the parnassians to true swallowtails, such as the old world swallowtail, is demonstrated by the osmeteria of their larvae. Osmeteria are eversible, brightly colored, and foul-smelling defensive organs located on the thorax near the head.

Fig. 10.17. Butterflies (Lepidoptera). ***Upper left:*** *Parnassius eversmanni,* male as indicated by only a single red spot on each hind wing. *P. eversmanni* is the only yellowish parnassian and the only species of the Parnassinae likely to be seen on the North Slope (Toolik Field Station, ADH). ***Lower left:*** *P. eversmanni* female as indicated by three red spots on each hind wing (Atigun Pass, ADH). ***Upper right:*** Underside of *P. eversmanni* female showing waxy "sphragis" attached by male to prevent further mating. ***Lower right:*** *Papilio machaon,* hilltopping male (Atigun Gorge, ADH).

Adults of *P. eversmanni* have a slow, fluttering flight, remaining near the ground and often stopping to bask with wings held flat on the ground. The preferred larval food plant is *Corydalus,* particularly *C. arctica* (Fumariaceae, Fig. 9c.6), which shares the same geographical range within Alaska. Alkaloids sequestered from this plant may be used as a chemical defense by larvae and adults. Larvae require two years for growth and development. Overwintering pupae are enclosed in silken cocoons concealed in soil. Curiously, adult males cement a conspicuous waxy structure (sphragis) to the female's abdomen once mating is completed (**Fig. 10.17**). This functions as a sort of chastity belt, making it impossible for females to mate with additional males.

The blues are identified by their small size (wingspan usually less than 2 cm). Their larvae feed primarily on flowers of the Fabaceae (*Astragalus, Lupinus*) as well as a diversity of other plant species (e.g., *Empetrum, Vaccinium, Rhododendron tomentosum, Saxifraga*). At least seven species of blues have been recorded from the North Slope, primarily in foothill and mountain habitats. Common species include the silvery blue

(*Glaucopsyche lygdamus*, **Fig. 10.18**), arctic blue (*Plebejus glandon*), and western tailed blue (*Cupido amyntula*).

Moths

Due to the continuous daylight of the brief arctic summer, there is little opportunity for the nocturnal activity typical of most moths of lower latitudes. Consequently, the moths of the North Slope are diurnal (day active) like butterflies. There are many families of arctic moths, but those most likely to attract attention are tiger moths (Arctiidae) and tussock moths (Lymantriidae). Larvae of both families are similar, being covered with long setae. Larvae of the Arctiidae are "bristly," however, due to clusters of black and/or orange setae arranged in rings about the body (**Fig. 10.18**). Adults are usually colorful with striking wing patterns (**Fig. 10.18**). The various species of the large and widespread genus *Grammia*, with geometric black-and-yellow patterns on their forewings and black dots on their red hind wings, will be familiar to many. In comparison to the Arctiidae, larvae of the Lymantriidae are "furry" rather than "bristly" due to microscopically plumose setae that form a dense fawn-brown pile that obscures the caterpillar's integument (**Fig. 10.19**). Only one species of tussock moth (*Gynaephora rossi*, the

Fig. 10.18. Butterflies and moths (Lepidoptera). *Upper left: Glaucopsyche lygdamus* (Atigun Gorge, ADH). The silvery blue is one of the largest blues of the North Slope. Its larvae feed on flowers of lupines and vetches. *Lower left:* Larva of tiger moth (Arctiidae, Toolik Field Station, ADH). *Upper right: Grammia philippiana*, male (Arctiidae, Toolik Field Station, ADH). *G. philippiana* is a true arctic species of the large and widespread tiger moth genus *Grammia*. *Lower right: Pararctia subnebulosa*, male (Arctiidae, Kuparuk River, ADH). In some years the tiger moth *P. subnebulosa* is common in foothills habitats of the North Slope. Females are flightless.

arctic wooly bear) is common on the North Slope. Larvae are active from May through August when they feed on dwarf Salix. Mature larvae spin cocoons and pupate shortly after emerging from hibernation in May (**Fig. 10.19**). The adults of *G. rossi* are much less conspicuous than those of most arctiids, being patterned with various shades of gray (**Fig. 10.19**). The females of *G. rossi* and many species of the Arctiidae are flightless because of heavy, egg-laden bodies and poorly developed wings. Males seek females by following aerial pheromone trails. Mating and oviposition usually occur near the female's cocoon. The males of *G. rossi* are conspicuous when they fly due to their rapidly buzzing wings as they search upwind for females.

   Although little is known about the larval biology of arctic tiger moths, much is known about the two species of arctic wooly bears, *G. rossi* and *G. groenlandica. Gynaephora groenlandica* is found only in the high Arctic (Canadian Archipelago, Greenland), where it is both the most northerly distributed member of the Lepidoptera and the largest terrestrial invertebrate. *G. rossi* has a much wider distribution, occurring across the North Slope and well to the south in alpine and boreal habitats. *G. groenlandica* arguably has the longest larval developmental

Fig. 10.19. Moths (Lepidoptera). *Upper left:* Cocoon of the arctic woolly bear, *Gynaephora rossi* (Atigun Gorge, ADH). A parasitic ichneumonid wasp (*Hyposoter*) emerged from this cocoon, rather than a moth. *Lower left: G. rossi*, male (Toolik Field Station, ADH). This male emerged from a cocoon collected along the Kuparuk River. Males are distinguished by their feathery antennae used to detect pheromone molecules released by the flightless females. *Right:* Larva of *G. rossi* basking in the morning sun on the tip of a *Betula* twig (Atigun Gorge, ADH).

period of any lepidopteran. Larvae require 7–14 years of growth before transforming to pupae. The life cycle of North Slope populations of *G. rossi* is shorter, probably not exceeding three to four years, but is still long compared with species from temperate regions. This extended life cycle is attributed to: 1) a short growing season; 2) low food quality due to anti-herbivore compounds; and 3) the energy required for synthesizing glycerol, a cryoprotectant required for overwintering (see "Freeze Tolerance and Freeze Avoidance"). The synthesis of cryoprotectants requires energy and nutrients that would otherwise be used for growth. Nevertheless, their production is essential for survival. This is illustrated by comparing the freeze tolerance of winter-hardened caterpillars in late summer (highest concentration of cryoprotectants) with caterpillars in early summer (lowest concentrations of cryoprotectants). The lower lethal-temperature limit for winter-hardened *G. groenlandica* caterpillars is –70°C while that of the same caterpillars in early summer is –15°C.

The *Gynaephora* species are large and conspicuous insects, and it should not be surprising that their caterpillars and pupae are important prey for insect parasitoids and birds (**Fig. 10.19**). At least two parasitoids use *G. rossi* as a host on the North Slope, a tachinid fly (*Chetogena gelida*) and an ichneumonid wasp (*Hyposoter*). It has been suggested that heavy parasitism is a factor contributing to the short growing season of *G. groenlandica*, with larvae spinning wintering cocoons (hibernacula) in soil litter as early as mid-July as a strategy to avoid the peak activity of parasitoids. Bird predation on egg masses laid on cocoons is also a significant cause of mortality, and it is not unusual to find the remnants of cocoons destroyed by songbirds scattered on the tundra in early June. The combined mortality of parasitoids and bird predation may be greater than 50 percent for a given cohort of larvae.

Thermoregulation by Arctic Moths and Butterflies

Gynaephora caterpillars spend as much as 60 percent of their time basking to gain sufficient body heat for foraging, so it is not surprising that they show behaviors that maximize the absorption of body heat. These behaviors include orienting the body perpendicular to sun rays and, in the case of *G. rossi*, climbing to the branch tips of shrubs. The dense pile of setae covering these caterpillars helps conserve body heat by reducing convective cooling, as shown by experiments comparing shaved caterpillars with controls. The combination of basking behaviors and insulation results in body temperatures reaching 13°C or more above ambient, and a significant increase in total heat absorbed cumulatively during the lengthy larval developmental stage. Such factors are critical for the success of any organism living on the "thermal edge" in the harsh environment of the Arctic.

The requirement for external heat sources has resulted in the evolution of several behaviors common to many North Slope butterfly species. Unlike the bumblebees and some moths (e.g., *G. rossi*), which produce heat by shivering their flight muscles, butterflies are unable to generate significant heat from internal physiological processes. This presents a serious challenge because the flight muscles of a typical butterfly—including those living in the Arctic—must be warmer than 28°C before voluntary flight is possible. Consequently, they must gain sufficient heat from their surroundings before flying. An excellent clue to understanding the close link between environmental temperature and butterfly activity in the Arctic is the effect of cloud cover on their flight behavior. On warm, sunny days in early summer numerous alpines and sulphurs may be observed flying about the tundra. When a cloud blocks the sun, however, even for a moment, flight ceases and does not resume until the sun reappears and the butterflies are able to warm their flight muscles. The sudden change in activity occurs because these butterflies live near the thermal edge.

Arctic butterflies tend to be fuzzy and dark. Their fuzziness is due to a dense covering of setae that provides insulation that reduces convective cooling of the thorax during flight. Their dark color facilitates the absorption of radiant heat. The wings of arctic butterflies typically have conspicuous areas of dark pigments on their undersides, particularly the hindwing. The darkest area is usually near the base of the wing that rests directly over the thorax and abdomen when the wings are closed. This enhances the absorption of heat by the butterfly's body. It is important to realize that heat must be absorbed directly by the body through the wing base as the wings themselves are poor conductors of heat. The circulation of haemolymph (insect blood) through wing veins is too slow to provide a viable mechanism for heat transfer along the wing.

Absorption of radiant heat by butterflies in the Arctic is further facilitated by lateral basking and dorsal basking. Lateral baskers (*Colias, Oeneis*) close their wings and tilt their bodies to present a profile that is perpendicular to the sun's rays (**Fig. 10.16**). This maximizes the solar radiation received per area and greatly enhances the efficiency of heat absorption, particularly in the basal region of the hind wing. Such heat-seeking behavior is initiated when thoracic temperatures fall below about 35°C. Studies have shown that darker individuals of arctic sulphurs are active for longer periods during the day and show more rapid rates of egg maturation than lighter individuals. This is critical for foraging and mating success during the short arctic summer. Unlike lateral baskers, dorsal baskers (*Boloria, Parnassius*) hold their wings flat against the ground when basking (**Fig. 10.16**). This enhances heating of the thorax by trapping warm air beneath the wings while simultaneously reducing the circulation of air around the body and thus convective cooling. By dorsal basking, butterflies are able to maintain body temperatures as high as 17°C above ambient.

Caddisflies (Trichoptera)

The larvae of caddisflies produce a spectacular array of portable cases from stones, plant fragments, and sometimes mollusk shells cemented together with silk (**Fig. 10.20**). Although some species are common in streams and rivers, the larvae of most arctic caddisfly species are found in pools and lakes. With the exception of free-living larva of *Rhyacophila mongolica,* which are predators, the larvae of the North Slope caddisflies feed primarily on algae and decaying leaves (detritus). Although caddisfly larvae are familiar to most, their terrestrial adults are usually mistaken for small drab moths. Twenty-three species of caddisflies have been

Fig. 10.20. Caddisflies (Trichoptera). *Upper left:* Adult of *Ecclisomyia conspersa* (Limnephilidae, Ivishak Hot Spring, ADH). *E. conspersa* is a common caddisfly of deep lakes and spring streams. *Lower left:* Larva of *Brachycentrus americanus* showing transparent case of silk with the remnants of a previous case made of organic particles toward the posterior (Kuparuk River, M.R. Kendrick). These larvae use a tab of silk (visible as a white material to the immediate lower right of the head) to attach the anterior lip of their case to a rock surface in relatively rapid flow. Once secured, they use their legs to intercept drifting organic particles and invertebrate prey. *Upper right:* Larva of *Dicosmoecus* (Limnephilidae) in case made of gravel and organic particles (Kuparuk River, ADH). These larvae feed on algal films growing on rock surfaces. *Lower right:* Adult of *Grensia praeterita* (Galbraith Lake, ADH). Larvae of *G. praeterita* inhabit tundra ponds and lakes, where they feed on decaying organic matter. Adults emerge shortly after snowmelt and are often found on snowbanks and aufeis.

Fig. 10.21. Beetles (Coleoptera). *Upper left:* Adult northern carrion beetle (*Thanatophilus lapponicus*, Silphidae, Toolik Field Station, ADH). *Upper center:* Adult and larvae of the northern carrion beetle feeding on caribou carrion (Kuparuk River, ADH). *Upper right:* Adult predacious diving beetle (*Rhantus*, Dytiscidae; floodplain pool, Kuparuk River, ADH). *Lower left:* Adult ground beetle (*Nebria nivalis*, Carabidae, Toolik Field Station, ADH). *Lower right:* Predacious diving beetle larva (*Dytiscus*, floodplain pool, Kuparuk River, ADH).

reported from the North Slope; about half of this diversity is contributed by the Limnephilidae (11 species).

Beetles (Coleoptera)

At least 185 species of beetles occur in arctic North America (**Fig. 10.21**), with about half of these being ground beetles (Carabidae, 42 percent) and predacious diving beetles (Dytiscidae, 10 percent). Ground beetles are primarily predators of other invertebrates and may be found beneath stones and other types of cover in well-drained tundra habitats. Predacious diving beetles are common in tundra pools and lakes, where they feed on zooplankton.

Spiders

More than 60 species of spiders occur on the North Slope, where they are predators of the abundant arthropod fauna. About half of their taxonomic richness is contributed by the Linyphiidae (**Fig. 10.22**), the diminutive sheet-web spiders. Their tiny, densely woven webs are spun on the ground where they are most conspicuous when coated with early morning dew. Although sheet-web spiders are the most abundant and species-rich family of spiders on the North Slope, the large and active wolf spiders (Lycosidae, **Fig. 10.23**) are the most conspicuous. These spiders are active hunters that either pursue or ambush prey without the aid of a web. Female wolf spiders are well known for the habit of carrying their silken egg cocoons and young on their abdomen while foraging. Egg-bearing females of one species of *Arctosa* build domed, silken retreats on the south-facing sides of tussocks in coastal plain habitats.

Fig. 10.22. Spiders (Arachnidae: Araneae). *Left:* A tiny sheet-web spider or money spider (Linyphiidae, Toolik Field Station, ADH). *Right:* Their tiny, dew-coated sheet webs (about 2 cm in diameter) resemble silver coins when viewed from a distance.

Fig. 10.23. Spiders (Arachnidae: Araneae). *Upper left:* Female wolf spider (*Arctosa*, Lycosidae) carrying egg cocoon (Dalton Highway, MP 395). *Lower left:* Female carrying young. *Right:* Domed silken retreat of female wolf spider (*Arctosa*, Dalton Highway, MP 395).

These retreats presumably function as microgreenhouses to enhance the availability of heat for egg development (**Fig. 10.23**).

Crustaceans

Major groups of the crustaceans likely to be encountered in ponds and lakes of the North Slope are the tadpole shrimp, fairy shrimp, and water fleas (Branchiopoda), amphipods (Amphipoda, **Fig. 10.24**), seed shrimp (Ostracoda), and copepods (Copepoda). Fairy shrimp, tadpole shrimp, water fleas, amphipods, and copepods are found in ponds and lakes. Amphipods, seed shrimp, and copepods are also found in the sediments of streams and rivers.

Fairy Shrimp, Tadpole Shrimp, and Water Fleas

Fairy shrimp, tadpole shrimp, and water fleas are members of the Branchiopoda, a diverse group of crustaceans that have in common a series of flattened thoracic appendages called phyllopods (gill legs) and a pair of tapering appendages or claws on their last body segment. Tadpole shrimp (**Fig. 10.24**) are distinguished from other North Slope branchiopods by the presence of a large oval carapace (the dorsal exoskeleton similar to the lobster's shell) that covers the thorax and much of the abdomen. Fairy shrimp (**Fig. 10.25**) lack such a carapace. Fairy shrimp and tadpole shrimp are also the largest freshwater crustacea of the region, with adults attaining more than 20 mm in length. By comparison, water fleas (**Fig. 10.26**) are tiny (less than 5 mm) with bodies enclosed in laterally flattened carapaces.

Tadpole Shrimp

The arctic tadpole shrimp (Notostraca, *Lepidurus arcticus,* **Fig. 10.24**) is distributed across the coastal plain, where it is found in shallow ponds with soft, organic sediments that freeze completely during winter. Like fairy shrimp, its requirement of fishless habitat (and thus freezing) appears to be related to a lack of mechanisms for avoiding predation. *L. arcticus* is a benthic (bottom-dwelling) omnivore that feeds on organic sediments and invertebrates. Most populations of *L. arcticus* reproduce asexually by self-fertilization. They overwinter as eggs that hatch shortly after snowmelt. Their young live within bottom sediments. Adults appear in early August and can be observed moving about on the sediment's surface or occasionally swimming in the water column in pursuit of zooplankton.

Fig. 10.24. Crustaceans. *Left: Lepidurus arcticus* (Notostraca, coastal plain pond, Dalton Highway, MP 385, ADH). *Right: Gammarus* (Amphipoda, Gammaridae, coastal plain pond, Dalton Highway, MP 385, ADH). On the North Slope amphipods are found in fishless coastal plain ponds, where they actively swim in the water column.

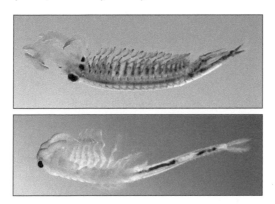

Fig. 10.25. Crustaceans. *Upper: Polyartemiella hazeni* (Anostraca), male. Note the bizarre single-segmented claspers formed from modified second antennae (floodplain pond, Kuparuk River, ADH). *Lower: Branchinecta paludosa*, male. The two segmented claspers of *B. paludosa* are relatively simple compared with those of *P. hazeni* (Toolik Field Station, ADH).

Fairy Shrimp

Two species of fairy shrimp (Anostraca, *Branchinecta paludosa* and *Polyartemiella hazeni*, **Fig. 10.25**) can be abundant in isolated, fishless ponds that freeze solid during winter in foothills and coastal plain habitats. They are usually found in fishless habitats because they lack mechanisms for avoiding fish predation. The different species are distinguished by the number of phyllopods. *B. paludosa* has no more than 11 pairs, whereas *P. hazeni* has at least 17 pairs. Male fairy shrimp have a pair of second antennae[5] that are grossly enlarged to form claspers used to hold females while mating. In the case of *P. hazeni*, these are downright bizarre, appearing as tiny replicas of caribou antlers!

Fairy shrimp feed by filtering organic particles from the water column or the bottom by rhythmic movements of their phyllopods. Their primitive feeding mechanism is similar to that of the extinct trilobites. So similar, in fact, that fairy shrimp have been used as models of probable trilobite feeding behavior. During mid- to late summer females deposit dormant eggs that settle to the sediment. These exceedingly tough resting eggs require a period of freezing or drying before development is activated. Hatching occurs when the ponds thaw. Adults mature in late June and are active until August.

Although primarily Arctic, populations of *B. paludosa* and *P. hazeni* also occur in isolated ponds in western Canada and the central and western United States. The distribution of these populations coincides with the interior North American migratory flyway, suggesting that waterfowl nesting in the Arctic have dispersed them to these southern ponds. This seems reasonable since viable resting eggs of fairy shrimp have been recovered from duck feces.

Water Fleas

Water fleas (Cladocera) are abundant zooplankton in probably every pond and lake on the North Slope. Unlike the other Branchiopoda, they are small, usually less than 5 mm in length. They are also distinguished by having a single eye and a transparent, laterally compressed carapace that contains the body. Some species use the second pair of antennae as oars, resulting in a characteristically jerky, "up-and-down" swimming motion. Others remain close to bottom sediments rather than swimming in open water. The phyllopods double as both gills and electrostatic filters that collect the phytoplankton and organic particles upon which they feed. *Daphnia pulex* and *D. middendorffiana* (**Fig. 10.26**) are among the most common and widespread zooplanktonic cladocerans on the North Slope. *Eurycercus* (**Fig. 10.26**) is a large (more than 5 mm long) bottom-feeding species common to shallow coastal plain ponds.

Two types of zooplankton communities occur on the North Slope. Large-body communities are dominated by large species, such as *D. middendorffiana* (about 3 to 5 mm in length), and are found in isolated ponds that freeze solid during winter and are thus fishless. Small-body communities occur in large lakes where fish predation reduces the abundance of large species. A typical member of the small-body community is *D. pulex* (about 1–2 mm in length). Exceptions to this pattern appear to be related to the abundance and species of fish present (e.g., grayling versus whitefish). Shorebirds such as red phalarope may feed preferentially on large zooplankton in shallow coastal plain ponds, resulting in a shift to small-body assemblages.

Cladocerans produce two types of eggs: those that hatch relatively quickly and those that require a dry "resting" period before development

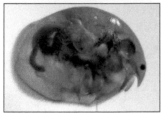

Fig. 10.26. Crustaceans. *Upper left: Heterocope septentrionalis* (Copepoda, coastal plain pool, Dalton Highway, MP 395, ADH). *Lower left: Eurycercus* (Cladocera, coastal plain pool, Dalton Highway, MP 385, ADH). Note developing young visible through carapace. *Right: Daphnia middendorffiana* (Cladocera, coastal plain pool, Dalton Highway, MP 395, ADH). The dark pigmentation is typical for arctic zooplankton living in shallow pools. It is believed to be an adaptation to reduce damage from ultraviolet radiation.

begins. The latter eggs, known as *ephippia*, are exceedingly tough blackish, triangular capsules. Ephippia can withstand years, even decades, of storage in dried sediments where they comprise egg banks.[6] Like the eggs of fairy shrimp, ephippia are relatively unaffected by passage through the guts of fish and birds, which are important agents for dispersal.

Copepods

Like water fleas, copepods are important members of freshwater food webs. They are about the same size as water fleas (less than about 3 mm in length) but differ by having cylindrical, obviously segmented bodies with equally obvious antennae. Some species feed on organic particles and phytoplankton; others are predators of other zooplankton. The largest copepod on the North Slope is *Heterocope septentrionalis* (**Fig. 10.26**). Mature females may exceed 3 mm in length and are often bright red or vivid green in color. Such bright pigments are typical for high-latitude zooplankton, and it has been suggested that they protect zooplankton from UV radiation. *H. septentrionalis* is the top predator in many fishless ponds, where it can have a large effect on the relative abundance of its zooplankton prey. In these habitats it usually co-occurs with *Daphnia middendorffiana,* which is safe from copepod predation when full grown. One scientist, in a fit of anthropomorphism, called adult *Heterocope* "infant killers" in recognition of their aggressive pursuit of recently hatched prey.

Mollusks

At least 19 species of mollusks are found on the North Slope, including snails, clams, and slugs. The great pond snail (*Lymnaea stagnalis*, **Fig. 10.27**) is the largest snail of the North Slope, attaining 30 mm or more in length. It is abundant in deep lakes, where it is important prey for lake trout. The tiny fingernail clams (Sphaeriidae, seven species) live in lake and pond sediments, where their shells may ultimately be used as case-making material by larvae of the caddisfly *Philarctus quaeris* (**Fig. 10.27**). The slug *Deroceras leave* (Agriolimacidae, Toolik Field Station, ADH) is found beneath stones in foothills habitats (**Fig. 10.27**). Its extraordinary geographical range encompasses all continents except Antarctica. Although inconspicuous, the potential importance of *D. leave* to the ecology of the North Slope should not be underestimated.

Fig. 10.27. Mollusks. *Upper left:* The slug *Deroceras leave* (Argriolimacidae, Toolik Field Station, ADH). *Upper right:* Shells of the great pond snail (*Lymnaea stagnalis*) cast ashore at Galbraith Lake (ADH). *Bottom:* Shells of the fingernail clam *Pisidium* attached to the larval case of the caddisfly *Philarctus quaeris* (coastal plain pond, Dalton Highway, MP 385, ADH).

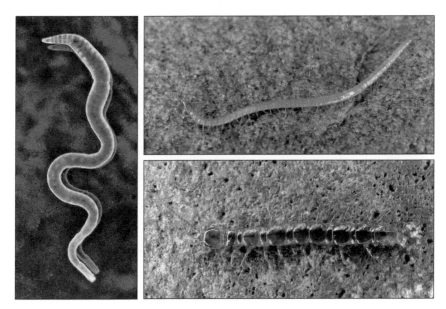

Fig. 10.28. Earthworms (Oligochaeta) and centipedes (Chilopoda). *Left:* An oligochaete from the sediments of a sedge wetland near the Kuparuk River (ADH). *Upper right:* Earth centipede (Chilenophilidae, Toolik Field Station, ADH). *Lower right:* Stone centipede (Lithobiidae, Toolik Field Station, ADH).

D. leave is the intermediate host of the muskox lungworm (*Umingmakstrongylus pallikuukensis*), a pathogenic nematode that impairs lung function. Although this parasite is endemic in the muskoxen herds of the Northwest Territories, it has not yet been reported from herds west of the Mackenzie River. Nevertheless, should an infected animal make its way west to the North Slope, two critical requirements for completing the complex life cycle of *U. pallikuukensis* are currently in place here, muskoxen and the diminutive slug *D. leave.*

Other Invertebrates

Given the abundance of permafrost, there are a surprising number of terrestrial and freshwater species of earthworms (Oligochaeta: Lumbriculidae) and potworms (Oligochaeta: Enchytraeidae) on the North Slope (**Fig. 10.28**). More than 15 species of potworms, for example, have been recorded from the coastal plain, with some individuals exceeding 60 mm in length. The relatively great diversity of oligochaetes here is attributed to the role of the Beringian refuge during the widespread glaciations of the Pleistocene. Despite total freezing during winter, they can be abundant with more than 10,000 individuals/m^2 reported from wetland soils. Apparently they tolerate freezing because of the controlled dehydration of their tissues. Centipedes (Chilopoda) are relatively common beneath stones in well-drained foothills habitats, where they are predators of the abundant arthropod microfauna (**Fig. 10.28**).

11

Fish

About 26 species of fish have been recorded from the freshwater habitats of the North Slope, if one includes coastal species only occasionally found in freshwater habitats (e.g., Pacific herring *Clupea pallasii*, arctic flounder *Pleuronectes glacialis*, four-horned sculpin *Myoxocephalus quadricornis*) and inland species that are uncommon or very local in distribution (e.g., inconnu *Stenodus leucichthys*, three-spine stickleback *Gasterosteus aculeatus*). Only 14 of these species, however, are widespread. This assemblage is dominated by the Salmonidae (ciscoes, whitefish, grayling, and char), with only the longnose sucker (*Catostomus catostomus*), burbot (*Lota lota*), nine spine stickleback (*Pungitius pungitius*), and slimy sculpin (*Cottus cognatus*) being from other families.

Whitefish, Cisco, Grayling, Char, and Salmon (Salmonidae)

Fish of the family Salmonidae have small cycloid scales,[1] conspicuous lateral lines,[2] and an adipose fin.[3] Three subfamilies of salmonids are found on the North Slope. Whitefish and ciscoes (Coregininae) have fewer than 100 scales along the lateral line, teeth that are small and weak or absent, and strongly forked tails. The arctic grayling (Thymallinae) resemble ciscoes and whitefish but have greatly enlarged dorsal fins, well-developed teeth, and young with parr marks.[4] The chars and salmon (Salmoninae) have more than 100 scales along the lateral line, well-developed teeth on their jaws and vomer (upper palate), caudal (tail) fins with shallow forks (with the exception of the lake trout), and young with parr marks.

Cisco and Whitefish

Fishes of the genus *Coregonus* are silver with two flaps of skin dividing the opening of each nostril (rather than a single flap), a broad snout, and no parr marks on their young. Five species are found on the North Slope (**Figs. 11.1, 11.2**): the arctic cisco (*C. autumnalis*), least cisco (*C. sardinella*), Bering cisco (*C. laurettae*), broad whitefish (*C. nasus*), and humpback whitefish (*C. clupeaformis* complex). Adult arctic ciscoes have upper and lower jaws of the same length and white pelvic fins with no dark coloration or speckling. The least cisco has a lower jaw that projects slightly beyond the upper jaw and dusky or black pelvic fins. The very pale pelvic and pectoral fins of the Bering cisco separate it from the least cisco, but the arctic cisco and Bering cisco can be distinguished reliably only by inspection of internal gill structures. Both the humpback whitefish and broad whitefish have lower jaws that are shorter than their upper jaws. The heads of humpback whitefish, however, have a concave lateral profile followed by a pronounced dorsal hump while those of broad whitefish have a convex lateral profile and they lack a dorsal hump. The Mackenzie and Colville Rivers are population

Fig. 11.1. *Top:* Least cisco, juvenile (*Coregonus sardinella*), Teshekpuk Lake (W.A. Morris). ***Center:*** Arctic cisco, adult (*C. autumnalis*, USGS National Digital Library). ***Bottom:*** Humpback whitefish (*C. pidschian*, USGS National Digital Library).

Fig. 11.2. *Upper left:* Arctic grayling (*Thymallus arcticus*, Kuparuk River, J.P. Benstead). *Upper right:* Arctic grayling (Oksrukuyik Creek, ADH). *Lower left:* Round whitefish (*Prosopium cylindraceum*, Oksrukuyik Creek, ADH). *Lower right:* Broad whitefish (*Coregonus nasus*, Oogrukpuk River, East Creek, W.A. Morris).

centers for most *Coregonus* species on the North Slope because they provide extensive reaches of deep water for overwintering. In contrast, shallow braided rivers such as the Sagavanirktok have limited areas of overwintering habitat.

The arctic cisco is more tolerant of saltwater than other members of the Coregininae. It is truly anadromous,[5] occurring in both marine and freshwater habitats, but requires freshwater for reproduction. Adults spend the autumn and winter at sea and ascend rivers to spawn in spring and summer. Most arctic cisco spawn in the Mackenzie River, where they may run 1,000 km or more upriver. There is no evidence indicating that they spawn in Alaska. Spawning females may broadcast up to 90,000 nonadhesive eggs that settle to the bottom gravel, where they stay until hatching in spring. Young-of-the-year descend to the Mackenzie River delta, where they either remain or continue westward, following near-shore currents to the Sagavanirktok River and other major rivers farther west. The rivers between the Mackenzie and the Sagavanirktok do not provide sufficient winter habitat, so migrating fish must reach the Sagavanirktok River to survive. Juveniles spend about three years in the lower Sagavanirktok River and then migrate farther west to the Colville River. It is thought that limited overwintering habitat in the Sagavanirktok stimulates the migration of juveniles to the Colville River, which contains 75 km of deep channel habitat. Once juveniles reach maturity (eight to nine years) they move to offshore habitats in the Beaufort Sea and return only semiannually to the Mackenzie River to spawn. Arctic ciscoes are critical to near-shore marine food webs, where they feed primarily on marine invertebrates (mysid shrimp, copepods, insects, small fish) and in turn are prey for larger fish and marine mammals. Arctic ciscoes may live for 13 years and attain lengths of 35–40 cm. Little is known about the biology of the Bering cisco. Unlike the other North Slope members of *Coregonus*, the Bering cisco only occurs in rivers west of Oliktok Point (just east of the Colville River delta).

The least cisco is one of the most abundant fish of the coastal plain, where it spawns in rivers and streams in late September and early October. Females broadcast about 9,800 to 93,500 eggs that settle into the gravel until hatching in early spring. Adults feed on aquatic insects, snails, fingernail clams, zooplankton, and sticklebacks. Although lake-dwelling populations of least cisco are apparently nonmigratory, populations dwelling in major rivers are diadromous.[6] Like other species of *Coregonus*, the population centers of diadromous least cisco in the Beaufort Sea region are the Colville and Mackenzie Rivers. Adults are common in Prudhoe Bay and the Sagavanirktok River delta, where juveniles may also be abundant in years when strong westward winds assist the migration of young-of-the-year from the Mackenzie River. Predators of adult least cisco include lake trout; burbot and grayling feed on their eggs. Least cisco mature at three or more years and may attain 11 years in age and 42 cm in length.

Unlike the ciscoes, the broad whitefish is primarily a freshwater species, inhabiting streams, rivers, ponds, and lakes of the Arctic Coastal Plain, although most individuals probably enter brackish water for short periods at least once each year. Broad whitefish require interconnected small streams and lakes during the summer and deep lakes in the winter. The populations in the Chipp and Ikpikpuk drainages and the Teshekpuk Lake region are likely the largest of the North Slope as these provide extensive, excellent habitat. Lake-dwelling broad whitefish disperse into streams and rivers during early summer floods. Their upstream spawning runs begin as early as June and continue into autumn. Spawning adults broadcast eggs and milt over gravel in relatively fast-flowing water and then return downstream to overwinter in deep river channels, deltas, or interconnected lakes. Broad whitefish feed on chironomids, snails, bivalves, other aquatic insect larvae, and crustaceans. They reach sexual maturity in 9–12 years and may attain lengths of 67 cm. Biological information about humpbacked whitefish is scarce due to difficulties in separating the species of the humpback whitefish complex. The species inhabiting the North Slope is believed to be *C. pidschian*, which is anadromous. It has been taken offshore near the Sagavanirktok River where it apparently spawns during summer and autumn. As the slowest maturing *Coregonus* of the North Slope, humpback whitefish attain sexual maturity in 10 to 13 years and reach lengths of 53 cm.

The round whitefish (*Prosopium cylindraceum*, **Fig. 11.2**) is the only species of *Prosopium* on the North Slope where they are widespread and common in river, stream, and lake habitats. *Prosopium* differs from *Coregonus* by having only a single flap (rather than two) of skin dividing the opening of each nostril; a body that is round in cross section (rather than laterally compressed); a narrow, pointed snout; and young with parr marks. Round whitefish spawn during September and October over gravelly shallows of rivers and rocky inshore lake habitats where females broadcast 1,000–12,000 eggs that settle to the bottom until hatching in spring. Round whitefish do not migrate significant distances, although movements over short distances between overwintering and spawning habitats may occur. They feed on insect larvae, mollusks, copepods, and fish eggs, reach sexual maturity in five to seven years, and attain lengths of 56 cm or more.

Inconnu or Sheefish

The inconnu (*Stenodus leucichthys*), or sheefish, is distinguished from ciscoes and other whitefish by its large mouth (extends posteriorly to the approximate position of the pupil) and protruding lower jaw. They are long-lived, attaining ages of 20 or more years while reaching nearly 5 to 11 kg and 1.4 m in length. During late September they broadcast spawn in streams with gravel bottoms, where females may release as many as 400,000 eggs that hatch in early spring. Adults feed primarily on least cisco. Inconnu winter near the mouths of large rivers and deltas and begin upstream migrations to spawning habitats after ice-out. Inconnu have been captured from the Colville and Meade Rivers but have not been reported from the North Slope in recent years.

Arctic Grayling

The arctic grayling (*Thymallus arcticus*, **Fig. 11.2**) is one of the most widespread and abundant fish species on the North Slope, where they are found in streams, rivers, and lakes of the coastal plain and foothills. During snowmelt, they may enter coastal waters to migrate among major drainages. Most arctic grayling winter in deep lakes and rivers. Juveniles, however, may winter in areas of perennially upwelling groundwater in relatively shallow stream habitats. The availability of a suitable volume of overwintering habitat is a primary factor affecting the abundance of grayling on the North Slope. Following breakup in May, arctic grayling migrate from wintering to spawning habitats—typically gravel riffles of streams and rivers where females broadcast about 400–13,000 eggs that hatch in June. Adults may summer in or near spawning habitats or move to the cooler waters of deep, connected lakes. In foothills habitats, they feed on aquatic and terrestrial insects trapped on the water's surface and on larvae drifting in the current. Coastal plain populations of arctic grayling also feed on sticklebacks. Abundant food during summer is critical for producing fat reserves for winter, when they must spend as long as eight months trapped beneath ice. Arctic grayling become sexually mature at about six to seven years with exceptional individuals living for 30 years and attaining 40 cm in length. In locations where they coexist, lake trout can be significant predators of arctic grayling.

Chars (Salvelinus)

Species of *Salvelinus* are colorfully marked with combinations of pink, red, or cream spots. They also have minute scales that are difficult to see without magnification; white leading edges on their pectoral, pelvic, and anal fins; and juveniles with parr marks. Three species of *Salvelinus* occur on the North Slope: Dolly Varden (*S. malma,* **Fig. 11.3**), arctic char (*S. alpinus,* **Fig. 11.4**), and lake trout (*S. namaycush,* **Fig. 11.4**). The Dolly Varden is distinguished by a scattering of orange to red spots on its flanks, all smaller than the pupil of its eye. Dolly Varden have more laterally compressed bodies (a probable adaptation for living in rivers) while the more closely lake-associated arctic char and lake trout tend to be more torpedo-shaped. The similar arctic char differs from the Dolly Varden by having pink to red spots on its back and flanks with the largest usually exceeding the size of its pupil. Lake trout are distinctive in having deeply forked tails and a dense scattering of small yellow spots on olive heads, bodies, and dorsal and caudal fins.

Dolly Varden are widely distributed across the North Slope, where they are the only stream- and river-spawning char. With the exception of scattered resident populations in headwater springs, the Dolly Varden of the North Slope are anadromous. Adults and subadults (about three to eight years) summer in the Beaufort Sea, where they feed on small fish and crustaceans, particularly mysid shrimp. Depending upon level of maturity, individuals may spend from one to three months at sea. The growth rates of Dolly Varden in coastal habitats are rapid, with some subadults doubling their weight over summer. In late summer, sea-run Dolly Varden migrate upstream to spawn and overwinter. Because of the requirement of flowing water year-round, arctic populations of Dolly Varden are able to spawn and overwinter only in rivers that

Fig. 11.3. *Upper left:* Dolly Varden (*Salvelinus malma*), mature, nonmigratory "sneaker" male, length ~18 cm (Ivishak Hot Spring, ADH). *Upper right:* Dolly Varden, young-of-the-year showing parr marks (Ivishak Hot Spring, ADH). *Center:* Dolly Varden, adult sea-run female, length ~67 cm (Ivishak River, M.R. Kendrick). *Bottom:* Dolly Varden, sea-run juvenile (unnamed stream west of Kuparuk River, W.A. Morris).

Fig. 11.4. *Upper:* Arctic char (*Salvelinus alpinus*, Fog Lakes, Toolik Lake Field Station, C. Leucke). *Lower:* Lake trout (*S. namaycush*, Green Cabin Lake, J.P. Benstead).

contain significant perennial springs. Because of the numerous springs in its eastern tributaries (e.g., Ivishak River, Echooka River, Lupine River), the Sagavanirktok River drainage harbors the largest Dolly Varden population on the North Slope, with the Ivishak River containing the bulk of this population, or about 8,000–26,000 fish. This population estimate includes overwintering spawners (of which some may have actually spawned in locations other than the Ivishak River), nonspawning adults, and juveniles. The number of spawning Dolly Varden in the Ivishak River in any given year is probably somewhere in the neighborhood of 1,500–5,000 fish.

Dolly Varden usually return to their birth streams to spawn, but may overwinter in non-natal streams during nonspawning years. Spawning occurs from late August to early October, with adult females spawning every second or third year. Spawning females use vigorous swimming motions to form bowl-shaped depressions (redds) in gravel riffles of braided streams and rivers into which they deposit as many as 6,000 eggs while accompanying males produce milt. Young emerge from the gravel the following May and migrate to headwater spring streams and off-channel habitats where they spend two to five years feeding on insects and other invertebrates. During their third to fifth year, females and most males convert to smolts (silvery juvenile forms that are physiologically prepared to enter saltwater) and begin their first migration seaward. Some males will remain in their headwater habitat after becoming sexually mature. These sneaker males, which seldom attain lengths greater than 22 cm, approach spawning sea-run fish and opportunistically contribute milt to their redds. Dolly Varden mature at about seven to nine years and make about three to five round-trips to sea before spawning. Once mature, some spawners may remain in freshwater habitats for as long as 18 months. Dolly Varden live as long as 16 years and attain lengths of 80 cm. These would be exceptionally large individuals on the North Slope, however, as most adults average 50–60 cm.

Arctic char (*Salvelinus alpinus*) are long-lived, slow-growing fish that attain ages of 24 years and lengths of 54 cm or more. Although they have been reported from isolated lakes on the coastal plain, arctic char are most abundant in the foothills, where they are typically found in headwater lakes at least 850 m in elevation and 6–7 m deep. Arctic char feed on insects, mollusks, and other fish. During August and September, they spawn over gravel shoals in lakes and pools of lake-outlet and -inlet streams. Spawning females prepare redds that receive 5,000–6,000 eggs that hatch in spring.

Mysteriously, some foothills lakes contain arctic char and sometimes sculpin but have outlet streams with gradients so steep that they are clearly impassable to fish. So…how did arctic char colonize these lakes? Apparently the scattered populations of arctic char on the North Slope are relicts of what was a more continuous distribution during the Pleistocene. At that time the lakes they now inhabit had outlet streams with more moderate gradients. These outlets became steeper over time, effectively isolating arctic char populations from further colonization by fish. This provides only a partial answer, however, because it raises a second question: Why are arctic char no longer present in lakes with moderately steep outlet streams? The key to this question is the recent colonization of the North Slope by lake trout. Although today they can be found in most lakes of suitable size and depth, lake trout were absent from the North Slope during the heyday of arctic char during the Pleistocene. As predators of arctic char, lake trout extirpate populations of arctic char from most lakes they colonize. By denying passage to lake trout, the steep outlet streams of the scattered lakes presently containing arctic char have protected them from complete extirpation from the North Slope.

On the North Slope, lake trout inhabit large lakes, usually 8 m or more in depth. They may also occur in shallower lakes containing sufficient dissolved oxygen (less than 4 mg O_2/L) year-round. They spawn in mid-September over rocky substrata at depths ranging from 3 to 5 m. Possibly because of limited spawning habitat, males congregate over suitable areas of lake sediments and clear away organic debris by vigorous twisting of body and tail along bottom and by rubbing with their snouts. Once the spawning habitat is prepared, females arrive to spawn with males en masse. As many as seven males and three females have been observed spawning together. During spawning their large eggs (5–6 mm diameter) fall to the lake bottom, where they are eventually moved into interstitial spaces by wave action. Here they remain until hatching in February and March. Females produce several hundred to 17,000 eggs, and probably spawn once every three years on the North Slope. Lake trout feed primarily on snails during summer and fish—particularly overwintering arctic grayling and round whitefish—during fall and winter. Lake trout grow slowly and attain relatively great ages. On the North Slope, they routinely reach lengths of 45 cm in five years, 73 cm in 10 years, and 96 cm in 15 years. One of the slowest growing populations yet documented for Alaska occurs in Campsite Lake in the Sagavanirktok River drainage. Here fish may reach lengths of 105 cm at 37 years of age. As is typical for large top predators, populations of lake trout are usually quite small. Toolik Lake, for example, contains only about 100 large lake trout ranging in age from 15 to 20 years even though it is a fairly large lake with an area of about 150 ha and a mean depth of 7 m.

Pacific Salmon (Oncorhynchus)

All five species of Pacific salmon have been recorded from arctic waters. Only pink (*Oncorhynchus gorbuscha*) and chum salmon (*O. keta*), however, have small, self-sustaining populations on the North Slope. Of the Pacific salmon, pink and chum salmon have the highest level of "preadaptation" to the Arctic because they show high levels of cold tolerance and they require freshwater habitats only for spawning and incubation; their young migrate to sea shortly after hatching. As of 2010, pink and chum salmon have been captured from North Slope rivers as far east as the Canning River, and at least eight self-sustaining populations of pink salmon and seven populations of chum salmon have been reported from the Colville River and westward. Spawning pink salmon have also been reported from the Kuparuk and Sagavanirktok Rivers, but there is no evidence that populations are self-sustaining in these rivers. Finally, spawning coho salmon (*O. kisutch*) have been observed on the far western North Slope in Kuchiak Creek.

Alaska Blackfish (Umbridae)

The Alaska blackfish (*Dallia pectoralis*, **Fig. 11.5**) is a stout little fish with a short, flattened snout, dorsal and anal fins located toward the tail, and strange stick-like pelvic fins. They are slow-growing invertivores with eight-year-old fish reaching only about 12 cm in total length. On the North Slope they are found in ponds and slow-moving streams with abundant vegetation on the coastal plain westward from the Colville River delta. Little is known about their biology on the North Slope. Populations in the Alaskan interior, however, spawn throughout spring and summer when females deposit 40–300 eggs in dense vegetation. Alaskan blackfish have been accorded legendary abilities of cold tolerance, with some reports suggesting an ability to tolerate complete freezing. Although such reports are untrue, Alaskan blackfish do have a high tolerance for anoxia (complete absence of oxygen) and are able to survive without oxygen for at least 24 hours at 0°C.

Northern Pike (Esocidae)

Northern pike (*Esox lucius*) have elongated, cylindrical bodies and broad, flattened snouts. Their jaws contain many large and sharp teeth and their dorsal and anal fins are located well toward the rear. Adults may attain large sizes with some males attaining 75 cm and exceptional

Fig. 11.5. *Upper:* Juvenile burbot (*Lota lota*, Dan Creek, J.P. Benstead). *Lower:* Alaskan black-fish (*Dallia pectoralis*, tributary of Mayoriak River and outlet for Teshekpuk Lake, W.A. Morris).

females exceeding 100 cm. Northern pike are found in lakes and slow rivers, where they seek cover in submerged vegetation. They winter in deep water but shortly after breakup they move to shallow wetlands (less than 50 cm in depth) to spawn. During spawning, large females may release as many as 600,000 eggs onto submerged vegetation, a process that may take several days. Eggs hatch in early summer. Adults feed on fish (including smaller pike), waterfowl, and swimming mammals. Young feed on aquatic insect larvae and other invertebrates. Although never abundant on the North Slope, northern pike are found in the Teshekpuk Lake region and the Colville, Meade, and Chipp River drainages.

Longnose Sucker (Catostomidae)

The longnose sucker (*Catostomus catostomus*) is a long, narrow fish with a cylindrical body and a protrusible, ventrally placed mouth used to vacuum organic sediments and associated invertebrates from stream and lake bottoms. This species has been reported from the Teshekpuk Lake, Chipp River, and Colville River drainages of the North Slope. Longnose suckers occur in both lakes and rivers, but lake residents make short migrations to streams and rivers where they spawn in early spring. Longnose suckers may attain ages of almost 20 years and lengths greater than 50 cm.

Burbot (Gadidae)

The burbot (*Lota lota,* **Fig. 11.5**) is the only truly freshwater cod in North America. They are widely distributed on the North Slope, where they are unlikely to be mistaken for any other freshwater fish. Burbot have long, sinuous bodies with extremely long anal and second dorsal fins, deeply embedded scales, and large heads with a distinctive barbel at the chin tip. Their color ranges from light brown to yellow with dark mottling. Burbot are primarily inhabitants of deep lakes but are also found in deep rivers. Juveniles feed on insect larvae, mollusks, and small sculpin. Adults feed on fish—their usual prey—and invertebrates, fish eggs, voles, ducklings, and carrion; cannibalism is also common. Spawning occurs in January or February. At this time males and females congregate over sand or gravel in shallow water (0.3–1.5 m beneath the ice cover), where they form a dense tangle, with individuals continuously writhing toward the center while releasing eggs and sperm. Single females may produce from 500,000 to 1 million eggs, which settle to the bottom until hatching in March or April. Burbot become sexually mature in six to seven years and may live 15 years. Fifteen-year-old fish average about 72 cm in length.

Sticklebacks (Gasterosteidae)

The ninespine stickleback (*Pungitius pungitius,* **Fig. 11.6**) is one of the most widespread and abundant fish on the Arctic Coastal Plain, where it is found in nearly all lakes and streams that remain unfrozen in winter (e.g., more than 2 m in depth). Ninespine sticklebacks are identified by 7–12 free spines before their dorsal fins and a keel on their caudal peduncle (the narrow body region just anterior of the tail). They are most abundant in ponds and streams with dense submerged plant beds and deep (more than 2 m) wintering habitat. In late spring sticklebacks move from wintering habitats to submerged plant beds (particularly those along the margins of pools of beaded streams), where they prey on zooplankton, midge larvae, and other small invertebrates. Prior to spawning in late June and early July, males construct tunnel-like nests of organic debris using an adhesive secreted from their kidneys. They then lead gravid females to their nests, where clutches of 50–80 eggs are deposited. Males fertilize the eggs and remain to tend them until young are able to survive independently. Male ninespine sticklebacks live for about three years, while females live for about five years and attain lengths of up to 8 cm. They are prey for least cisco, grayling, Dolly

Varden, lake trout, burbot, and birds. In turn, sticklebacks are predators of fish eggs and larvae, particularly those of arctic grayling. Three-
spine sticklebacks (*Gasterosteus aculeatus*) are also found on the North
Slope in brackish water habitats near the coast from the Sagavanirktok
River delta westward.

Sculpins (Cottidae)

Slimy sculpins (*Cottus cognatus*, **Fig. 11.6**) are abundant in lakes, rivers, and streams throughout the North Slope. They are distinguished
by a slender, light brown body with two conspicuous saddles posteriorly, a relatively large head and mouth, and large, fan-like pectoral fins. Slimy sculpins spawn in shallow-water habitats in streams
and lakes in May and June. Spawning males excavate nests beneath
cobbles overlying sandy substrates to which they sequentially lead as
many as two to three gravid females. Once within the nest, females
cement clutches of about 150–600 eggs to its ceiling; the male then
fertilizes them and remains to tend the eggs until hatching. Slimy sculpin feed primarily on aquatic insects, although small fish may also be

Fig. 11.6. *Upper:* Ninespine stickleback (*Pungitius pungitius*, Fawn Creek, just west of
Prudhoe Bay, W.A. Morris). *Lower:* Slimy sculpin (*Cottus cognatus*, Toolik Lake, ADH).

taken. They mature in about four years and may live for as long as seven years while attaining lengths of 12 cm. The four-horned sculpin (*Myoxocephalus quadricornis*) is common in coastal marine habitats and the lower reaches of streams and rivers near the Beaufort Sea. It can be distinguished from the slimy sculpin by the presence of four blunt protuberances ("horns") on the top of the head (two between the eyes, two at the rear of the head).

12

Reptiles and Amphibians

The only amphibian species reported from the North Slope in historical times is the wood frog (*Rana sylvatica*), which has been
occasionally found along the Canning River and elsewhere in the extreme eastern North Slope. There are many reports of wood frogs from
above the Arctic Circle in Canada, which presumably is the source of
those found on the North Slope. The presence of wood frogs in the
Arctic should not be surprising. During winter, they hibernate below
the surface of the soil and can survive relatively long periods with as
much as 65 percent of their body water in a frozen state. This ice forms
in extracellular fluid compartments while cell contents are protected
from freezing by massive quantities of glucose produced during the onset
of freezing. Rather than winter temperatures per se, the major factor
apparently limiting the northern range of the wood frog appears to be
the length of time that breeding habitats (shallow pools) remain ice-free,
allowing development and metamorphosis of tadpoles.

Although today there are no reptiles on the North Slope, this has
not always been the case. Exposures of the Prince Creek Formation
along bluffs overlooking the lower reaches of the Colville River have revealed abundant dinosaur and turtle fossils ranging in age from 66 to 76
million years ago. These fossils, which include bones, skin impressions,
and tracks, provide evidence that a diverse community of hadrosaurid
(duck-billed), tyrannosaurid, pachycephalosaurine (dome-headed), and
troodontid (bird-like) dinosaurs once lived on the North Slope of Alaska
(seven families, eight genera total). Associated plant fossils indicate that
the environment of the North Slope during the mid- to late Cretaceous
was temperate floodplain or delta forest. The high latitude of the North
Slope at this time (70–85°N) shows that dinosaurs could persist in habitats with dramatic seasonal fluctuations in day length and temperature.
It is tempting to imagine that the North Slope dinosaurs coped with the

extreme seasonality of their environment by migratory behavior, such as that shown by the present-day bird fauna and caribou. Paleontologists have found no evidence indicating that this occurred, however.

13

Birds

It's stunning to think that one of the thrush species that we saw there (Kenya), the northern wheatear, migrates thousands of miles across Siberia to nest in Alaska's Arctic. Imagine this remarkable insect-eating bird perched next to elephants on the savannah in the winter, and then standing near caribou on the tundra in the summer.
—President Jimmy Carter, *Arctic Wings*

Over 150 species of birds visit the North Slope annually, and of these nearly 100 species also nest here. Only a handful—fewer than 10 species—are year-round residents, however. These include willow and rock ptarmigan, ravens, gray jays, the American dipper, and possibly gray-headed chickadees and redpolls. Gyrfalcons and snowy owls may also overwinter depending upon the abundance of prey. Most of these hardy species show specialized adaptations to cope with the extremes of the arctic winter. The remaining species simply avoid the North Slope winter by migrating elsewhere. As a consequence, the North Slope is an important focal point for the annual migratory cycles of numerous bird species. If one plots their migration routes on a map, similar to those showing the routes of airliners between major international airports, the North Slope appears to be a hub, gathering numerous converging flight paths across the globe—from Antarctica, New Zealand, Africa, India, China, Japan, North America, and South America.

The geographical scope of the migration routes followed by birds nesting on the North Slope is nothing short of astonishing. The arctic tern, a small bird often observed hovering over North Slope ponds, makes the longest migration of any bird in the world—Arctic to Antarctic, a round-trip of about 30,000 km. The journey between its wintering habitat at sea near Antarctica (antarctic summer) and its summer nesting habitat on the North Slope is about 15,000 km and requires three months. The fall migration route of the American golden plover is similarly spectacular. After leaving the North Slope, it crosses the Hudson Bay and New England and continues directly over the Atlantic Ocean to the dry plains of Argentina and Patagonia. Similar migration routes are found for other species of shorebirds nesting on the North Slope, such as the wandering tattler and the semipalmated sandpiper. Such marathon migrations are not restricted to shorebirds, however. The northern wheatear, a thrush that nests on the North Slope—believe it or not—winters in Africa. In fact, northern wheatears summering on the North Slope follow the longest migration route known for any songbird. Although migration routes for the birds of the North Slope are well documented, little is known about why so many of them are so lengthy and complex, and why the North Slope is such a critical hub. Answers concerning the "why" of such dramatic migratory behavior are undoubtedly wrapped in layers of evolutionary, biogeographical, and ecophysiological theory.

Loons (Gaviidae)

Loons are remarkable birds. Their ability to compress air from their feathers, combined with dense bones, results in a low level of buoyancy, allowing them to ride unusually low in the water and enhancing their ability to dive deeper than 60 m in pursuit of prey. Another remarkable feature is the posterior position of their legs. Although excellent for paddling, they are useless for standing. When moving about on shore, loons must slide on their breast while pushing with their feet. When they arrive on the North Slope in late May or early June, loons must stage[1] on open river deltas until ice melts sufficiently to allow access to ponds and lakes that provide foraging and nesting habitats. Their nests are simple scrapes near the water's edge or on mounds of vegetation protruding from the water near shore. They usually lay clutches of two eggs that males and females incubate cooperatively. Young leave the nest shortly after hatching and are able to fly within a month. Because they nest near the water's edge, flooding is a common cause of nest failure; loons usually nest relatively late in the spring to reduce this risk. Late nesting, however, exposes young birds to the risk that an early fall freezeup may trap them before they fledge. Predation is another important cause of mortality. Eggs and young are often lost to glaucous gulls, parasitic and pomarine jaegers, and arctic and red foxes. Predation by arctic foxes is a major cause of nest failure near Prudhoe Bay. Both parasitic and pomarine jaegers have been observed thieving food from loons ferrying fish to their young.

Four species of loons are found on the North Slope. The yellow-billed loon (*Gavia adamsii*, **Fig. 13.1**), the largest, is distinguished by its size, extensive white markings on its back, and a yellow bill. The common loon (*G. immer*) is similar but has a black bill. Despite its name, the

Fig. 13.1. *Upper left:* Pacific loon (*Gavia pacifica*, Sagavanirktok River, ADH). *Upper right:* Red-throated loon (*G. stellata*, Ice Cut, ADH). *Lower left:* Tundra swan (*Cygnus columbianus*, Ice Cut, ADH). *Lower right:* Yellow-billed loon with young (*G. adamsii*, Toolik Lake, JWS).

common loon is relatively uncommon on the North Slope. Red-throated loons (*G. stellata*, **Fig. 13.1**) are the smallest and have gray necks, red throats, and a dark back when in breeding plumage. The intermediate-size Pacific loon (*G. pacifica*, **Fig. 13.1**) has a broad, rounded head, an eerie pale-gray nape, and extensive white markings on its back.

Pacific loons are abundant on the coastal plain, where they nest near the shores of small (more than 2.0 ha), shallow (less than 2 m) ponds. Their young feed on invertebrates captured in their nesting habitat. The smaller red-throated loons are also abundant on the coastal plain where they nest near even smaller (less than 0.5–2.0 ha) and shallower (less than 1 m) ponds. Such shallow ponds freeze solid during winter and so lack fish. Because red-throated loons feed almost exclusively on fish regardless of age, adults must capture fish from nearby water bodies and ferry them to their nesting lakes to feed their young. Unlike Pacific and red-throated loons, the piscivorous yellow-billed loons nest near the shores of relatively large (more than 13 ha) and deep (more than 2 m) foothills lakes. Loons depart the North Slope by early September to stage briefly in coastal waters before migrating south to wintering habitats. The Pacific loons of the North Slope winter offshore from southern Alaska to northern Mexico, while the red-throated loons winter on the western Pacific as far west as Korea, and the yellow-billed loons winter offshore from southern Alaska to British Columbia and from Japan to China and Korea.

Swans, Ducks, Geese, and Mergansers (Anatidae)

Swans

The tundra swan (*Cygnus columbianus*, **Fig. 13.1**) is the only swan likely to be found on the North Slope, where it is unmistakable, given its large size (maximum length about 139 cm, mass about 9 kg), white plumage, and long neck. Six thousand to 10,500 swans nest here, with most inhabiting major river deltas, where they feed on aquatic plants, upland plants such as *Vaccinium* and *Empetrum*, and invertebrates. Migrating swans first arrive on the North Slope in May, when they begin to nest in tussock tundra and sedge meadows near lakes with beds of emergent plants. Their nests are large mounds of vegetation topped by a hollow bowl. Clutches of three to four eggs are laid in early June and incubation is shared by both parents. Shortly after hatching, cygnets (young swans) are led to brood-rearing lakes, where the adults molt. Egg predators include parasitic jaegers, arctic and red foxes, and grizzly bears; golden eagles may attack adults. Because of the long period required for fledging, the timing of breakup is critical to nesting success. Cool springs and a late thaw result in a high percentage of nest failure. Tundra swans depart the North Slope in September for winter habitats along the coasts of Maryland, Virginia, and North Carolina.

Dabbling Ducks and Divers

Common dabbling ducks of the North Slope include the northern pintail (*Anas acuta*, **Fig. 13.2**), American wigeon (*A. americana*), northern shoveler (*A. clypeata*, **Fig. 13.2**), green-winged teal (*A. creca*), and mallard (*A. platyrhynchos*). The breeding males of these species are readily identified. Male mallards and northern shovelers are distinguished by green heads. The mallard has a distinctive chestnut breast, however, while the breast of the northern shoveler is white. The northern shoveler is also a relatively small duck and has a distinctive, shovel-like bill. Male northern pintails have long, tapering tail feathers (the "pin"), brown heads, and white breasts. Male green-winged teal, the smallest duck of the region, are identified by brown heads with large green patches on either side. Male American wigeon have a white pate, a light-brown breast, and extensive white panels on their upper wings. Males of the greater scaup (*Aythya marila*, **Fig. 13.2**), a diving duck, are identified by dark heads and breasts offset by striking white flanks. In flight their wings display extensive white bands.

Fig. 13.2. *Upper left:* Northern pintail, male and female (*Anas acuta*, Toolik Field Station, ADH). *Upper right:* Northern shoveler, male (*A. clypeata*, Ice Cut, ADH). *Lower left:* Greater scaup, male (*Aythya marila*, Toolik Lake, JWS). *Lower right:* Long-tailed duck, male (*Clangula hyemalis*, Sagavanirktok River near Happy Valley, ADH).

With the exception of the northern shoveler, dabbling ducks feed by "tipping up" over sediments in shallow ponds and wetlands. Their diet is primarily sedge and grass seeds, supplemented with other vegetation, invertebrates, and occasionally small fish. Shovelers use their unique bill to filter zooplankton as they skim the surface of the water while swimming; they also feed on snails, aquatic insects, and seeds. Unlike the dabblers, scaup dive to depths of 6 m or more to capture snails, other invertebrates, and small fish. They also feed on vegetation.

The northern pintail can be the most abundant duck on the North Slope, where in some years its abundance may equal or exceed that of all other duck species combined. Years of exceptional pintail abundance on the North Slope are often attributed to drought conditions in southern Canada and the north-central United States. Green-winged teals and greater scaup are also abundant in some years, while northern shovelers, American wigeon, and mallards are usually less common. In general, dabbling ducks and scaup first arrive on the North Slope during mid-May. Although they reach their greatest abundances on the coastal plain, they can be found on almost any significant body of water on the North Slope. Nests, which receive clutches of 8–12 eggs, are bowls formed from dry grasses or sedges and lined with down, and usually concealed among dense grasses or sedges, often in riparian habitats or on the edges of frost polygons. Although nests are often near open water, they may also be relatively far from the water's edge (as much as a kilometer for northern pintails). Males abandon the nest once incubation by the female begins and migrate to large "molting" lakes. After young hatch, adult females lead them to creeks, ponds, lakes, and river deltas. Here the adult females molt while tending their brood. Young fledge by late August or early September and migrate to wintering grounds shortly thereafter. Dabbling ducks of the North Slope generally migrate south along the Pacific Flyway, with most wintering in Washington, Oregon, and California. Greater scaup winter along the Pacific coast from the Aleutian Islands to Baja California and along the Atlantic coast from Newfoundland to the Gulf of Mexico and the West Indies.

Sea Ducks

The common sea ducks of the North Slope interior are long-tailed ducks (*Clangula hyemalis,* **Fig. 13.2**) and scoters (black scoter *Melanitta nigra,* white-winged scoter *M. fusca*). Male long-tailed ducks have very long, thin central tail feathers (much longer than those of pintails) and extensive white markings on otherwise chocolate brown heads. Male surf scoters have dark plumage and orange ornamented bills. Male white-winged scoters are similar to surf scoters but have a large, trailing white wing panel and a white "comma" near the eye.

The long-tailed duck is one of the most abundant breeding ducks on the North Slope, rivaled only by the pintail in some years. Migrants arrive in mid- to late May and stage on open water near the arctic coast. As the spring thaw proceeds, pairs move inland to ponds and wetlands, where they nest. Clutches of five to nine eggs are laid in a deep bowl formed from dry sedges and grasses lined with down. Males abandon females once incubation begins and move to coastal bays and lagoons, where they molt. Once hatching occurs, adult females move with their brood to molting lakes. Long-tailed ducks feed on invertebrates (mollusks, insect larvae, crustaceans). These excellent divers have been entangled in fishing gear at depths exceeding 60 m in the Laurentian Great Lakes. Prior to migrating in late August and September, adults and young stage along the arctic coast before wintering at sea as far north as the Bering Strait, where leads or polynyas[2] provide open water, and as far south as the coasts of Washington and Japan.

White-winged scoters arrive on the North Slope in late May, when they begin to nest in shrubby foothill habitats. Their nests, which receive clutches of 7–11 eggs, are simple hollows lined with down. As with most other ducks, males migrate to molting habitat once incubation begins. Females abandon their young to join molting males one to three weeks after hatching their eggs. Abandoned young often congregate in groups of 20 or more, occasionally accompanied by straggling adult females. White-winged scoters feed on aquatic snails, insect larvae, and small fish captured by diving to depths of up to 12 m. They depart the North Slope in late summer to winter along the Pacific coast from the Aleutians to Baja California and along the Atlantic coast from Newfoundland to South Carolina. Little is known about the biology of the surf scoter.

Eiders

Four species of eiders (*Somateria*) occur in northern coastal plain habitats. Males of the common eider (*S. mollissima*) have white heads capped with black and a greenish nape. King eiders (*S. spectabilis,* **Fig. 13.3**) have a bizarre tubercle at the base of their bill, and the spectacled eider (*S. fischeri,* **Fig. 13.3**) has a greenish head with white, black-rimmed "spectacles." The threatened Steller's eider (*Polysticta stelleri*) occurs only near Barrow.

King eiders arrive on the North Slope in late May, followed by common eiders and spectacled eiders in June. The Prudhoe Bay region is the eastern limit of concentrated breeding habitat for king and spectacled eiders, while common eiders nest along the entire coast. They first appear offshore in open leads, where they stage until nesting habitats become snow-free. Their nests are shallow bowls pressed into tundra or sand and lined with dry grasses and down. These receive clutches of 1–11 eggs depending upon species. King eiders and spectacled eiders are solitary nesters that nest inland on the coastal plain along ponds and lakes. Common eiders, however, nest in colonies, often among accumulations of driftwood on barrier or river delta islands. The islands of the Sagavanirktok River delta support large colonies. Once incubation commences in early summer, males of all three species leave to molt offshore while females lead newly hatched brood to foraging habitat, where they feed on invertebrates. Eiders are excellent divers, with king eiders reaching depths of 55 m. In late summer, female king and spectacled eiders leave the coastal plain with their newly fledged young to molt offshore before eventually joining males on wintering grounds in the Bering Sea. Timing of migration is crucial for king eiders, the first species to arrive in spring. If the sea ice is unbroken and shore-fast, tens of thousands of eiders may die of starvation. Predators of eggs and young include glaucous gulls, parasitic jaegers, and arctic foxes, with gull predation being the primary cause of hatchling mortality.

Fig. 13.3. *Upper left:* King eider, male (*Somateria spectabilis*, Deadhorse, JWS). *Upper right:* Spectacled eider, male (*S. fischeri*, Deadhorse, JWS). *Lower left:* Harlequin duck, male (*Histrionicus histrionicus*, Toolik Lake, JWS). *Lower right:* Harlequin duck, female with young (Ivishak River, ADH).

Harlequin Duck

The harlequin duck (*Histrionicus histrionicus*, **Fig. 13.3**) is found along mountain and foothills streams. Breeding males are identified by slate-blue, rufous, and white markings that are the basis for the name *harlequin*. Both males and females have a distinct round white spot behind the eye. Harlequin ducks arrive here in late May and early June. Nests are on the ground near small streams, often among tree roots or in crevices. Once incubation begins in early summer, males migrate to the coast, where they join nonbreeders to molt. Following hatching, young forage for insect larvae and small fish in streams along with adult females. In late summer females and newly fledged young migrate to wintering grounds along the coast of British Columbia.

Geese

Four species of geese nest on the North Slope. Taverner's cackling goose (*Branta hutchinsii taverneri*, **Fig. 13.4**) is identified by its black head and neck, white cheek patches, and dark gray breast. Brant (*B. bernicula*) are similar to cackling geese but lack white check patches and have a white necklace. Greater white-fronted geese (*Anser albifrons*, **Fig. 13.4**) are light brown with pink bills and orange legs. Snow geese

(*Chen caerulescens,* **Fig. 13.4**) are white with black wing tips and pink legs and bills.

Adult geese feed on roots and shoots of cotton grass and sedges in spring, and seeds and berries in summer and fall. Hatchlings, however, feed primarily on invertebrates. Snow geese and brant prefer seashore habitats, whereas greater white-fronted geese and Taverner's cackling geese are more generalized. Their nests, which are simple depressions or scrapes lined with down, receive clutches of four to seven eggs (**Fig. 13.4**). Following hatching of young, the brood and parents move to feeding and molting habitat. Since geese do not reach sexual maturity until three years of age, and all members of a flock migrate, numbers of nonbreeding birds associated with nesting habitats can be large. Mortality due to predation on eggs, nestlings, and young may be high. Arctic foxes, which prey on eggs and young, are particularly important predators in coastal plain habitats. During years with a combination of a late spring and numerous lemmings, arctic foxes may be both unusually abundant and able to gain access to islands supporting nesting colonies due to persistent late spring ice. During such years entire colonies of snow geese and brant may abandon nests due to fox predation. Wolverines and grizzly bear prey on brant eggs. Glaucous gulls prey upon

Fig. 13.4. *Upper left:* Taverner's cackling geese (*Branta hutchinsii taverneri,* note dark breast, Deadhorse, ADH). *Upper right:* Cackling goose nest (Toolik Field Station, JWS). *Lower:* Snow geese (*Chen caerulescens*) and greater white-fronted geese (*Anser albifrons,* Dalton Highway, MP 372, ADH).

young brant and young snow geese. Golden eagles have been observed killing adult snow geese.

Taverner's cackling geese arrive on the North Slope in early to mid-May, when they begin nesting along rivers, small braided streams, and ponds. They are not colonial nesters, but their nests may become clustered in ideal habitat. Taverner's cackling geese are not widespread on the North Slope but may be abundant in the Prudhoe Bay region. In some years lesser Canada geese (*B. canadensis parvipes*) may be numerous on the North Slope when nonbreeding migrants join summer residents in molting habitat. Taverner's cackling geese begin to stage along the coast during August prior to migrating to wintering habitat from Washington to California by mid-September.

Greater white-fronted geese arrive on the North Slope in early to mid-May, where they are the most abundant and widespread goose species. They nest singly on sedge and grass tundra near sloughs, lakes, or ponds. A typical nest is within 2–3 m of water, often on the raised ridges of low-centered polygons. The brooding habitat of greater white-fronted geese is usually a small beaded stream, which provides transportation routes for flightless young and molting flightless adults. The white-fronted geese nesting on the North Slope are members of the mid-continent population that winters in Texas and northern Mexico.

Unlike greater white-fronted and Taverner's cackling geese, snow geese and brant are colonial nesters. Snow geese first arrive on the North Slope in early May, when they stage on snow-free tundra to await the spring thaw. The largest colony of nesting snow geese on the North Slope is found on Howe Island in the Sagavanirktok River delta. Other smaller colonies are scattered across the coastal plain. The snow geese nesting on Howe Island migrate to wintering grounds in central California, New Mexico, and northern Mexico during September. Brant arrive in late May or early June. Major colonies nest in wet sedge meadows and on sand and gravel spits on Howe and Duck Islands in the Sagavanirktok and Kuparuk River deltas. Family groups feed and molt in coastal salt marshes. During late summer brant migrate to wintering habitats off the Pacific coast, from southern Alaska to Mexico.

Mergansers

The red-breasted merganser (*Mergus serrator*) is the only merganser likely to be found on the North Slope. They are distinguished by a ragged crest of feathers near the back of their heads, thin saw-toothed bills, and a white speculum or wing patch. Breeding males have green heads, white necks, and a rufous breast. Red-breasted mergansers arrive on the North Slope in late May. In late June they begin to nest along rivers and lakes, where they feed on fish and invertebrates. Nests receive clutches of 7–12 eggs and are depressions lined with dry vegetation, usually in dense brush or among rocks near open water. Females abandon young shortly after hatching to join molting males offshore. In late summer, adults and newly fledged young migrate to wintering habitats along the Pacific coast from the Aleutians to northern Mexico and along the Atlantic coast from Newfoundland to the southern United States.

Raptors (Accipitridae)

Eagles

The golden eagle (*Aquila chrysaetos*, **Fig. 13.5**) is the largest raptor of the North Slope. It is likely to be confused only with immature bald eagles (*Haliaeetus leucocephalus*, **Fig. 13.5**), which are rare summer visitors, and rough-legged hawks (*Buteo lagopus*). Although there is little chance of misidentifying an adult bald eagle, immature bald eagles are notoriously difficult to distinguish from golden eagles—even by experts. At a distance, immature bald eagles tend to show raggedy and highly variable white patches within their otherwise brown plumage. Adult golden eagles are uniformly brown and immatures have sharply bordered white patches beneath their wings and tail. The golden eagle is much, much larger than the rough-legged hawk and has different plumage. The underwings of adult golden eagles are brown and those of juveniles are brown with central patches of white on the outer half of their wings. In comparison, the posterior half of the wing of rough-legged hawks is white. When resting, the breast of the golden eagle is brown and the back of its neck shows golden overtones, while the breast of the rough-legged hawk is usually light with a conspicuous dark band and its neck shows no sign of a golden overtone.

Golden eagles may be encountered anywhere on the North Slope but are most common in mountain and foothill habitats. They are often seen soaring above the Atigun Gorge. Golden eagles begin nesting in late April and May. Clutches usually consist of two eggs, and about 135–145 days post-laying are required for fledging. As a consequence, eggs must be laid no later than the first week of May to ensure that young can depart the North Slope as independent subadults by mid-September. Both early nesting and good weather are required for successful reproduction. Because of this tight schedule it may take a pair of eagles 10 years to successfully produce a pair of fledged young. Their massive nests, perched on mountain cliffs, may be as large as 3 m in

Fig. 13.5. *Upper left:* Bald eagle, juvenile (*Haliaeetus leucocephalus*, coastal plain along Dalton Highway, JWS). *Upper right:* Immature golden eagle (*Aquila chrysaetos*) showing white band on tail (coastal plain along Dalton Highway, JWS). *Lower left:* Golden eagle nest (Roche Moutonnee Creek, JWS). *Lower right:* Northern harrier, male (*Circus cyaneus*, Toolik Field Station, JWS).

diameter and more than 1 m high (**Fig. 13.5**). These nests may be reused for decades. Golden eagles take ground squirrels (their primary prey), snowshoe hare, Dall sheep lambs, caribou calves, foxes, and birds, particularly owls and ptarmigan. In late autumn, they presumably migrate to wintering habitats from British Columbia to Mexico.

Northern Harrier

The northern harrier (*Circus cyaneus*, **Fig. 13.5**) is a medium-size raptor often seen soaring lazily over the tundra. They are long-winged, long-tailed, and long-legged, with conspicuous white rumps. Their flight is often described as "buoyant" and they usually rock from side to side with wings held in a shallow V (dihedral). Unlike most raptors, male and female harriers differ in size and color. Males are small and gray; females are large and brown. Harriers have well-defined facial disks similar to those of owls. These are formed by a rim of stiff feathers that aids in

Fig. 13.6. *Upper:* Light-phase rough-legged hawk (*Buteo lagopus*) in flight showing conspicuous dark "wrist patches" (Ice Cut, JWS). *Lower left:* Dark-phase rough-legged hawk in flight (Toolik Field Station, JWS). *Lower right:* Rough-legged hawk (Ice Cut, JWS).

sound perception and orientation to its source, a critical system used to detect prey. On the North Slope harriers are likely to be confused only with short-eared owls, which share similar habitats and flight behavior.

Northern harriers arrive on the North Slope in May to nest on the foothills and coastal plain. Their nests receive clutches of four to six eggs and are shallow bowls of sticks, moss, and grasses on the ground, usually well concealed in wet, shrubby tundra. Females remain on their nests during incubation and early brooding while males provide food. Under optimal conditions, males may mate with more than one female but must provide food for each nest. Harriers prey upon voles, lemmings, young snowshoe hare, songbirds, and ptarmigan. They begin their migration south by mid-September and winter from southern Canada to Central America and the West Indies.

Rough-Legged Hawk

The rough-legged hawk (*Buteo lagopus*, **Fig. 13.6**) is often observed soaring in high, lazy circles or perching on mileposts along the Dalton Highway. They are large raptors that, on the North Slope, are second in size only to the eagles. The rough-legged hawk has relatively long wings

Fig. 13.7. *Upper left:* Peregrine falcon (*Falco peregrinus*, Dalton Highway, MP 308, JWS). *Upper right:* Peregrine falcon young in abandoned hawk nest (Galbraith Lake, JWS). *Lower left:* Gyrfalcon (*F. rusticolus*, Ice Cut, ADH). *Lower center:* Gyrfalcon nest on cliff ledge (Ice Cut, JWS). *Lower right:* Merlin (*F. columbarius*) feeding on ground squirrel (Toolik Field Station, JWS).

with extensive white posterior margins. When observed from below, its wings may appear almost completely white except for dark brown and diagnostic "wrist" patches. When perched, rough-legged hawks show a dark zone or band across their upper breast.

Rough-legged hawks arrive on the North Slope in early May to construct nests on cliffs and steep bluffs along streams and rivers. Their nests, which receive two to five eggs, are large and bulky structures constructed of sticks (**Fig. 13.7**). Rough-legged hawks feed primarily upon lemmings, voles, and ground squirrels, although snowshoe hare, shorebirds, and ptarmigan are also taken. Once likely prey are detected, a hawk may hover in place before plunging in pursuit. Rough-legged hawks migrate to winter habitats from southern Canada and throughout the United States in late September.

Falcons

Although never abundant on the North Slope, falcons are conspicuous. The merlin (*Falco columbarius*, **Fig. 13.7**) is the smallest of the three species of falcon occurring here and is identified by a slate-blue back and upper wings, a long banded tail, and a breast colored by

Fig. 13.8. *Left:* Carcass of rock ptarmigan (*Lagopus mutus*) killed by raptor (Galbraith Lake, ADH). Raptors typically consume the head and breast muscles and leave the wings and legs, as shown. *Right:* Peregrine falcon feeding on ptarmigan (Toolik Field Station, Edward Metzger).

alternating dark, longitudinal streaks. The peregrine falcon (*F. peregrinus,* **Fig. 13.7**) is distinguished by its familiar dark mustache. When viewed from below, its tail has much narrower bands than the merlin and adults have breasts that are streaked transversely rather than longitudinally. The gyrfalcon (*F. rusticolus,* **Fig. 13.7**) is very large, with a stocky body and broad wings. The coloration of the gyrfalcon is variable, but most North Slope birds range from pale gray to almost white.

Gyrfalcons and peregrine falcons gather no nesting materials. Consequently, they must either nest directly on cliff ledges or co-opt a nest constructed by ravens, rough-legged hawks, or golden eagles (**Fig. 13.7**). Merlins may show similar behavior but also nest on the ground, typically in willow or birch scrub. All three species produce clutches of three to five eggs in early spring and incubation is mostly by the female. Merlins are predators of small shorebirds, songbirds, and large flying insects. Peregrine falcons take ptarmigan (**Fig. 13.8**), shorebirds, ducks, and songbirds. Gyrfalcons prey on ptarmigan, shorebirds, ducks, geese, jaegers, gulls, smaller raptors, ground squirrels, and snowshoe hare. The migration of North Slope gyrfalcons is linked to population cycles of their major prey—ptarmigan. In years of high ptarmigan abundance, gyrfalcon may overwinter near their nesting cliffs. In years when ptarmigan are scarce, they may migrate to wintering habitats as far south as the northern United States. Peregrine falcons and merlins presumably follow their migrating prey southward in September. Peregrine falcons winter from southern Canada as far south as Chile and Argentina. Merlins winter from the northwestern United States to South America and the West Indies.

Ptarmigan (Phasianidae)

Two species of ptarmigan occur on the North Slope: the willow ptarmigan (*Lagopus lagopus,* **Fig. 13.9**) and the rock ptarmigan (*L. mutus,* **Fig. 13.9**). Both species show extreme seasonal changes in plumage, being white with black tails during winter and a cryptic mottled brown in summer. Breeding male willow ptarmigan (April–June) have rufous heads and necks and white bodies. In contrast, breeding male rock ptarmigan retain their white winter plumage, which contrasts strongly with their exaggerated red eyebrow wattles. During winter, ptarmigan aggregate into flocks of dozens to hundreds of birds; during summer, they disperse into individual territories. Although they are year-round residents of the North Slope, ptarmigan may show a vague migratory behavior. Female willow ptarmigan near Anaktuvuk Pass, for example, move southward to winter in the interior valleys of the Brooks Range and return to summer on the North Slope. There are numerous reports of 6–10-year population cycles for ptarmigan, but causes of such cycles are unclear.

Willow ptarmigan are widely distributed on the North Slope. Rock ptarmigan, however, are confined to the foothills and mountains. Both

Fig. 13.9. *Upper left:* Willow ptarmigan, male (*Lagopus lagopus,* Toolik Field Station, ADH). *Upper center:* Willow ptarmigan, female (Toolik Field Station, ADH). *Upper right:* Willow ptarmigan, female (Toolik Field Station, ADH). *Lower left:* Rock ptarmigan, male (*L. mutus,* Toolik Field Station, ADH). *Lower center:* Rock ptarmigan, female (Ivishak River, ADH). *Lower right:* Willow ptarmigan (Oksrukuyik Creek, ADH).

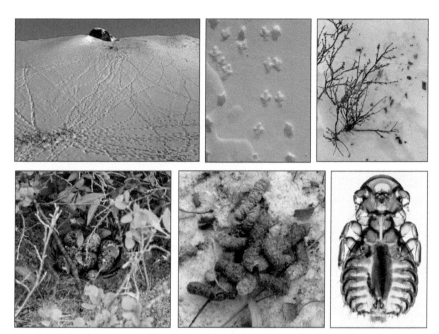

Fig. 13.10. *Upper left:* Ptarmigan tracks (Galbraith Lake, ADH). *Upper center:* Ptarmigan tracks (Happy Valley, ADH). *Upper right:* Ptarmigan feeding sign (Ivishak River, ADH). *Lower left:* Rock ptarmigan nest, abandoned following hatching of eggs (Toolik Field Station, JWS). *Lower center:* Ptarmigan scat in winter with willow fibers (Trevor Creek, ADH). *Lower right:* Chewing louse (Phthiraptera) from rock ptarmigan (Galbraith Lake, ADH).

species produce clutches of 6–10 eggs in early June. The nests of willow ptarmigan are shallow depressions on tussock or shrubby tundra. Those of rock ptarmigan are scrapes in carpets of moss and lichen (**Fig. 13.10**). Male willow ptarmigan are monogamous and tend nesting females and brood. Male rock ptarmigan, however, abandon the female shortly after incubation commences. The precocial[3] young of both species remain with adults through the summer, feeding primarily on insects. In spring and summer adults feed on leaves and flower buds of willow, birches, and alder, supplemented by seeds and berries. During winter, ptarmigan shelter in dense, riparian willow thickets, where they feed on willow buds and twigs (**Fig. 13.10**). The fact that ptarmigan often gain weight on such a low-quality diet—when many other animals wintering on the North Slope are effectively starving—provides evidence of their impressive adaptation to the Arctic.

Cranes (Gruidae)

The sandhill crane (*Grus canadensis,* **Fig. 13.11**) is unlikely to be confused with any other bird on the North Slope, given its gray plumage, red "cap," long legs and neck, and large size (length about 104 cm, wingspan about 185 cm). Sandhill cranes first arrive in May and begin nesting in wet tundra along rivers and sloughs in early June, often within a few kilometers of the arctic coast. Their nests are broad platforms (0.5–1.0 m in diameter) of vegetation topped by shallow depressions lined with dry grass and feathers. Clutches usually consist of two eggs that are incubated cooperatively and their precocious young usually fledge by late August. Sandhill cranes are omnivorous, feeding on voles, lemmings, invertebrates, roots, tubers, and berries. Those nesting on the North Slope are members of the lesser sandhill crane complex that summers from Siberia to northern Canada and winters in Texas, New Mexico, and northern Mexico.

Shorebirds (Scolopacidae)

Shorebirds comprise a diverse family of small to medium-size birds with long legs and thin bills. Eleven genera of shorebirds are widespread on the North Slope. These include plovers (*Pluvialis, Charadrius*), "peep" sandpipers (*Calidris*), yellowlegs (*Tringa*), the spotted sandpiper (*Actitis*), curlews (*Numenius*), turnstones (*Arenaria*), tattlers (*Heteroscelus*), dowitchers (*Limnodromus*), snipes (*Gallinago*), and phalaropes (*Phalaropus*). A number of other shorebirds are common near the coast but are rarely encountered inland (dunlin *Calidris alpina*, pectoral sandpiper *C. melantos*, stilt sandpiper *C. himantopus* [**Fig. 13.12**], red phalarope *Phalaropus fulicaria*). Shorebirds are usually found along streams, rivers, wetlands,

Fig. 13.11. *Left:* Sandhill crane (*Grus canadensis*, Toolik Field Station, JWS). *Right:* Sandhill crane (Ice Cut, ADH).

Fig. 13.12. Flock of peeps, including semipalmated (*Calidris pusilla*, small) and stilt (*C. himantopus*, large) sandpipers (Deadhorse, JWS).

ponds, and lakes, where they capture prey, usually invertebrates, by picking or probing. Spring migrants usually arrive in May and June to nest in habitats that are snow-free early in the season. Their nests (**Fig. 13.13**) are shallow scrapes or hollows sparsely lined with vegetation in habitats ranging from the banks of mountain streams to coastal marshes. Clutches invariably consist of four eggs and, with a few exceptions (Wilson's snipe, spotted sandpiper, red-necked phalarope), incubation is shared. Adults of many species feign injury to lure would-be predators away from nests. Their young are precocial.

Plovers

Three species of plovers are found on the North Slope: the American golden plover (*Pluvialis dominica,* **Fig. 13.13**), black-bellied plover (*P. squatarola,* **Fig. 13.13**), and the semipalmated plover (*Charadrius semipalmatus,* **Fig. 13.13**). Breeding golden and black-bellied plovers both have black breasts. The underside of the American golden plover is entirely black, however, while that of the black-bellied plovers is white from legs to tail. The semipalmated plover has a single dark breast band and orange legs.

American golden plovers nest on the dry heaths of well-drained ridges and kames adjacent to moist tussock and wetland habitats; they can be relatively conspicuous and abundant in these habitats. American golden plovers winter in Argentina and Patagonia. Black-bellied plovers are relatively uncommon on the North Slope but can be found on the

Fig. 13.13. *Upper left:* American golden plover (*Pluvialis dominica*, Toolik Field Station, JWS). *Lower left:* American golden plover, young (Toolik Field Station, JWS). *Upper center:* Black-bellied plover (*P. squatarola*, Ice Cut, ADH). *Upper right:* Semipalmated plover (*Charadrius semipalmatus*, Ivishak River, JWS). *Lower right:* Semipalmated plover nest (Toolik Field Station, JWS).

coastal plain in areas of dry tundra. They winter along the Pacific coast from southeastern Alaska to Chile and the Atlantic coast from New England to Brazil. Semipalmated plovers occur along large braided rivers where they nest on gravel bars, stony beaches, or dry heaths. Fall migrants depart in mid-August to winter along the coasts of California and North Carolina to southern South America and the West Indies.

"Peeps"

Four species of *Calidris* or "peep" sandpipers regularly occur inland on the North Slope: Baird's sandpiper (*Calidris bairdii*), the western sandpiper (*C. mauri*), semipalmated sandpiper (*C. pusilla*, **Figs. 13.12, 13.14**), and the least sandpiper (*C. minutilla*, **Fig. 13.14**). The least sandpiper, the world's smallest (length about 15 cm, mass about 20 g), is identified by yellow-greenish rather than black legs. The remaining *Calidris* sandpipers are difficult to distinguish. Those interested in their

Fig. 13.14. *Upper left:* Least sandpiper (*Calidris minutilla*, Ivishak River, JWS). *Upper right:* Semipalmated sandpiper (*C. pusilla*, Deadhorse, JWS). *Lower left:* Red-necked phalarope, female (*Phalaropus lobatus*, Deadhorse, JWS). Note droplet of water being "ratcheted" up the bill. *Lower right:* Trio of long-billed dowitchers (*Limnodromus scolopaceus*, Ice Cut, ADH).

identification should consult specialized field guides. The peeps are most common in coastal plain habitats.

Semipalmated sandpipers are one of the most abundant shorebirds of the inland North Slope. They usually nest within a few kilometers of the coast in moist to wet tundra habitats. Females abandon males and young shortly after hatching and begin their southward migration to wintering habitats off the coasts of Central and South America and the West Indies. Adult males remain to brood their young until late July, when they too migrate south, followed by fledged juveniles in August. The least sandpiper also nests on the coastal plain but usually farther inland than semipalmated sandpipers. They winter from the southern United States to central South America and the West Indies. Western sandpipers are most abundant on the western coastal plain. They winter in coastal habitats from the southern United States to South America. Unlike the previous three species, Baird's sandpiper nests on well-drained, stony ridges and riparian habitats throughout the North Slope. Individuals of this uncommon species may be found foraging along rocky streambeds. Adults begin their southward migration to wintering habitats in South America in July, followed by juveniles in August.

Other Shorebirds

Lesser yellowlegs (*Tringa flavipes*) are distinguished by long yellow legs and a white rump that is conspicuous in flight. They nest on well-drained slopes and ridges, sometimes far from water. Yellowlegs feed in shallow wetlands, sometimes submerged to their bellies while stalking invertebrates and small fish. They winter along the Pacific coast from California to Chile and the Atlantic coast from North Carolina to Argentina and the West Indies.

The spotted sandpiper (*Actitis macularia*) is found in the foothills and mountains, where solitary individuals forage along stream and riverbanks. Spotted sandpipers are identified by their spotted breast, orange bill, and diagnostic "bobbing" behavior. They nest on gravel bars and other sparsely vegetated habitats, usually within 30 m of open water. They winter along the Pacific coast south of British Columbia and the Atlantic coast from South Carolina to South America. Like the red-necked phalarope, female spotted sandpipers mate with and lay eggs in the nests of more than one male (polyandry). Eggs are incubated exclusively by males.

The whimbrel (*Numenius phaeopus*) is a large shorebird identified with a strongly down-curved bill about two times as long as its head. Unlike most species of North Slope shorebirds, the whimbrel is most abundant in open tussock-tundra valleys of the foothills where it nests on well-drained ridges. They winter along the southern coast of the United States to Brazil.

The ruddy turnstone (*Arenaria interpres*) is found along large braided rivers and on coastal mudflats. Their short, slightly upturned bills are used to flip rocks as they forage for insects on gravel bars. Breeding males are unmistakable, having striking black-and-white markings on their heads, rufous wings, and orange legs. Ruddy turnstones nest on riverbanks, upland heaths, dry tundra, or similar sparsely vegetated habitats. In the Prudhoe Bay region they nest on saline tundra near the Arctic Ocean. Ruddy turnstones winter along the California coast and the Atlantic coast from Maryland to South America.

Wilson's snipe (*Gallinago delicate*) is small, stocky, long-billed, and short-winged. It is one of the few shorebirds found more frequently in foothills habitats than on the coastal plain. Wilson's snipe is extraordinarily cryptic and is usually detected only by the aerial display of breeding males. Such displays consist of the rapid ascent of a male immediately followed by a rapid circling descent while extending specialized tail feathers laterally. These feathers cause an eerie "winnowing" sound often heard near foothills lakes and wetlands. If one is particularly observant, the specialized feathers of male snipes can be observed in flight. Wilson's snipes nest in habitats ranging from wet sedge meadows to riparian willow thickets and upland tundra. Unlike most shorebirds, females incubate eggs alone. Wilson's snipe winters from southern Canada to South America and the West Indies.

Red-necked phalaropes (*Phalaropus lobatus,* **Fig. 13.14**) are common on the coastal plain and foothills, where they nest in sedge meadows, near the shores of ponds, or on margins of low-centered polygons. Unlike most other shorebirds, breeding female phalaropes have the more striking color pattern consisting of slate gray breasts, rufous necks, and white throat patches. Both males and females have needle-like bills. The reversed pattern of coloration between male and female phalaropes is related to their reversed nesting roles compared with other shorebirds. Males incubate eggs and rear the brood alone. In some cases, a single female may lay clutches of eggs in as many as four separate nests, each tended by a different male (serial polyandry). Females return to their wintering habitat at sea once eggs are laid. Phalaropes are highly aquatic; if not flying they are usually swimming. They feed on zooplankton, which they capture by swimming in tight circles to generate vortices that draw suspended prey toward the surface. They then capture and swallow droplets of water containing prey. This is possible because their remarkable beaks function as capillary ratchets that move droplets from the beak's tip to their mouths. Red-necked phalaropes winter in small flocks offshore off the western coast of South America.

The long-billed dowitcher (*Limnodromus scolopaceus,* **Fig. 13.14**) is a stocky shorebird with a long, straight bill that is about twice the length of its head and a white rump that is conspicuous when in flight. They are most abundant on the coastal plain, where they nest in wet tundra, but they are also regular visitors to the foothills, where they may be found foraging for invertebrates along rivers and streams. They feed by probing with their bills, often while fully immersing their heads. Long-billed dowitchers winter along the southern coast of the United States, Mexico, and Central America.

The wandering tattler (*Heteroscelus incanus,* **Fig. 13.15**) nests in foothills and mountain habitats. They are distinguished from other North Slope shorebirds by yellow, relatively short legs; gray backs and tails; and heavily white-and-black barred breasts. Wandering tattlers are found along rocky foothills and mountain streams in which they forage for insects, often submerging their heads in the process. They nest in gravelly, riparian habitats. The wandering tattler winters along the Pacific coast from southern California to Ecuador and in the South Pacific as far south as New Zealand.

Jaegers, Gulls, and Terns (Laridae)

Jaegers

Jaegers are predators and kleptoparasites.[4] Unlike raptors, jaegers lack clawed talons—their feet are webbed for swimming—and must kill prey on the ground with their bills alone. They are also unable to carry prey with their feet. Prey must be either consumed on the ground or dismantled and carried in their crops. Jaegers arrive from their oceanic wintering habitats in May and, in years of successful nesting, begin their return migration in August and September. When on the tundra they feed on lemmings, voles, young birds, eggs, small fish and invertebrates, and carrion. When at sea they feed on fish robbed from other seabirds. Their nests are shallow depressions lined with fragments of lichen or moss (**Fig. 13.15**). Clutches usually contain two eggs and are incubated by both parents. In years when tundra prey are scarce they may abandon their nests and return to sea.

Three species of jaegers occur on the North Slope—the long-tailed jaeger (*Stercorarius longicaudus,* **Fig. 13.15**), the parasitic jaeger (*S. parasiticus,* **Fig. 13.15**), and the pomarine jaeger (*S. pomarinus*). Breeding long-tailed jaegers are identified by long central tail feathers and white heads topped with black caps. Long-tailed jaegers nest in tussock tundra and dry heath habitats over which they often hover as they search for lemmings, voles, and other prey. Long-tailed jaegers are prey for peregrine falcons, gyrfalcons, and foxes. Predation by arctic foxes is an important cause of mortality of eggs and young, particularly in years following peaks in lemming abundance when foxes are numerous. Long-tailed jaegers winter at sea along the Pacific coast of South America from Ecuador to Chile and along the Atlantic coast of Argentina.

Parasitic jaegers have short central tail feathers that form a "spike." They occur in two different color morphs, light and dark. The light morph is similar to the long-tailed jaeger. The dark morph is uniformly slate gray. Parasitic jaegers are common on the coastal plain and are regular visitors to the foothills. They nest in wet sedge tundra, often placing nests on the dry ridges separating low-centered polygons. Like many shorebirds, parasitic jaegers may feign injury to lure would-be predators away from their nests and young. They are proficient at catching peeps and phalaropes on the wing. As kleptoparasites, parasitic jaegers have

Fig. 13.15. *Upper left:* Parasitic jaeger (*Stercorarius parasiticus*, Toolik Field Station, JWS). *Upper right:* Long-tailed jaeger (*S. longicaudus*, Toolik Field Station, ADH). *Lower left:* Wandering tattler (*Heteroscelus incanus*, Ivishak River, ADH). *Lower right:* Long-tailed jaeger nest (Toolik Field Station, ADH).

been observed harassing red-throated loons until they drop fish, which are then taken. Parasitic jaegers winter at sea in the Atlantic Ocean from the British Isles south to southern Africa and Argentina and in the Pacific Ocean from Baja California south to Chile and New Zealand.

The pomarine jaeger is the largest jaeger of the North Slope and has spatula-shaped central tail feathers that are curiously twisted. Pomarine jaegers nest in sedge tundra along the arctic coast, often on the ridges separating low-centered polygons. Their abundance varies dramatically from year to year, depending on lemming population cycles. Unlike other jaegers, pomarine jaegers will hunt on foot, systematically removing the roofs of lemming runways as they become exposed by the spring thaw. They are also proficient hunters of shorebirds, often taking them on the wing. Pomarine jaegers winter off the shores of Peru and the Galapagos Islands.

Gulls

Only two species of gulls are common in inland habitats of the North Slope, the glaucous gull (*Larus hyperboreus*, **Fig. 13.16**) and the mew gull (*L. canus*, **Fig. 13.16**). The glaucous gull is a large, conspicuous, and very pale bird, lacking black wing tips. The mew gull is smaller, with conspicuous black wing tips. Sabine's gull (*Xema sabini*), which

Fig. 13.16. *Upper left:* Arctic tern (*Sterna paradisaea*, Toolik Field Station, JWS). *Upper right:* Mew gull (*Larus canus*, Ivishak River, JWS). *Lower left:* Glaucous gull nest (*L. hyperboreus*, pond at MP 284, Dalton Highway, ADH). *Lower right:* Glaucous gulls (Toolik Field Station, JWS).

has a black head during summer, is abundant along the coast but rarely ventures inland.

Glaucous and mew gulls first appear on the North Slope in early May, often well before snowmelt. Glaucous gulls nest in large colonies along the arctic coast (e.g., 300 nests). Those nesting inland on coastal plain and foothills lakes and ponds, however, nest alone on small islands or on narrow peninsulas. Their nests are placed on top of conical mounds of vegetation and receive two to three eggs that are incubated by both sexes (**Fig. 13.16**). Glaucous gulls are predators of the eggs and young of ducks, shorebirds, lemmings, voles, invertebrates, and fish. They also scavenge fresh carrion and compete with ravens and jaegers for the heaps of entrails discarded by caribou hunters and road-killed arctic ground squirrels that litter the Dalton Highway. Predators of glaucous gulls include ravens and parasitic jaegers, which take their young and eggs, and other glaucous gulls. They migrate to winter habitats along the Pacific coast from southeastern Alaska south to California and the Atlantic coast from New England to Florida in late September. Like glaucous gulls, mew gulls nest on islands, peninsulas, and gravel bars of foothills lakes and rivers. They may co-opt abandoned nests of glaucous gulls if available. Mew gulls are predators of aquatic invertebrates and small fish. North Slope birds migrate to winter habitats along the Pacific coast from Alaska to Baja California in late August.

Fig. 13.17. *Left:* Short-eared owl in flight showing dark wrist patch, male (*Asio flamme-us*, Toolik Field Station, JWS). *Center:* Short-eared owl, male (Toolik Field Station, JWS). *Right:* Short-eared owl showing ear tufts, female (Oksrukuyik Creek, ADH).

Terns

The arctic tern (*Sterna paradisaea*, **Fig. 13.16**) is the only tern found inland on the North Slope. Adults arrive in May to nest in wet tundra along the shores of rivers, marshes, and lakes. Their nests are simple scrapes that are usually detected only by the presence of eggs. Clutches consist of two eggs that are incubated by both parents. Arctic terns often hover over lakes and ponds, searching for fish that are captured by plunging through the water's surface. Young are fed fish that adults carry with their bills. Arctic terns have the greatest range of any bird breeding on the North Slope. After departing in mid- to late August, they migrate to wintering habitat off the coast of Antarctica. While migrating, one banded bird flew approximately 13,750 km in three months. For their size, arctic terns are exceptionally long-lived, with some wild birds reaching ages greater than 30 years.

Owls (Strigidae)

Two species of owls occur on the North Slope: the short-eared owl (*Asio flammeus*, **Fig. 13.17**) and the snowy owl (*Bubo scandiacus*, **Figs. 13.18, 13.19**). Short-eared owls are large, pale birds with dark "wrists" and wing tips. Their low, buoyant flight causes them to be confused with harriers, which hunt over similar terrain. Females are distinguished from males by their darker plumage. Their nests are shallow grass-lined bowls on the ground in shrubby or wet sedge tundra. Clutches of four to eight eggs are brooded by females. Short-eared owls are predators of voles, lemmings, and songbirds. The contents of their owl pellets[5]

Fig. 13.18. *Left:* Snowy owl, male (*Bubo scandiacus*, Deadhorse, ADH). *Center:* Snowy owl, female (Deadhorse, ADH). *Right:* Snowy owl in flight showing densely feathered legs (Deadhorse, ADH).

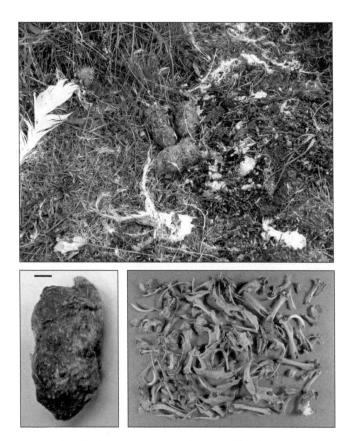

Fig. 13.19. *Upper:* Detail of snowy owl roost showing three "owl pellets" (center), guano splashes, and molted feathers (Deadhorse, ADH). *Lower left:* Close-up of owl pellet from snowy owl roost (scale line = 1 cm, Deadhorse, ADH). *Lower right:* Remains of five collared lemmings from pellet shown at left.

during May 2011 indicated that they may feed on snow buntings when the tundra is snow-covered. Short-eared owls are prey for rough-legged hawks, snowy owls, gyrfalcons, and red foxes, which are particularly effective predators of young owls. Short-eared owls arrive on the North Slope in May and return to wintering habitats in the United States and Mexico in September.

The snowy owl—the heaviest North American owl—is very large and very white. They are most abundant on the coastal plain, where they may be conspicuous while perching on the tundra. As with short-eared owls, the plumage of males and females differs; females have breasts that are heavily barred with brown, whereas males are mostly white. Like the arctic fox, snowy owls show high cold tolerance due to effective insulation. The conductance of body heat through the plumage of the snowy owl is lower than that of any other bird except the Adélie penguin (*Pygoscelis adeliae*) and is equivalent to that of the winter pelt of arctic fox. The nests of snowy owls are simple scrapes on hummocks or low ridges that receive clutches of 4–10 eggs incubated by the female. They prey upon lemmings, voles, other birds including ducks and eiders, and possibly fish. Lake trout have been found cached in their nests in the Canadian Arctic. Snowy owls arrive on the North Slope by March and return to winter habitats in southern Canada and the northern Great Plains by late September, although some birds may occasionally over-winter. They are exceptionally wide-ranging creatures with some individuals breeding in Siberia, Alaska, and Canada in successive summers. The year-to-year abundance of both snowy and short-eared owls on the North Slope shows high year-to-year fluctuations due to regional migrations in response to fluctuating prey availability. The cyclical appearances of the snowy owl are particularly pronounced at Barrow.[6] Here no snowy owls can be found during most summers. In years when lemmings are abundant (about every three to five years), however, as many as a dozen snowy owl nests may be observed from a single location.

Tyrant Flycatchers (Tyrannidae)

Two species of flycatchers are regular but uncommon visitors of the North Slope. The alder flycatcher (*Empidonax alnorum*) is a typical *Empidonax* flycatcher with an olive-green back and white wing bars. Say's phoebe (*Sayornis saya*) is a colorful flycatcher with a rufous belly and black tail that has been described as a "small robin-like bird that behaves like a flycatcher," referring to a stereotyped feeding behavior consisting of rapid darting flights from conspicuous perches to capture or "hawk" flying insects. Say's phoebe occurs locally in the mountains and foothills, where it nests on the ledges of cliffs and outcrops over-looking rivers and streams. Their nests, which receive clutches of three to seven eggs, are bowls of grasses or moss lined with feathers, fur, or willow down. They arrive in late May and depart in July for winter-ing habitats in the southwestern United States and Mexico. The alder flycatcher is an uncommon visitor to willow thickets along foothills streams; there are no nesting records for the North Slope.

Shrikes (Laniidae)

The northern shrike (*Lanius excubitor,* **Fig. 13.20**) is a robin-size bird with a hooked bill, gray back, and black wings with conspicuous white patches. Adults arrive on the North Slope in May to nest in riparian willow thickets in the foothills and mountains. Their nests are bowls of twigs, often lined with ptarmigan feathers, and usually 2–3 m above the ground (**Fig. 13.20**). Females produce clutches of two to nine eggs. Shrikes are predators of small mammals and birds but may attack prey

Fig. 13.20. *Upper left:* Northern shrike, adult (*Lanius excubitor,* Galbraith Lake, ADH). *Upper center:* Field sparrow carcass cached by shrike (Toolik Field Station, JWS). *Upper right:* Singing vole carcass cached by shrike (Ivishak River, ADH). *Lower left:* Shrike nest with egg photographed on May 30, 2008 (Galbraith Lake, ADH). *Lower right:* Same nest with six young photographed on June 26, 2008 (Galbraith Lake, ADH).

as large as American robins. Because they lack talons, they often wedge prey in the forks of shrubs to facilitate butchering. Macabre examples of cached prey, usually singing voles, may be observed near nests (**Fig. 13.20**). Northern shrikes migrate to wintering habitats in southern Canada and the northern United States in late August or September.

Jays and Ravens (Corvidae)

Two species of Corvidae occur on the North Slope, the common raven (*Corvus corax*, **Fig. 13.21**) and the gray jay (*Perisoreus canadensis*, **Fig. 13.21**). As both the largest songbird and the largest all-black bird in the world, ravens are conspicuous. Gray jays, with white faces, black caps, and small beaks, resemble overgrown chickadees.

The raven is one of a handful of birds that are year-round residents of the North Slope. Although little is known about the ecology of ravens here prior to the development of Prudhoe Bay, it is likely that they were

Fig. 13.21. *Upper left:* Ravens (*Corvus corax*, Happy Valley, ADH). ***Upper right:*** Raven nest (Happy Valley, ADH). ***Lower left:*** Bird's-eye view of raven nest lined with caribou hair and muskoxen underfur (*qiviut*) containing five young. This picture was taken by leaning over the rail of the Atigun River 1 Bridge (ADH). ***Lower right:*** Gray jay (*Perisoreus canadensis*, Oksrukuyik Creek, February 2009, ADH).

restricted to foothills and mountain habitats because cliffs and steep bluffs are required for nesting. Ravens are now widely distributed on the coastal plain, however, due to an abundance of man-made structures providing nest supports (**Fig. 13.21**). At least 20–25 pairs of ravens nest in Deadhorse and the Kuparuk and Prudhoe Bay oil fields each year, where there were probably none prior to development. These nests produce an average of 60–75 successfully fledged young annually.

The ability of ravens to flourish over a wide range of latitudes without modifying their behaviors is astonishing. On the North Slope ravens commence building nests in mid-March, begin laying eggs in late March, and fledge young in June—a timing essentially identical to those nesting in more temperate environments south of the Canadian border. Their nests are bulky platforms constructed of sticks or, in the oil fields, industrial materials (**Fig. 13.21**). These platforms contain a deep bowl lined with hair, lichens, and mosses that receives clutches of three to seven eggs incubated by the female while tended by the male. Ravens are long-lived birds (some wild individuals achieve 20 years or more in age) that pair for life. They are well known for scavenging carrion, but they are also effective predators. Like owls, ravens regurgitate pellets containing the undigested remains of their prey. An analysis of raven pellets collected in the vicinity of Deadhorse showed that 55 percent contained mammal remains, including those of northern collared and brown lemmings and tundra and singing voles. Bird feathers, duck bills, and eggshells (goose, duck, and ptarmigan) were also abundant. In addition to carrion and prey, ravens feed opportunistically on berries. Ravens will cache food by covering it with soil or snow. Although considered year-round residents of the North Slope, individuals may move widely. One female marked in Deadhorse was later observed in Fairbanks. Most breeding adults, however, remain on the North Slope.

The gray jay is an uncommon, likely year-round resident of the North Slope (in February 2009 a pair of birds was observed in a willow thicket along Oksrukuyik Creek, **Fig. 13.21**). Although well known for their conspicuous behavior, gray jays are secretive when nesting. Their nests are relatively bulky bowls of twigs, grass, and moss lined with hair that are constructed in tall shrubs (3 m or more) from late February through April. Females produce clutches of three to four eggs. Gray jays feed opportunistically on invertebrates, berries, flowers, and carrion. They have also been observed killing young snowshoe hares and songbird nestlings. Like ravens, gray jays will cache food in times of surplus. Unlike any other North American bird, however, gray jays cache food in trees by gluing it to tree bark with sticky saliva that coagulates rapidly when exposed to air. This behavior prevents their caches from becoming buried in snow.

Larks (Alaudidae)

The horned lark (*Eremophila alpestris,* **Fig. 13.22**) is relatively common on foothill heaths where adults feed on seeds and invertebrates. Although their "horns" (feather tufts) are apparent only at close range, they can be identified by conspicuous, dark masks and a dark breast band. Horned larks arrive on the North Slope in early May. Their nests are shallow cups of fine grasses that are constructed on the ground, often in natural hollows in barren, stony habitats. Clutches consisting of two to five eggs are incubated by the females. Horned larks begin their southward migration to wintering habitats in southern Canada and the northern United States by mid-August.

Chickadees (Paridae)

The gray-headed chickadee (*Poecile cincta*) is rare, very local, and possibly a year-round resident of the North Slope. It is similar to other chickadee species from which it is distinguished by its large size, long tail, and decidedly grayish cap. It is widespread across Russia and northern Europe. Populations on the North Slope and the Yukon and arctic Canada represent the eastern limit of its range. Most reports of gray-headed chickadees in Alaska are from the Canning River region of the Arctic National Wildlife Refuge, where breeding pairs occur in scattered balsam-poplar groves that are large enough to provide tree cavities in which they nest.

Swallows (Hirundinidae)

Two species of swallows are regularly found on the North Slope: the bank swallow (*Riparia riparia,* **Fig. 13.22**) and the cliff swallow (*Petrochelidon pyrrhonota,* **Fig. 13.22**). Bank swallows, the smallest North American swallow, have a dark band across their white breasts and conspicuously notched tails. Cliff swallows are larger, have buffy rumps, and lack a notched tail. Bank and cliff swallows fly in loose, wheeling flocks along bluffs and cliffs overlooking rivers. They feed on flying insects, particularly the terrestrial adults of otherwise aquatic insects. Swallows arrive on the North Slope in late May and depart in mid-August.

Fig. 13.22. *Upper left:* Horned lark (*Eremophila alpestris*, Toolik Field Station, JWS). *Upper right:* Arctic warbler (*Phylloscopus borealis*, Ivishak River, JWS). *Lower left:* Cliff swallow feeding young at nest at Atigun River 2 Bridge (*Petrochelidon pyrrhonota*, MP 271, JWS). *Lower right:* Bank swallows at burrow entrance (*Riparia riparia*, Ice Cut, JWS).

Bank swallows nest in burrows in steep bluffs and tall banks along rivers. Their burrows are approximately 70–90 cm long with deceptively small (about 3 by 5 cm) openings containing nests of dry grasses lined with hair or feathers. Bank swallows produce clutches of four to eight eggs that are incubated cooperatively. Small colonies of bank swallows (e.g., 8–10 birds) have been reported from burrows along the Sagavanirktok River at Ice Cut, Sagwon Bluffs, and Happy Valley. They winter in Central and South America.

Cliff swallows build jug-shaped nests of mud lined with fine grass or hair and attached to sheer cliffs, outcrops, and bridge supports. They produce clutches of three to six eggs that are incubated cooperatively. Although regarded as uncommon on the North Slope, a large colony (about 100 nests) was reported from cliffs along the upper Kuparuk River early in the 20th century and scattered nests have been found on cliffs along the Atigun River. A colony occurs beneath the Atigun 2 Bridge and pipeline crossing. Cliff swallows winter in South America as far as southern Argentina.

Old-World Warblers (Sylviidae)

The arctic warbler (*Phylloscopus borealis*, **Fig. 13.22**) is primarily a Eurasian species with a range that includes the North Slope as its eastern limit. They are small, drab olive in color, and have prominent pale "eyebrows." They inhabit dense, riparian willow thickets from which they glean insects. Their nests, which receive clutches of five to seven eggs, are hair-lined domes of grasses and moss constructed on the ground. Arctic warblers have recently been reported from the Ivishak River and from willow thickets near the Sag River DOT camp (Dalton Highway, MP 305) and Ice Cut. They begin migrating to wintering habitats in Southeast Asia, the Philippines, the Moluccas, and the East Indies by mid-August.

Dippers (Cinclidae)

The American dipper (*Cinclus mexicanus*, **Fig. 13.23**) is an extremely local, permanent resident of the North Slope. Dippers are stocky, slate gray, long-legged birds with stubby tails. On the North Slope dippers are found only near perennial springs and groundwater-fed rivers, where they are conspicuous as they fly to and fro just above the water's surface. Dippers are truly aquatic birds that may submerge their entire bodies and swim or walk about on the stream bottom as they forage for aquatic insects and larval fish. When on land they show a stereotyped "dipping" behavior, explaining their common name. Their nests, constructed in May, are spherical enclosures of moss with a small, slightly downward-facing opening on one side (**Fig. 13.23**). These are attached to cliff faces, usually behind waterfalls. Clutches of four to five eggs are incubated by females. Once their eggs have hatched, adults are conspicuous as they ferry insect larvae from stream to brood. Dippers show several adaptations to their aquatic habitat. Their uropygial (preen) gland, which provides oils used to waterproof feathers, is 10 times larger than those of other songbirds. They also have movable flaps that seal their nostrils when underwater, and thick nictitating membranes ("third eyelid") that protect their eyes from spray (**Fig. 13.23**). Finally, when compared with songbirds of similar size, they have an unusually high density (about 1.4 times greater) of short, contour feathers that, when coated with oils from the uropygial gland, provides a water-repellent overcoat that

Fig. 13.23. *Upper left:* American dipper (*Cinclus mexicanus*, Ivishak River, JWS). *Upper right:* American dipper showing well-developed nictitating membrane (Ivishak River, JWS). *Lower left:* A pair of American dippers have nested beneath this overhang almost every year since 2001 (Ivishak Hot Spring, ADH). *Lower right:* American dipper nest with brood (Ivishak Hot Spring, ADH).

protects a dense undercoat of down. This undercoat is an obvious pre-adaptation to the North Slope winter, where they have been observed actively foraging in spring streams and open leads in rivers when air temperatures are below −40°C.

Thrushes (Turdidae)

Four species of thrushes are found on the North Slope: the bluethroat (*Luscinia svecica*, **Fig. 13.24**), northern wheatear (*Oenanthe oenanthe*, **Fig. 13.24**), gray-cheeked thrush (*Catharus minimus*, **Fig. 13.24**), and American robin (*Turdus migratorius*). Bluethroats have a rufous rump divided by a dark longitudinal band that is conspicuous in flight. Males have a unique blue and rufous throat patch; females have a pale throat bordered with black. Northern wheatears have conspicuous white rumps and a black inverted T-shaped patch at the tip of their tails. The gray-cheeked thrush is a typical forest thrush—brown with a heavily

Fig. 13.24. *Upper left:* Gray-cheeked thrush (*Catharus minimus*, Ivishak River, JWS). *Upper center:* Bluethroat nest with eggs (*Luscinia svecica*, Toolik Field Station, J. Wingfield). *Upper right:* Bluethroat, male (Toolik Field Station, JWS). *Lower left:* Northern wheatear (*Oenanthe oenanthe*, Atigun Gorge, ADH). *Lower center:* American pipit (*Anthus rubescens*, Toolik Field Station, JWS). *Lower right:* Eastern yellow wagtail (*Motacilla flava*, Toolik Field Station, JWS).

spotted breast. The familiar American robin is a large thrush with an orange breast. Thrushes arrive on the North Slope in May and depart for wintering habitats by mid-August. Their diet is primarily insects and other invertebrates, supplemented by seeds and berries.

Bluethroats inhabit willow and alder thickets, often near streams and lakes. They are secretive, mouse-like skulkers that creep about in thick brush, where they glean invertebrate prey from low vegetation and from beneath leaves and soil. They are usually observed only when flying to and from willow thickets or when they occasionally break cover to "hawk" insects from the air. Their nests are cups of finely woven grasses lined with hair or willow down that are carefully concealed on the ground (**Fig. 13.24**). These nests receive five to six eggs that are incubated by females who "mouse away" over the ground when disturbed. Bluethroats have been reported nesting near Happy Valley (MP 368) and Toolik Lake. They are excellent mimics. A single bird may string together phrases from other birds, such as the fox sparrow, Lapland longspur, American golden plover, and arctic tern, and—believe it or not—mammals, such as the "sik-sik" call of the arctic ground squirrel. They winter across a large region from northern Africa to Southeast Asia. Birds nesting on the North Slope probably winter in southeast China.

Northern wheatears are common in mountain and foothills habitats. Their nests, which receive clutches of five to seven eggs, are loose cups of grass lined with hair or willow down in natural cavities of cliffs, outcrops, or talus slopes of mountain habitats. They begin their autumn migration in mid-August, when flocks of staging birds gather in the foothills and coastal plain. Northern wheatears winter in Eurasia, Southeast Asia, and northern Africa. The wheatears of the North Slope winter in Africa.

Gray-cheeked thrushes and American robins are found in tall riparian willow thickets in the foothills and mountains. The nests of gray-cheeked thrushes receive clutches of three to six eggs and are cups of dry grasses in thickets on or near the ground. They winter from southern Mexico south to Peru or Brazil. American robins typically nest in tall riparian willow thickets. They also nest in man-made structures. Their nests receive clutches of three to six eggs and are stout cups of dry grasses, fine twigs, and mud about 1 m or more above the ground. American robins winter from southern Canada through much of the United States to Mexico, Guatemala, and Bermuda.

Wagtails and Pipits (Motacillidae)

The eastern yellow wagtail (*Motacilla flava,* **Fig. 13.24**) is an Old World species that reaches the eastern limit of its range on the North Slope, where it is found in riparian foothills habitats. Eastern yellow wagtails are recognized by their yellow undersides and white-bordered tails. Their nests, which receive clutches of four to seven eggs, are cups of grasses concealed on the ground in shrubby willows or tussock tundra, typically near lakes and rivers, and often lined with feathers and hair. Wagtails feed primarily on insects that are either gleaned from vegetation or "hawked" from the air. Wagtails arrive on the North Slope in May and depart for winter habitats in Southeast Asia and Indonesia by mid-August.

American pipits (*Anthus rubescens*) arrive on the North Slope in May, when they begin nesting on heaths and barren alpine tundra. They are distinguished by their small size, narrow bills, buffy undersides, and lightly streaked breasts. Their nests receive clutches of four to five eggs and are small cups of fine grasses, hair, and feathers in sheltered locations on open, often barren ground. American pipits feed on invertebrates and small seeds. They begin their southward migration to wintering habitats along the Pacific coast from southern British Columbia and the Atlantic coast from New York to Central America in August.

Wood Warblers (Parulidae)

Two species of wood warblers nest in the foothills and mountains of the North Slope: Wilson's warbler (*Wilsonia pusilla*, **Fig. 13.25**) and the yellow warbler (*Dendroica petechia*, **Fig. 13.25**). Wood warblers are small, often brightly colored birds with tiny, thin beaks. They are active and conspicuous as they glean invertebrates from shrubs or "hawk" them from the air. Male Wilson's warblers have plain greenish-yellow breasts and yellow heads with thin black caps. Male yellow warblers are bright yellow with red-streaked breasts. Wilson's warblers arrive on the North Slope in early June, where they can be locally common in riparian willow thickets. Their nests receive clutches of four to six eggs and are cups of dry grass and moss sunken into beds of moss or sedges,

Fig. 13.25. *Upper left:* Savannah sparrow nest (*Passerculus sandwichensis*, Toolik Field Station, JWS). *Upper right:* Savannah sparrow (Toolik Field Station, JWS). *Lower left:* Wilson's warbler (*Wilsonia pusilla*, Toolik Field Station, JWS). *Lower center:* Yellow warbler (*Dendroica petechia*, Toolik Field Station, JWS). *Lower right:* White-crowned sparrow (*Zonotrichia leucophrys*, Toolik Field Station, JWS).

usually at the base of a shrub. Yellow warblers arrive on the North Slope in May, where they can be locally abundant in tall riparian willow thickets where they nest. Their nests are small cups of grass, willow catkins, hair, and fine bark lined with feathers, hair, or willow down, and within 2 m of the ground. Both species depart for wintering habitats from Mexico to South America in late July or early August.

Sparrows, Buntings, and Longspurs (Emberizidae)

Sparrows

Five species of sparrows nest on the North Slope: the Savannah sparrow (*Passerculus sandwichensis*, **Fig. 13.25**), white-crowned sparrow (*Zonotrichia leucophrys*, **Fig. 13.25**), golden-crowned sparrow (*Z. atricapilla*), fox sparrow (*Passerella iliaca*, **Fig. 13.26**), and American tree sparrow (*Spizella arborea*, **Fig. 13.27**). Adult American tree sparrows have plain gray breasts with a conspicuous central dark spot; their gray heads have sharply defined rufous crowns. Savannah sparrows have white breasts heavily streaked with brown and distinctive yellow markings at the base of the upper bill. Adult golden-crowned sparrows are large, with gray heads topped by a sharp black cap divided dorsally by a yellow-to-white crown stripe. The similar white-crowned sparrow has a black cap with three conspicuous white stripes and a pink bill. The fox sparrow is also a large sparrow but has a white breast marked with strong dark stripes, a gray rump, and a distinctive rufous color.

Sparrows arrive on the North Slope in May. Their nests are compact cups of grasses, sedges, or mosses, often lined with feathers or hair, and usually in low shrubs or concealed on the ground by overhanging vegetation (**Figs. 13.25, 13.27**). Females usually produce clutches of three to six eggs, which they incubate alone. Sparrows are often observed scratching the soil to uncover the seeds, berries, and invertebrates upon which they feed. They depart the North Slope for wintering habitats by late August, although some birds may linger until the first snow in September.

The American tree sparrow is locally abundant in riparian willow thickets and shrubby tussock tundra in the foothills. They winter from southern Canada to northern Arizona, Texas, Arkansas, and North Carolina. The Savannah sparrow is one of the most abundant songbirds in the foothills, particularly in riparian thickets and shrubby tussock tundra. It is also one of the few songbirds nesting along the arctic coast. They winter from southern British Columbia through the southern United States to the West Indies, Guatemala, Belize, and Honduras. White-crowned sparrows are also common in riparian willow thickets.

They winter from southwest British Columbia south through the central and southern United States into Mexico. The golden-crowned sparrow is locally common in tall willow and alder thickets, where they may co-occur with white-crowned sparrows. They winter from southern British Columbia to Baja California east to Colorado and New Mexico. Fox sparrows may be locally common in dense willow thickets along foothill streams, where they skulk on the ground. They winter from southwest British Columbia to Baja California and east to Virginia.

Buntings

Snow buntings (*Plectrophenax nivalis*, **Fig. 13.26**) arrive on the North Slope in April, where, with flashing white-and-black wings, they cannot be confused with any other bird. During summer they disperse widely across the Arctic, with individuals occasionally observed within 240 to 320 km of the North Pole. They nest in cavities in cliffs, scree slopes, and boulder fields, as well as man-made structures. Snow buntings are common at Atigun Pass, Deadhorse, and the major oil fields due to

Fig. 13.26. *Upper left:* Smith's longspur (*Calcarius pictus*, Toolik Field Station, JWS). *Upper center:* Lapland longspur (*C. lapponicus*, Toolik Field Station, ADH). *Upper right:* Snow bunting (*Plectrophenax nivalis*, Atigun Pass, ADH). *Lower left:* Lapland longspur nest with young (Toolik Field Station, JWS). *Lower right:* Fox sparrow (*Passerella iliaca*, Ivishak River, JWS).

Fig. 13.27. *Upper left:* Male and female common redpolls (*Carduelis flammea*, Toolik Field Station, ADH). *Upper right:* Hoary redpoll (*C. hornemanni*, Ivishak River, JWS). *Lower left:* American tree sparrow (*Spizella arborea*, Toolik Field Station, JWS). *Lower center:* Bird's-eye view of American tree sparrow nest in fork of felt-leaf willow shrub (Ivishak River, ADH). *Lower right:* Gray-crowned rosy finch (*Leucosticte tephrocotis*, Atigun Pass, JWS).

concentrations of either natural or man-made nesting cavities. They are also common along the arctic coast, where they nest beneath driftwood. Snow bunting nests are thick-walled bowls of mosses and grasses, lined with fine grass, hair, and feathers. Clutches of four to six eggs are incubated by the female while being tended by the male. During summer they feed on invertebrates and seeds. Most snow buntings remain on the North Slope until late September, when they migrate to southern Canada, the northern United States, southern Eurasia, and Japan. Some birds, however, remain until October or November.

Longspurs

The Lapland longspur (*Calcarius lapponicus*, **Fig. 13.26**) is the most abundant songbird and the most abundant nesting bird on the North Slope. Here their densities range from about 20 to more than 100 birds per km^2, with highest densities occurring in upland tussock tundra. When Lapland longspurs arrive in May, they feed on berries and seeds but switch to insects—primarily crane flies and midges—as summer proceeds. Their nests are cup-like hollows in dense grasses, lined with fine grass, hair, or feathers in tussock-heath tundra (**Fig. 13.26**). Lapland longspurs produce clutches of four to six eggs that are incubated by the female. Following hatching the parents may divide their brood and rear them separately. Predators include foxes, jaegers, bears, lemmings, weasels, ravens, and glaucous gulls. Ground squirrels are important egg predators. By late August, most Lapland longspurs have departed the North Slope to winter from southern Canada to northern California east to Maryland and south to northeastern Texas. Smith's longspur (*Calcarius pictus,* **Fig. 13.26**) is locally common in the foothills, particularly the Atigun and Sagavanirktok River valleys as far north as Sagwon Bluffs. They arrive in May to nest on the ground in sedge and tussock tundra. Their nests receive clutches of four to six eggs and are grass hollows lined with fine grasses, feathers, hair, or plant down. In late July to mid-August they migrate to the south-central United States from Kansas and Iowa south to Oklahoma, east-central Texas, and northwestern Louisiana.

Finches (Fringilidae)

Rosy Finches (Leucosticte)

The gray-crowned rosy finch (*Leucosticte tephrocotis,* **Fig. 13.27**) is a medium-size finch with a gray crown and brown body with pinkish flanks. Rosy finches are common in mountain habitats such as scree slopes, boulder fields, and meadows, where they forage for seeds, often in the company of wheatears and snow buntings. Rosy finches arrive on the North Slope in May. Their nests, which receive four to five eggs, are bulky structures of moss and grass, lined with fine grasses, feathers, or hair and concealed within rock crevices and among boulders. Nesting adults develop a pair of peculiar throat sacs used to carry food. Rosy finches begin their southward migration in late August and September to winter from the Aleutian Islands east to southern Saskatchewan and south to central California and northern New Mexico.

Redpolls (Carduelis)

Redpolls are small finches with red forecrowns and pale flanks that are heavily streaked with brown. The breasts of breeding males are washed with pink. There are two North American species, the common redpoll (*Carduelis flammea,* **Fig. 13.26**) and the hoary redpoll (*C. hornemanni,* **Fig. 13.26**). The hoary redpoll is paler than the common redpoll; some individuals may appear almost white at a distance. On the North Slope, redpolls are the second most abundant passerine after the Lapland longspur. They arrive in May to congregate in riparian willow and birch thickets. Redpoll nests are bowls of grasses lined with cottongrass and willow down, feathers, or hair. Common redpolls nest aboveground in shrubs, usually willows. Hoary redpolls nest on the ground or in low shrubs. Females incubate clutches of three to five eggs while being tended by the male. Their diet consists of seeds of birches, alders, willows, and grasses, particularly cottongrass, subsidized by insects during summer. Redpolls have the greatest cold tolerance of any passerine yet studied. This is due to unusually high rates of energy intake from their diet of high-calorie seeds combined with a unique storage pouch in their esophagus that provides a continuous supply of food during darkness. They depart the North Slope for wintering habitats in southern Alaska and the Yukon to the central United States in late August or September.

14

Mammals

At least 26 species of terrestrial mammals are residents of the North
Slope.[1] Of these, only the Alaska marmot has a range that is largely
restricted to this region. Arctic specialists (those specially adapted to
the Arctic) here include the collared lemming, the arctic fox, and the
polar bear. Perhaps equally notable are other species with no apparent
specialized adaptations, such as the red fox, that flourish alongside the
specialists during brutal winters.

The common megafauna of the North Slope include the caribou
(about 1 caribou per km²) and red fox (about 1 fox per 10 km²). At the
other end of the spectrum of abundance are species such as the grizzly
bear (about 1 bear per 150 km²) and gray wolf (about 1 wolf per 500
km²). The most abundant mammals on the North Slope, however, are
the voles and lemmings, which are also the smallest and least conspicuous. Populations of voles on the North Slope can attain densities as high
as 5,000 per km² of tundra,[2] and it is not surprising that these small,
secretive, but plentiful herbivores can have major effects on tundra communities. To put these statistics in perspective, consider a 200 m wide
swath of the North Slope along the Dalton Highway from Atigun Pass
to Prudhoe Bay. This swath, which provides 100 m of easily scanned
terrain on either side of the road, will likely contain as many as 250,000
voles and lemmings, 54 caribou, five red fox, three moose, one wolverine, and even fewer muskoxen, grizzly bears, and wolves. Although
simplistic, due to an assumption of uniform distribution that ignores
factors such as habitat quality and herding behavior, this exercise provides insight into the probability of spotting different mammals while
exploring the pipeline corridor. The chance of seeing large, relatively
common animals from the road, such as caribou, red fox, and moose, is
pretty high, as is that of seeing voles and lemmings when hiking on the
tundra in years of peak abundance. On the other hand, the probability

of encountering rare animals, such as a bear or a wolf, or both rare and inconspicuous animals, such as a wolverine, is quite low.

Voles and Lemmings (Cricetidae)

Voles

Voles are stocky mice with short muzzles, tails, and ears. They are similar to lemmings but have longer tails and larger ears. Voles are preyed upon by bears, wolves, wolverines, foxes, weasels, owls, harriers, rough-legged hawks, falcons, jaegers, gulls, and shrikes. The singing vole (*Microtus miurus*) and the tundra vole (*M. oeconomus*) are the most common and widespread voles on the North Slope (**Fig. 14.1**). The less common northern red-backed vole (*Myodes rutilus*) is found in mountain and foothills habitats (**Fig. 14.1**). Singing voles have gray-brown backs and buffy flanks. Tundra voles are larger than singing voles, show less contrast between the color of their backs and flanks, and have coarse, black-tipped guard hairs, while northern red-backed voles have brightly colored orange-red backs and brown flanks.

Fig. 14.1. *Upper left:* Singing vole (*Microtus miurus*) feeding on fireweed (Toolik Field Station, JWS). *Upper center:* Winter tunnel complex of tundra vole exposed by melting snow (*Microtus oeconomus*, Atigun Gorge, ADH). *Upper right:* Seeds cached in abandoned wasp nest (Ivishak River, ADH). *Lower left:* Northern red-backed vole (*Myodes rutilus*, Atigun Pass, JWS). *Lower center:* "Hay pile" of singing vole (Toolik Field Station, ADH). *Lower right:* Tundra vole winter nest exposed by melting snow (Atigun Gorge, ADH).

Singing voles are usually found in moist habitats on slopes and low, rocky areas where they construct extensive runways connecting feeding and nesting areas (**Fig. 14.1**). In late summer they sit at exposed locations and produce a weak metallic trill, hence their name. The function of this behavior is unknown but may signal territory boundaries or danger from predators. Reproduction occurs during spring and summer when litters of 4–12 young are produced. Females may reproduce in the summer of their birth but rarely survive more than two years. Like most small arctic mammals, the abundance of singing voles fluctuates dramatically. A population of singing voles near Toolik Lake, for example, varied from 5 to 50 voles per hectare over a four-year period. Their diet includes bistort, cottongrass, horsetails, fireweed, coltsfoot, bearberry, willows, and licorice root. During early August they prepare "hay piles" of green vegetation for winter forage (**Fig. 14.1**). These can be quite large, ranging up to 30 liters, and are constructed above the soil in a variety of well-drained spots such as on rocks and in the bases of shrubs.

Tundra voles prefer wetter habitats than singing voles, such as wet lowland tundra and riparian areas with a dense cover of rhizomatous sedges. Tundra voles breed from May to September, when females may produce two to three litters of four to eight young. Like singing voles, they construct extensive networks of burrows and runways that connect grazing areas with nests of fine grasses (**Fig. 14.1**). Their summer diet consists of sedges, grasses, bistort, and horsetails. During autumn they provision caches with seeds and rhizomes (**Fig. 14.1**). These caches are large enough to have been sought as food by the Iñupiat.

Lemmings

Lemmings are stout, vole-like mammals about 110–180 mm in length with very short tails, blunt muzzles, and short round ears. Two species of lemmings occur on the North Slope: the collared lemming (*Dicrostonyx groenlandicus*, **Fig. 14.2**) and the brown lemming (*Lemmus trimucronatus*, **Fig. 14.2**). The collared lemming is a truly arctic mammal. It ranges farther north than any other rodent and has unique specializations. As winter approaches, collared lemmings produce a coat of thick white fur and develop double-tined claws on their forefeet that are used to burrow through snow. They also store enormous amounts of fat, resulting in a late-autumn weight (50–112 g) nearly twice their early spring weight (30–50 g). As spring approaches, collared lemmings lose their double-tined claws and produce a gray coat with a dark chest band and a thin black dorsal stripe from nose to rump. In summer they construct nests of grasses, fur, and feathers in burrows or beneath rocks in upland tundra,

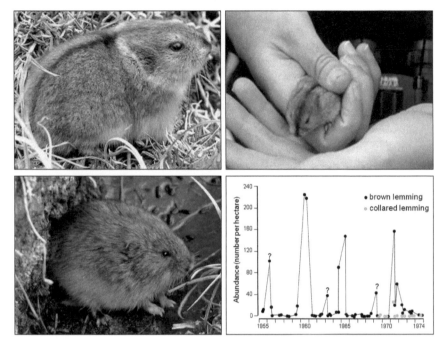

Fig. 14.2. *Upper left:* Collared lemming (*Dicrostonyx groenlandicus*, E. Weiser, with permission). *Upper right:* Collared lemming (Guardhouse Rock, J.E. Hobbie). *Lower left:* Brown lemming (*Lemmus trimucronatus*, E. Weisner, with permission). *Lower right:* Population cycle of brown lemmings at Barrow (redrawn from Batzli et al. 1980). Left axis shows abundance (individuals per hectare); bottom axis shows year. Dashed lines indicate changes in abundance during winter when essentially all activity occurs beneath the snow. Question marks indicate likely peak winter population size estimated from grazing damage and number of winter nests. The remaining estimates were based upon captures of actual lemmings. Compared with brown lemmings, collared lemmings were relatively scarce except during 1971.

where they feed on willow leaves, forbs, and sedges. During winter they migrate to meadows at lower elevations, where they feed on willow buds and bark and construct winter nests and runways. These nests are beneath the snow, directly on the surface of the frozen tundra within the relatively open layer of depth hoar (**Fig. 1.1**), which provides access to frozen vegetation and allows successful breeding activity.

The brown lemming is less specialized and more widely distributed than the collared lemming, occurring in both arctic and boreal regions, where they are found in tundra and meadow habitats. They are the dominant grazer in the Barrow region, which is distinctly different from the Prudhoe Bay region where caribou, brown lemmings, and collared lemmings are co-dominant grazers. The fur of the brown lemming, not surprisingly, is brown year-round and the specialized double-tined winter claws of the collared lemmings are lacking. They construct runways

Fig. 14.3. *Left:* Summer runways of brown lemmings in lawn of *Dupontia fisheri* (Barrow, G.O. Batzli, with permission). *Upper right:* Winter nest of brown lemming (Barrow, G.O. Batzli). *Lower right:* Sedge and grasses cropped by brown lemming beneath winter snow (Barrow, G.O. Batzli).

and burrows that connect feeding areas with nests of dried vegetation in low-lying, wet habitats with sedges, grasses, and mosses (**Fig. 14.3**). The burrows and nests are just beneath the moss layer in low, wet areas. The nests, however, are kept dry by their strategic placement on higher spots of microtopography. Like collared lemmings, brown lemmings construct winter nests beneath the snow within the depth hoar layer (**Figs. 1.1, 14.3**). Brown lemmings feed on leaf sheaths, shoots, rhizomes, and mosses.

Lemming Population Cycles

The legendary fluctuations of lemming populations are attributed to the attainment of reproductive maturity in only three to six weeks, coupled with multiple large litters (about eight young) during long breeding seasons. These characteristics drive cycles of population booms that occur roughly every three to six years with abundances being extremely low during intervening years (**Fig. 14.2**). Of the two lemming species of the North Slope, the population cycles of the brown lemming are best understood because the population of the Barrow region has been the focus of research since the mid-1950s. Studies there have shown that the abundance of brown lemming ranges from highs of 225 animals per hectare attained while the lemmings breed beneath the winter snow to lows of 0.02 animals per ha (one animal per 50 ha).[3] Population cycles of the brown lemming occur synchronously within a 50 km radius of Barrow. Although long-term studies of lemming populations at locations other than Barrow are lacking, there is limited evidence indicating that lemming cycles may occur elsewhere on the North Slope (Atqasuk, Wainwright, Pitt Point, Inaru River, and Umiat).

Why do lemmings show such dramatic cycles of abundance? At least 22 hypotheses have been offered to explain this phenomenon, but the current consensus is that lemming population cycles at Barrow result from combined overgrazing and predation. First, overgrazing by brown lemmings severely damages the grasses and sedges upon which they feed during winter (**Fig. 14.3**). In years of population peaks nearly 100 percent of sedges and grass stems may be clipped during winter. Once this occurs, lemmings begin to dig and feed upon underground rhizomes, causing additional and long-term damage. During years of peak abundance, lemming populations eat virtually all available vegetation during winter, causing a precipitous decline in abundance until sedge and grass productivity recovers. Second, lemmings are important prey in coastal plain food webs so it should not be surprising that their population cycles have enormous consequences for their predators, many of which breed successfully only during years of lemming abundance. In such years, lemmings are extremely vulnerable, particularly during snowmelt when their winter tunnels become exposed. At this time, great numbers of migratory predators—primarily snowy owls and pomarine jaegers but also short-eared owls, glaucous gulls, parasitic jaegers, and long-tailed jaegers—cause further losses to what may already be a declining population due to food limitation. Least weasels are also effective predators. In years of high weasel abundance (e.g., 25 animals per ha) populations of brown lemmings can decline precipitously well before snowmelt.

In a nutshell, the population cycles of brown lemmings at Barrow result from a catastrophic decline in reproduction rate caused by the lack of food due to overgrazing during winters of peak abundance. The influx of predators following snowmelt then continues to deplete the lemming population during the following spring and summer even while vegetation starts to recover and lemming reproduction resumes. Once lemming populations are so reduced, three to six years are required for a return to peak abundance. Although not considered a factor specifically affecting population cycling, inclement weather can further affect lemming abundance. Wet summers with extensive flooding of lemming habitat (standing water depths as shallow as 2–3 cm have significant negative effects on lemming foraging behavior), freezing rains, and winter thaws can all effectively reduce food availability during crucial periods of the lemming life cycle.

Squirrels and Marmots (Sciuridae)

Two species of the Sciuridae occur on the North Slope: the arctic ground squirrel (*Urocitellus parryii*, formerly *Spermophilus parryi*, **Fig. 14.4**) and the Alaskan marmot (*Marmota broweri*, **Fig 14.4**). These colonial species live in underground burrows.

Fig. 14.4. *Upper left:* Arctic ground squirrel (*Urocitellus parryi*, Galbraith Lake, ADH). *Upper right:* Alaskan marmot (*Marmota broweri*, Toolik Field Station, JWS) showing "black cap" and with clay on nose from digging. *Lower left:* Arctic ground squirrel burrow entrance (Toolik Field Station, ADH). *Lower right:* Alaskan marmot hibernation burrow with mosquitoes hovering near entrance.

Ground Squirrels

During summer, arctic ground squirrels are, without doubt, one of the most commonly observed mammals on the North Slope. Their fur is reddish brown to tawny yellow and their backs are ornamented with faint rows of light spots. They also have inconspicuous ears and short tails tipped with black. Arctic ground squirrels, the largest species of ground squirrel, reach 300–500 mm in total length and 500–900 g in weight.

Extensive colonies of ground squirrels occur in habitats with well-drained sandy soils and a thick active layer (e.g., permafrost 1 m or more below the surface). Such habitats are found on river terraces, kames, moraines, and talus slopes. Ground squirrels construct several types of burrows (**Fig. 14.4**). *Home burrows* have multiple entrances and enlarged chambers for sleeping and nesting. Their entrances are often on rises providing good visibility, allowing squirrels to scan for danger before leaving to forage. Squirrels hibernate in hibernation burrows that have a single, well-concealed entrance and a sleeping chamber lined with dry grass. Hibernation may also occur in home burrows. Shallow flight burrows provide refuge when a squirrel is threatened while away from its home burrow.

Ground squirrels forage primarily on forbs, seeds, and willow leaves. Berries, insects, bird eggs, baby mice, and carrion are also consumed, and cannibalization of young by males is not uncommon. Ground squirrels in turn are important prey for foxes, bears, wolves, wolverines, gyrfalcons, rough-legged hawks, golden eagles, jaegers, snowy owls, and glaucous gulls. Given their importance as prey, it is not surprising that ground squirrels have developed sophisticated anti-predator behaviors. They are vigilant, often standing at burrow entrances for long periods scanning for predators. Neighbors are alerted to the presence of aerial predators by a shrill whistle and to the danger of terrestrial predators by a sharp "sik-sik."

Ground squirrels are deep hibernators—an adaptation allowing energy conservation during periods of predictable food shortage. While in deep hibernation, which lasts about seven to eight months, their heart rate and metabolism stabilize at about 1 percent of normal basal levels and their body temperatures supercool to as low as −2.9°C, which is the lowest spontaneously attained body temperature measured for any mammal or bird on Earth. During hibernation, when their body temperatures are near ambient, ground squirrels are not asleep. They are rather in a state of torpor and lack the organized brain waves and periods of rapid-eye movement (REM) that indicate sleep—in essence, they appear to be "brain dead." Every two to three weeks, however, hibernating ground squirrels arouse spontaneously for short periods (about 15 hours). During arousals their body temperatures return to active levels (about 37°C) and they begin to sleep (i.e., organized brain waves and REM begin). Although the function of such arousals is unknown, they may be related to the maintenance of memory and synaptic connections required for complex behaviors. Hibernation is terminated when fat stores are reduced to about one-third of pre-hibernation levels during mid-April to early May. Females lose as much as one-third of their body mass during winter. Males, however, may show only minor weight losses because they use their cheek pouches to cache as many as 2 kg of seeds in their burrows during late summer and autumn. By feeding on these caches before emergence, males restore body condition and thus their ability to compete for mates. If a male fails to cache sufficient winter food, it will be forced to forgo reproduction that year. Mating occurs shortly after emergence and litters of two to six young are born in late May or early June. Young squirrels must attain body weights sufficient to sustain them through their first winter by the summer's end. Given the short active season, it is not surprising that the growth rates of juvenile ground squirrels are rapid compared with species from temperate regions. Ground squirrels may live up to six years.

Marmots

Colonies of Alaskan marmots are scattered in mountain and foothills habitats, where they occur on well-drained rocky slopes adjacent to meadows. Colonies easily accessible from the Dalton Highway are on moraines southeast of Toolik Lake and on Slope Mountain. On the North Slope the Alaskan marmot may be confused only with the arctic ground squirrel, which occupies similar habitats. This is unlikely, however, because marmots are much larger (total length 540–650 mm, weight 2–4 kg or more) and have black caps on their heads and black noses. Marmot colonies are based on family groups, with males occupying burrows adjacent to those of females and young. As for ground squirrels, various types of burrows are constructed. Home burrows may extend for many meters and provide shelter at night, nests for young, and a refuge from predators. Flight burrows provide additional refuge for foraging away from the home burrow. Hibernation burrows are used for hibernation by family groups and are usually on exposed ridges that remain relatively snow-free during winter, allowing early emergence during snowmelt (**Fig. 14.4**).

Alaskan marmots feed on grasses, herbs, forbs, berries, roots, mosses, and lichens and occasionally insect larvae, carrion, and small rodents. Because they require large fat stores to survive months of hibernation, marmots eat massive quantities of vegetation. The digestive tract of a well-fed animal may make up 33 percent of its weight. The behavior of marmots is strongly influenced by mosquito activity. When mosquitoes are abundant they remain in their burrows unless the wind is sufficient to keep mosquitoes at bay. Marmots are preyed upon by red foxes, wolves, grizzly bears, wolverines, and raptors, especially golden eagles. The entrances to their dens are often protected by boulders to prevent digging by grizzly bears. When on the surface, marmots spend significant time searching for predators. When a predator is sighted, they produce a loud and sharp whistle that alerts other members of their colony.

Like ground squirrels, Alaskan marmots spend as much as two-thirds of their lives in deep hibernation. They often hibernate in family units of as many as 8–12 individuals. Such communal hibernation reduces energy requirements due to social temperature regulation and allows mating prior to emergence from dens in spring. Emergence occurs when the plug of ice sealing their den thaws. Mated females produce litters of about six young within two weeks of emergence. The age at first reproduction is unknown but is likely to be about three years. Wild marmots may live for 10 years or more.

Porcupines (Erethizonyidae)

The North American porcupine (*Erethizon dorsatum*) occasionally strays onto the North Slope and has been found as far north as the arctic coast.

Hares (Leporidae)

The snowshoe hare (*Lepus americanus*, Leporidae) is the only hare species likely to be found on the North Slope (**Fig. 14.5**). They are identified by their long ears and enlarged hind feet. They range from 36 to 52 cm in total length and weigh up to 1.7 kg for males and 2.2 kg for females. Their typical color during summer is grayish brown above and cream below. During winter, they are white except for the tips of their ears. Although snowshoe hares appear inarguably white during winter, the guard hairs of their fur have gray bases. This distinction is significant because it allows separation of snowshoe hare from the Alaskan hare (*L. othus*), which has winter guard hairs that are totally white. Alaskan hares are also much longer (56–69 cm total length) and heavier (3.9–7.2

Fig. 14.5. *Upper left:* Snowshoe hare, winter (*Lepus americanus*, Ivishak River, S.M. Parker). *Upper right:* Snowshoe hare, summer (Ivishak River, ADH). *Lower left:* Willow stems killed by snowshoe hare girdling (Oksrukuyik Creek, ADH). *Lower right:* Willows stripped of bark by snowshoe hare (Oksrukuyik Creek, ADH).

kg). Although there are historic records of Alaskan hare from the North Slope west of the Colville River, there have been no credible records north and east of the Seward Peninsula since 1951.

Snowshoe hares were documented on the western North Slope in the early 1900s but appear to have only recently colonized the Colville River drainage, where a population irruption was documented during the late 1990s, and the Sagavanirktok River drainage, where a population irruption occurred during 2007–2009. During these years snowshoe hares were abundant in the riparian willow thickets of Oksrukuyik Creek (access road at Dalton Highway, MP 305) and the Ivishak River, and signs of activity were documented at the Toolik Field Station and along the Atigun River from Dalton Highway MPs 255–266. By the summer of 2010, however, there was little sign of hare activity in these areas. Snowshoe hares feed on willow bark and buds during winter and leafy vegetation during summer. Dense populations, such as that along Oksrukuyik Creek during 2007–2009, cause significant damage to willows by girdling (**Fig. 14.5**).

Snowshoe hares tend to move along well-defined runways, which provide evidence that they are using a particular thicket as habitat. They shelter beneath brush rather than burrows, a behavior typical of hares in general. Snowshoe hares give birth to litters of four to six young (leverets) in simple, unlined depressions. Young are born fully haired and are capable of unassisted movement shortly after birth. They mature rapidly and breed in about one year, after which they may produce as many as three litters each summer under optimal conditions. Snowshoe hare populations in boreal regions are dynamic, showing large fluctuations every 8–11 years, and similar fluctuations may occur on the North Slope.[4] Factors driving fluctuations of snowshoe hare populations are not well understood but are probably predator-driven. Numerous studies have shown that predation is the major cause of death for snowshoe hares, with some estimates of annual mortality as high as 75 percent. Predators of young include ground squirrels and ermine. Wolf, red fox, wolverine, golden eagle, hawks, falcons, and raven are predators of adults. The Canadian lynx (*Lynx canadensis*), an important predator of snowshoe hare in interior Alaska, may stray as far north as Wainwright and Barrow during years of snowshoe hare population irruptions.

Shrews (Soricidae)

Shrews are tiny mammals with long pointed snouts, long tails (about 30 percent of total length for North Slope species), and a velvety pelage. The activity of these secretive beasts is usually concealed by vegetation and organic debris. Shrews are primarily invertivores, feeding on small arthropods (sawfly larvae, caterpillars, grasshoppers, crane flies, beetles, spiders), but they also eat small amounts of vegetation (seeds, berries) and will feed on carrion if available. In northern Yukon Territory they are known to feed on fish used to bait traps. Shrews remain active beneath the snow during winter. At this time they use the space provided by depth hoar (**Fig. 1.1**) to access food, as do lemmings, voles, and weasels. Nevertheless, it's a mystery how these tiny, nonhibernating animals manage to survive the arctic winter. Their summer food—arthropods—is frozen into the soil and they cannot survive on vegetation alone. It is possible that they survive on carrion during this time. Major predators of shrews include weasels and fox. Because of foul-smelling secretions produced by the flank glands of males, they are often discarded after being killed. These secretions may be used to attract females.

Four species of shrews have been reported from the North Slope. The dusky shrew (*Sorex monticolus*) and the tiny shrew (*S. yukonicus*) are rare or restricted in distribution and will not be treated further here.[5] The tundra shrew (*S. tundrensis*) and barren ground shrew (*S. ugyunak*), however, are common and widespread. The tundra shrew (total length 83–120 mm) inhabits dense grasses and thickets on well-drained hillslopes. In summer, their pelage consists of a dark-brown back, pale-brown flanks, and a pale gray belly. In winter, this pattern is reduced to a brown back with gray flanks and belly. Mating and reproduction apparently occur from May through September, when litters of 8–12 young are born in grass-lined nests. They probably produce several litters in a season and are capable of breeding in their first summer. Their maximum longevity is probably 12 to 18 months. Although smaller than the tundra shrew, the barren ground shrew (74–103 mm total length) is otherwise very similar. It prefers lowland sedge tundra with thickets of dwarf willow and birch, habitats decidedly less well drained than those preferred by tundra shrews. The identification of shrews is difficult and requires their capture and careful examination.

Wolves and Foxes (Canidae)

Wolves

Wolves (*Canis lupus,* **Fig. 14.6**) are year-round residents of the North Slope, where they vary widely in color from nearly white to black with gray most common. The much smaller coyote (*C. latrans*) also occurs on the North Slope but is restricted to the extreme south-central portion of this region (although individuals have been occasionally spotted as far north as Barrow). Wolves may be distinguished from coyotes at a distance by the position of their tails while running. Wolves tend to hold their tails horizontally, while coyotes usually hold their tails down toward the ground. Wolves are secretive and rarely seen. Perhaps the most rewarding assessment of their presence is a search for their tracks in soft sediments along streambanks (**Fig. 14.6**). The banks of the Atigun River at the Atigun River 2 Bridge are a particularly good place to search for wolf tracks. Wolf tracks, along with those of foxes and ground squirrels, may be abundant when fine river sediments are exposed in summer (**Fig. 14.7**).

Wolves are highly social animals and their packs—which, at minimum, contain a mated pair and their pups—are organized around gender-specific dominance hierarchies. Wolves mate in late winter and litters of 2–10 pups are born in dens in May or June. Dens, which may be used for many years, are excavated in sandy, well-drained soil and can be 3 m deep. After about 8–10 weeks the pups are moved from the birth den to a series of rendezvous sites. By October, pups are able to

Fig. 14.6. *Left:* Gray wolf (*Canis lupus*, Kuparuk River, ADH). *Right:* Wolf tracks (Galbraith Lake, boot provides sense of scale, ADH).

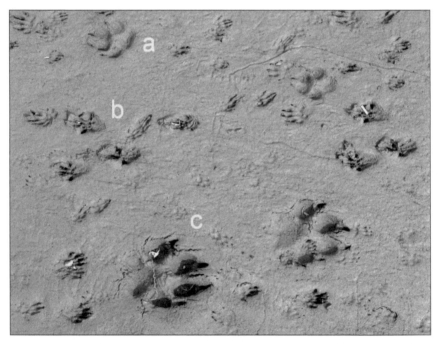

Fig. 14.7. Medley of mammal tracks in sediment of Galbraith Lake outlet stream ("Fox Creek") near Atigun River 2 Bridge (ADH): (a) red fox, (b) arctic ground squirrel, (c) wolf.

travel and hunt with the pack. Females become reproductively active during their second year and may breed for 10 years or more.

The present-day abundance of wolves on the North Slope is a legacy of federal efforts to reduce their populations during the mid-20th century. An aerial survey of the region from the Itkillik to the Canning River in April 2003 indicated the presence of about 25 animals divided among five or more packs, or about two wolves per 1,000 km². A more recent 2008 survey of the foothills region between the Killik and Anaktuvuk Rivers indicated the presence of about 78 animals divided among 17 packs of two to eight individuals, or about 4.4 wolves per 1,000 km². Recent studies have shown that wolf packs on the eastern North Slope do not follow herds of caribou to their winter ranges as was commonly believed, but rather remain in the same territory year-round preying on migrating caribou in spring and autumn and Dall sheep and moose in winter. This diet is subsidized by voles, lemmings, ground squirrels, and snowshoe hare where available. The relatively recent appearance of moose on the North Slope allows wolf packs to overwinter in foothills habitats that apparently were previously only used in summer. Kill rates probably average five caribou or moose per wolf every 100 days, with a wolf pack remaining with a carcass for two days or so. Wolves prefer caribou and switch to moose or small game when caribou are scarce. The longevity of wolves on the North Slope, where rabies and cannibalism are probably the greatest causes of their mortality, is probably less than 16 years. Deaths due to rabies are generally restricted to wolves of the coastal plain, where the virus is endemic in the arctic fox population.

Foxes

The arctic fox (*Vulpes lagopus,* **Fig. 14.8**) is distinguished from the wolf and red fox by its small size (average body length about 85 cm, average tail length about 30 cm), short legs and ears, and pelage. During winter (November to March) they are white except for the tips of their noses, which are black. During summer (June to September), their upper body is brown and their flanks and belly are yellowish brown. Arctic foxes are truly arctic mammals. Their dense winter fur provides excellent insulation, allowing their basal metabolism to remain constant until temperatures fall below –7°C. In addition, remarkable levels of fat accumulation during summer and autumn allow them to maintain moderate activity for up to a month without food during winter. The most likely place to find arctic fox from the Dalton Highway is Deadhorse. Although they stray farther south (a roadkill was found at MP

Fig. 14.8. *Upper left:* Arctic fox, winter (*Vulpes lagopus*, Deadhorse, JWS). *Upper right:* Arctic fox, summer (Deadhorse, JWS). *Lower left:* Red fox pup at burrow entrance (*V. vulpes*, Toolik Field Station, JWS). *Lower right:* Red fox hunting voles (Slope Mountain, ADH).

290 during November 2008), no dens have been reported south of the coastal plain (e.g., MP 360, near Pump Station 2). The southern boundary of their range may be controlled by the northern range of the red fox, a dominant competitor.

Arctic foxes are monogamous and females may become reproductively active as early as their first year. In years when lemming abundance is high, litters of as many as 11 pups may be produced in early June. In years when lemming abundance is low, litters are smaller and the probability of their failure is high. Arctic fox dens are typically on low, well-drained sandy hillocks or ridges 1–4 m high. Because such habitats are relatively sparse on the coastal plain, individual dens may be used for centuries. These are often conspicuous due to numerous burrow entrances (more than 25 in some cases) and unusually lush vegetation due to fertilization by fox urine and feces.

Compared with wolves and red foxes, arctic foxes show wide fluctuations in year-to-year abundance. This has been attributed to several factors, including early maturity and the production of large litters, high mobility and large home ranges, hunting pressure by humans, and population cycles of lemmings, their main prey. Fluctuations of arctic fox populations have indeed been linked to lemming population cycles in some areas. In other areas, however, their abundances show extraordinary year-to-year fluctuations that cannot be attributed to population cycles of their prey. Instead, such local population variation may be due to their high mobility, with individuals commonly moving hundreds of kilometers from one area to another in search of food—a behavior similar to that of the snowy owl. An alternative explanation for the lack of an apparent relationship between fox abundance and population cycles of their prey is hunting pressure. In places such as Barrow, where hunting pressure is high, arctic fox population dynamics may simply be controlled by human harvest rather than food supply.

Although lemmings are their main prey in years of abundance, arctic foxes are able to switch to other prey species when lemmings are scarce. For example, when lemmings are scarce during summer, arctic foxes may prey on the eggs and young of nesting waterfowl if these are available. In the vicinity of Prudhoe Bay they have prevented breeding of colonially nesting geese by taking and scatter-hoarding[6] hundreds of eggs. When lemmings are scarce in winter, arctic foxes may venture onto sea ice, where they trail polar bears for hundreds to thousands of kilometers to scavenge carrion from their seal kills. Here they may also prey opportunistically on juvenile seals. Major predators of arctic foxes are grizzly bears and golden eagles, which may kill large numbers of pups; red foxes have been observed killing and eating arctic foxes near Deadhorse, although this is not believed to be a major source of mortality. Populations of arctic foxes near settlements are also subject to trapping and hunting by humans. Probably the most significant cause of mortality for arctic foxes, however, is rabies, which is endemic in North Slope populations.

There is a good chance of encountering a red fox (*Vulpes vulpes,* **Fig. 14.8**) almost anywhere on the North Slope, with the best opportunities being in riparian foothills habitats. On the North Slope red foxes may be confused only with arctic foxes from which they are distinguished by long legs and ears and white-tipped tails. Two color phases of red fox occur here. The first is the familiar red coat with a white belly and black ear tips, lower legs, and feet. The second is the black-silver phase in which a red undercoat is obscured by black guard hairs with silver tips. The density of red fox on the eastern North Slope is about 100 animals per 1,000 km^2, with densities being greatest in productive riparian habitats. The northern limit of their range is believed to be restricted by the low productivity of the coastal plain. Evidence for this lies in the northward extension of their range primarily along the productive riparian habitats of the Sagavanirktok River to the Arctic Ocean. There is anecdotal evidence that red foxes have expanded their range northward on the North

Slope in recent decades. If true, such an expansion may indicate a general increase in the productivity of the tundra. Unlike the arctic fox, which shows special adaptations for arctic habitats, the red fox has no obvious morphological or physiological specializations. They are rather excellent ecological generalists, explaining their widespread distribution.

Red foxes are usually monogamous and may reach sexual maturity in their first year. Litters of three to six pups are born in spring in grass-lined dens that are usually in modified burrows of marmots and ground squirrels. These dens, which may be active for many generations, are used primarily for bearing and rearing young and are accessed by burrows that can be as long as 20 m with multiple entrances. Red foxes feed on voles and lemmings, hares, other small mammals, and birds and their eggs, any of which may be cached for later use. They also feed on invertebrates, berries, and carrion. In turn, red foxes are prey for wolves, wolverines, and bears. Most red foxes do not live more than five years in the wild, although some may reach ages of eight years. Red fox populations on the coastal plain are periodically reduced by outbreaks of rabies, which is endemic in the arctic fox population.

Bears (Ursidae)

The grizzly bear (*Ursus arctos*, **Fig. 14.9**) is one of two bear species of the North Slope. The short nose, disk-like face, and prominent hump above the shoulders are diagnostic for grizzly bears in general, and the "barren-ground" grizzly bears of the North Slope are further distinguished by color and size. Their fur tends to be light golden brown to almost blond, particularly the head, shoulders, back, and upper flanks. The light pelage can surprise those accustomed to seeing bears elsewhere in North America. North Slope bears are also small, averaging about 100 kg for females and 150 kg for males—about two-thirds the size of bears living elsewhere in Alaska. Grizzly bears are active on the North Slope for only six months of the year, spending mid-November to mid-April in hibernation dens (**Fig. 14.10**). Grizzly bears mate in May and June. Females usually produce their first litter at seven to eight years and may produce a pair of cubs every four years thereafter, with birth occurring while hibernating. In the northern Yukon, grizzly bears have been reported to live for as long as 28 years and one of the longest-living nonhuman mammal on the North Slope.

Although grizzly bears are regularly spotted on the North Slope, the chance of an encounter is low. During 2004–2005 the density of bears in the vicinity of the Dalton Highway was about seven animals

Fig. 14.9. *Left:* Grizzly bear (*Ursus arctos*, Toolik Field Station, JWS). *Center:* Grizzly bear tracks (Toolik Field Station, Edward Metzger). *Right:* Grizzly bear scat (Ivishak River, ADH).

Fig. 14.10. *Top:* Hibernation den of grizzly bear (Itkillik River, C. Johnson). The opening is about 1 m wide. *Bottom left:* Tundra soil overturned by foraging grizzly bear (Ivishak River, ADH). *Bottom right:* Ground squirrel burrow excavated by grizzly bear (Atigun Gorge, ADH).

per 1,000 km², which is slightly lower than the estimate of bear density for the entire North Slope (about eight animals per 1,000 km²). The density of bears is not uniform, however, with animals more numerous in the foothills and mountains than the coastal plain. Such differences in density are related to food availability; foothills habitats provide a greater abundance and diversity of food.

North Slope grizzly bears are omnivores. During spring and early summer they graze on sedges and horsetails and dig vetch roots (*Hedysarum*). In autumn they feed on blueberries, bearberries, and soapberries. Grizzly bears are also important predators of ground squirrels (**Fig. 14.10**) and caribou but will feed opportunistically on muskoxen, marmot, foxes, lemmings and other small rodents, bird eggs and nestlings, and carrion. Almost all (more than 90 percent) observed kills of caribou by grizzly bears have been calves captured during the post-calving migration. By mid-July calves are large enough to avoid becoming easy prey. Bears living near the arctic coast may venture onto sea ice to scavenge carcasses of marine mammals. Although adult grizzly bears have few natural predators, the killing and cannibalization of cubs by males is common.

Like the collared lemming and the arctic fox, the polar bear (*Ursus maritimus*, **Fig. 14.11**) is one of the few mammals of Alaska's North Slope that are uniquely Arctic. Well known for their white pelage, they are the largest bear species. Alaskan males may weigh more than 800 kg and, when standing on hind legs, may approach 4 m in height. Peak weights of females are only about half those of males. Polar bears are occasionally sighted in the vicinity of Prudhoe Bay during winter and spring, when females enter or leave maternity dens. They are much more common near Barrow and Kaktovik, however. On rare occasions, polar bears may move significant distances inland. In August 1999, for example, a young polar bear was observed about 60 km south of the coast along the Colville River (D. Norton, pers. comm.), and on 10 November 2002 a polar bear was observed near MP 297.1 of the Dalton Highway (about 170 km south of the coast, **Fig. 14.11**). This bear was feeding on caribou carrion; its fate is unknown.

Polar bears are specialized predators of seals, ringed seals in particular. About 1,800 bears (about 7 percent of the global population) live on pack ice on the Arctic Ocean within 300 km of the North Slope. Satellite tracking has shown that these are primarily marine creatures that spend only about 7 percent of their time on the northern coastal plain. The year-round availability of seals has resulted in the evolution of a hibernation strategy that differs markedly from that of grizzly bears. Only pregnant polar bears hibernate; males and nonreproductive females spend the winter wandering in search of new ice where seals are

Fig. 14.11. Polar bear (*Ursus maritimus*) in foothills along the Dalton Highway (MP 297, November 10, 2002, A. Balser and M. Sommerkorn).

ambushed at breathing holes. Their movements are extensive, ranging up to 3,000 km or more; the movement of one bear from Prudhoe Bay to Greenland has been documented.

Why do only pregnant female polar bears hibernate? Rather than hibernating as a strategy to survive periods of food scarcity, as used by grizzly bears, ground squirrels, and marmots, polar bears hibernate as a strategy to ensure survival of their young. Female polar bears enter dens in mid-November and give birth to one or a pair of cubs in early January. Polar bear cubs are hairless and weigh less than 700 g and would be unable to survive the arctic winter without constant shelter. Pregnant polar bears excavate hibernation dens during autumn in shore-fast ice, river bottoms, islands, and near-shore pack ice. In the Beaufort Sea region, their dens have been located on pack ice as far as 700 km north of the coast, and on land as far as 61 km south of the coast. The majority of terrestrial dens discovered on the North Slope have been distributed from the Colville River east to the Yukon Territory. Cubs are weaned during their third summer and females become reproductively active at six years. Mating occurs in March to June but implantation of eggs is delayed until autumn. With the exception of occasional cannibalism, polar bears have no natural predators. The maximum age for wild polar bears is about 30 years.

Weasels, Wolverines, and Otters (Mustelidae)

Weasels

Two species of weasels (*Mustela*) occur on the North Slope: the ermine (*M. erminea*, **Fig. 14.12**) and the least weasel (*M. nivalis*). Weasels have long, sinuous bodies that allow access to the burrows and runways of

Fig. 14.12. *Upper left:* Snow burrow (diameter of entrance is about 2 cm) and trackway of least weasel (*Mustela nivalis*, Ivishak River, ADH). *Left center:* Ermine at entrance of abandoned ground squirrel burrow (*Mustela erminea*, Atigun River near Atigun 2 Bridge, summer pelage, J. Dobkowski). *Lower left:* Ermine, summer pelage showing black tail tip (Green Cabin Lake, C. Mackenzie). *Right:* Trackway of ermine (Ivishak River, ADH).

lemmings and voles, their main prey. Although optimal for pursuing rodents, such a body shape is not optimal for conserving heat. Consequently, weasels have metabolic rates 50–100 percent higher than less slender mammals of similar mass (e.g., brown lemmings) when cold stressed. This high energy demand requires the almost continuous pursuit of prey during winter, when they must capture about one vole daily or one lemming every two days to survive. When prey are abundant, weasels will cache food for later use. Weasel abundance fluctuates dramatically in response to prey availability. Rapid changes in population size are possible due to short life spans and high reproductive rates. On the North Slope weasels inhabit dry, rocky uplands and well-drained streambanks. They are usually not found in low-lying, wet habitats unless lemmings are abundant. Weasel activity is most easily assessed in winter, when their trails and tunnels are readily observed (**Fig. 14.12**).

Ermine are the larger of the two North Slope weasels (male total length of 219–343 mm, female total length of 190–292 mm). Their relatively long, black-tipped tails (20–25 percent of total length) are probably their best diagnostic feature. During summer ermine have brown backs, white bellies, and white chins. During winter they are entirely white except for the black tail tip. This color pattern is thought to be a ploy to confuse predators, which see only the black tail tip moving against the snow. By attacking only an ermine's tail tip, would-be predators may allow it to escape. Ermine mate in summer but embryonic development does not occur until March due to delayed implantation of eggs. In April four to nine young are produced in fur-lined nests that are often modified vole nests. Females become reproductively active in as little as 60–70 days but rarely survive two years. In addition to rodents, ermine prey on birds, eggs, and young hare. Least weasels are much smaller than ermine and have short tails lacking a black tip (male total length of 180–205 mm, female total length of 165–180 mm; tail is 13–19 percent of total length). During summer their backs are dark brown and their bellies white; during winter they are entirely white. Mating occurs throughout the year and litters are produced year-round except December and January. Unlike ermine, least weasels do not delay implantation of eggs, allowing for more than one litter each year and explaining the lack of comparable reproductive seasonality. Females mature at four months and live for about one year. Least weasels are predators of lemmings, voles, and young hares, and may scavenge carrion.

Wolverines

The wolverine (*Gulo gulo,* **Fig. 14.13**) is the largest mustelid in North America, with exceptional males weighing up to 18 kg. They are dark brown with a light band extending over the brow and another extending from shoulder to rump. They also have trailing guard hairs that hang skirt-like from their flanks and short, brush-like tails. Wolverines are never abundant even under optimal conditions. Their densities on the North Slope are less than two animals per 100 km^2; they are usually less abundant than grizzly bears in similar habitats. Given their scarcity and relatively small size, spotting a wolverine is truly a once-in-a-lifetime experience even for those regularly visiting the North Slope. A visit to the North Slope during winter will provide the opportunity to find evidence of their presence in the form of tracks in the snow.

The main prey of North Slope wolverines are ground squirrels (about 60 percent of their diet), with the balance of their diet being ptarmigan and their eggs, marmots, voles, shrews, and caribou carrion. Although wolverines may pursue caribou or moose, they are rarely successful unless these are in poor condition or trapped in snow. Nevertheless, they

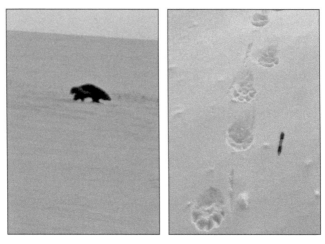

Fig. 14.13. *Left:* Wolverine (*Gulo gulo*, Sagwon Hills, ADH). *Right:* Wolverine trackway (Sagwon Hills, ADH). Length of pencil is 14 cm.

have been observed successfully killing moose on the North Slope. During winter wolverines feed primarily on caribou carrion (usually bone and hide) and the carcasses of ground squirrels cached the previous summer. A diet of bone can be surprisingly nutritious. Bones may contain as much as about 40 percent organic matter and wolverines are able to pulverize bone with their massive jaws and teeth, allowing them to access nutritious materials contained within. Wolverines are well known for their large home ranges. On the North Slope, the average summer range is about 100 km² for females and 700 km² for males. Wolverines are almost constantly on the move, with some males traveling about 50 km per day. Although solitary, they pair for short periods while breeding during late spring and summer. During late winter females excavate snow dens up to 7 m in length in which they bear a litter of two to four kits. Wolverines may reproduce in their second year and attain ages of 8–10 years in the wild.

Otters

The northern river otter (*Lontra canadensis*) is an uncommon resident of the North Slope, where it is associated with perennial spring streams providing year-round access to open water and Dolly Varden char as prey. River otters have been documented from tributaries of the Ivishak and Colville Rivers.

Caribou and Moose (Cervidae)

Since the New World caribou, because of its migrations, is subjected to snow factors for two-thirds of its annual cycle and because it exhibits behavioural and morphological adaptations to snow . . . the name "snow caribou" would be more suitable for this species than is the term "Barren Ground caribou."

—William O. Pruitt, Jr., *Arctic* 12 (1959): 172

Caribou

Barren-ground caribou (*Rangifer tarandus*) are identified by their color and antler structure (**Fig. 14.14**). The ground color of the winter coat is dark brown with portions of the neck, rump, and muzzle being cream to almost white. The hollow, air-filled hairs of the winter coat provide excellent insulation and buoyancy that assists river crossings during migration. During the summer molt they present a raggedy patchwork of light-brown and cream fur (**Fig. 14.14**). Unlike other deer, both genders

Fig. 14.14. *Upper left:* Male caribou (*Rangifer tarandus*, Toolik Field Station, ADH) with fully developed antlers during late summer. *Upper right:* Molting female caribou with developing ("velvet stage") antlers and yearling calf during late summer (Ivishak River, ADH). *Lower left:* Pregnant female caribou during late winter with fully developed antlers (Happy Valley, ADH). *Lower right:* Male caribou during late winter with developing antlers (Kuparuk River, ADH).

produce antlers (**Fig. 14.14**). Males' antlers have a peculiar shovel-like structure projecting forward toward their muzzle. Although many uses have been suggested (ice pick, snow shovel, eye guard), the true function of this structure is unknown. Males shed their antlers in October following the rut. Cows shed their antlers after calving in June. Perhaps the most unusual feature of the caribou is the least conspicuous. Their hooves are formed in such a way that the two toes together produce a structure much like an inverted bowl. Their dew claws[7] are also particularly well developed. When walking on snow their bowl-like toes and dew claws become splayed to increase their load-bearing capability in a manner identical to snowshoes. In fact, the load-bearing capability of caribou feet is greater than that of any other hoofed mammal occurring in the Arctic. During summer, caribou feed on the leaves of shrubs, sedges, and grasses. Mushrooms are consumed during late summer and autumn. During winter, lichens constitute about 90 percent of their diet and are obtained by pawing craters ("cratering") through the snow (**Fig. 14.15**). Barren-ground caribou are relatively small, standing 1.1 m tall at their shoulders. Females average about 80 kg and may live for 10 or more years. Males average about 110 kg and may live for seven to eight years.

On the North Slope caribou are dispersed among herds that are distinguished by the areas where females bear their calves. On the North Slope, four main herds are recognized: the Western Arctic, Teshekpuk, Central Arctic, and Porcupine. To simplify things, we will focus only on the behavior of the Central Arctic and Porcupine herds. Most caribou occurring along the Dalton Highway are members of the Central Arctic herd (25,000 or more animals); a few may belong to the Porcupine herd (120,000 or more animals). Cows from the Central Arctic herd calve on

 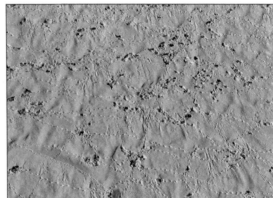

Fig. 14.15. *Left:* Caribou snow craters and tracks (Galbraith Lake, ADH). *Right:* Network of caribou craters with connecting tracks (Sagavanirktok River near Pump Station 3, ADH).

the coastal plain as far east as the Canning River and as far west as the Colville River, a region that includes the Prudhoe Bay oil fields. Cows from the Porcupine herd calve on the eastern coastal plain south of Barter Island. When calving is completed in mid-June, cows, newborn calves, yearlings, and bulls begin to disperse both eastward and westward along the coastal plain. During post-calving dispersal, mosquitoes, bot flies, and warble flies are abundant. To avoid these insects—mosquitoes in particular—caribou seek windy, exposed areas. This behavior tends to keep the herd concentrated into compact groups on exposed ridges or aufeis and also prevents them from feeding optimally. By mid-July the mosquito population is usually reduced to a level that allows caribou to disperse to habitats with abundant vegetation where they can begin to accumulate winter fat reserves.

During mid- to late July, the Central Arctic herd begins to migrate south toward the Brooks Range. Depending upon snow conditions, they may winter in the foothills (shallow snow) or they may move through passes, such as Atigun and Anaktuvuk, to winter south of the divide (deep snow). Pregnant cows begin to migrate north to calving grounds in early March and arrive in mid-May (**Fig. 14.16**). Yearlings, non-breeding cows, and bulls eventually follow the pregnant cows north but usually do not arrive at the calving grounds until the dispersal of females and newborn young has begun. The Porcupine herd follows a similar cycle but has migration pathways generally east of the Saga-vanirktok and Atigun Rivers in the Arctic National Wildlife Refuge and the Yukon Territory. Members of both herds intermingle where their

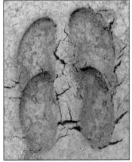

Fig. 14.16. *Left:* Female caribou migrating to calving grounds west of Prudhoe Bay (May 2011, Happy Valley, ADH). The characteristic single-file columns of migrating caribou herds is an adaptation thought to reduce the energy required to break paths through fresh snow. *Right:* Caribou tracks (Ice Cut, ADH). When compared with those of other hoofed mammals, the hooves of the caribou support significantly less weight per area because they function in a manner similar to snowshoes.

ranges overlap east of Prudhoe Bay and along the Sagavanirktok River. Although the migratory cycles for the different herds are relatively predictable, details of the timing and specific pathways followed can vary substantially from year to year.

Moose

Moose (*Alces americanus*, **Fig. 14.17**) are the largest cervids (antlered ungulates) on the North Slope. During the early 1900s they were relatively rare here, but they have become increasingly common during the latter half of the 20th century. Censuses of moose between the Sagavanirktok and Kuparuk Rivers indicate that the moose population was stable at about 50–70 animals during 1996–2002, and then increased to 150 animals or more from 2003–2008. Although moose are occasionally observed on open tundra, they usually are found in willow thickets that provide food and shelter and where abundant signs of their activity

Fig. 14.17. *Upper left:* "Broomed" felt-leaf willow shrubs resulting from moose browsing. Note bark stripping by snowshoe hare at base of shrub (Oksrukuyik Creek, ADH). *Upper right:* Male moose (*Alces americanus*, Toolik Field Station, JWS). *Lower left:* Moose tracks (Oksrukuyik Creek, ADH). *Lower right:* Herd of 18 moose in riparian willow thicket during late winter (Oksrukuyik Creek, ADH).

may be found in the form of browsed ("broomed") willows, trails, tracks, and scats (**Fig. 14.17**). During summer moose feed on the shoots and leaves of willow, particularly felt-leaf willow, birch, and alder. During winter they browse twigs, a low-quality diet causing them to lose as much as 20–55 percent of their weight during this time.

The familiar antlers of male moose are massive, weighing as much as 35 kg, and are shed each year following the rut in September and October. Males mature sexually as yearlings but mating is usually delayed until they reach a size allowing competition with dominant bulls for receptive females. The antlerless females become sexually active in their second year, after which they may give birth to single or twin calves every spring (**Fig. 14.18**). Mature North Slope males may attain more than 770 kg with weights of females being about 40 percent less. Major predators of moose on the North Slope are grizzly bears, which prey primarily on calves less than six months in age, and wolves, which prey on calves and adults.

Dall Sheep and Muskoxen (Bovidae)

Dall Sheep

Dall sheep (*Ovis dalli*, **Fig. 14.18**) are identified by their white fur and the massive spiral horns of mature rams. They are found throughout the Brooks Range, where they inhabit windswept habitats in dry, mountainous terrain containing forage in the form of sparse grasses, willows, and *Dryas*. Unlike other mammals of the North Slope, access to mineral licks is essential for their survival. Dall sheep are migratory to some degree, and herds may move 10–50 km between summer and winter ranges. Although summer ranges may be quite large, winter ranges are usually limited to snow-free ridges, which provide both escape routes to cliffs that are inaccessible to wolves and access to protected valley bottoms where sheep can forage by digging through snow. Because summers are short, most of the year is spent on the winter ranges.

Dall sheep spend much of the year in same-sex herds of about 4–10 animals. Rams and ewes intermingle only during the rut (mating season) in late November and December. Mature rams can be identified by fully curled horns. They average 82 kg in weight and may stand 1 m tall at the shoulder (**Fig. 14.18**). Dall sheep mature by their third year, but males do not participate in the rut until they are large enough to compete with dominant rams (about seven to eight years). Such competition has resulted in the evolution of differences in size between sexes, with ewes being much smaller than rams and having relatively inconspicuous

Fig. 14.18. *Upper left:* Female moose and calf (Oksrukuyik Creek, S.M. Parker). *Upper right:* Dall sheep ewes and lambs (*Ovis dalli*, Guardhouse Rock, S.M. Parker). *Lower Left:* Dall mountain sheep on slope east of entrance to Galbraith airstrip road (ADH). *Lower right:* Dall sheep ram (Atigun Pass, JWS).

horns. Once the rut is completed, rams and ewes segregate into separate herds to overwinter. In early spring, pregnant females move to "lambing cliffs" (lambing ranges) in steep, rugged terrain with abundant forage where they bear young in mid-May. This early date allows time for lambs to develop sufficiently for successful overwintering. Wolves are major predators; other predators include grizzly bears, wolverines, and golden eagles. During 1985 the number of Dall sheep throughout the entire Brooks Range was estimated at 13,000 individuals. Since this time this population has declined by about 40 percent due to severe winters, which reduce lamb production, and wolf predation, which is assisted by deep snow. Dall sheep are long-lived. Exceptional rams attain 16 years and ewes attain 19 years.

Muskoxen

Historically, muskoxen (*Ovibos moschatus,* **Fig. 14.19**) were distributed throughout the North Slope. At present, however, they are restricted to the east and far west. Lone males have been observed along the Dalton

Fig. 14.19. *Left:* Muskox skull showing protective "boss" (bumper) formed by the base of horns (Noatak River, ADH). *Upper right:* Muskoxen (*Ovibos moschatus*, Pump Station 3, ADH). *Lower right:* Muskoxen (Happy Valley, ADH).

Highway as far south as Atigun Pass and small herds are often seen along the Sagavanirktok River from Slope Mountain to the Sagwon Hills. Muskoxen are stocky animals with a long skirt of dark-brown guard hairs reaching from their flanks to at least half the length of their legs. Beneath the guard hairs is a layer of exceedingly fine light-brown wool (*qiviut*) that surpasses even cashmere wool in insulating efficiency. The guard hairs are retained for several years, but the *qiviut* layer is shed every spring. Like all bovids (horned ungulates), both sexes of muskoxen have keratinized horns formed as sheaths covering outgrowths (cores) of their skulls. The horns of bulls meet in the center of the forehead to form a massive "boss" used in fights deciding access to breeding females (**Fig. 14.19**). For those accustomed to seeing only photographs of muskoxen, live animals are surprisingly small, with the largest bulls only 135 cm high at the shoulder. They are stocky, however, and exceptionally large bulls attain weights of 400 kg. Breeding occurs in September, when dominant males mate with most of the females in their herds. Calving occurs during spring. Herds of about 12–30 individuals feed on windswept rises and river bluffs during winter where snow depth is shallow (less than 20–40 cm), allowing access to dried grasses. They disperse to lowland habitats during May to feed on legumes and sedge and willow shoots.

Wild muskoxen may attain ages of 12–15 years. Their primary predators are wolves, although in recent years grizzly bears have become a

major agent of muskoxen mortality on the eastern North Slope. Muskoxen show a unique defensive behavior when faced with circling wolves.
Mature animals of small herds will press their rumps together while
facing away from one another to form a defensive star configuration.
Larger herds of 20 or more animals will form a continuous outward-
facing circle. Young seek protection in the center of these formations.
As a consequence of this behavior, circling wolves must continuously
face the sharp, upswept tips of the horns of adults. Bulls and occasionally females may also make short, unpredictable charges, providing an
offensive dynamic to their otherwise defensive stance. Such behaviors
are apparently an effective deterrent against wolves, which have been
gored to death as a result. Sources of natural muskox mortality, in addition to predation, include drowning in rivers during ice breakup, falling
through thin ice, and starvation while stranded on sea ice.

The muskox herds of the North Slope are a true conservation success. First colonizing Alaska during the Pleistocene by migrating over
the Bering land bridge, muskoxen were extirpated by hunters during
1890–1910. The present-day muskoxen of the North Slope are descen-
dants of 34 animals from Greenland that were purchased by the U.S.
Biological Survey (now the U.S. Fish & Wildlife Service) and shipped to
Fairbanks in 1931. In 1935 and 1936 these muskoxen and their prog-
eny were moved to the Bering Sea island of Nunivak near the Yukon-
Kuskokwim delta. In 1969, 52 muskoxen from Nunivak were released
into what is now the Arctic National Wildlife Refuge near Kaktovik.
Thirteen additional animals were released along the Kavik River (about
70–80 km east of Deadhorse) in 1970. These are the ancestors of the
present-day herd of the eastern North Slope. As recently as 2007–2008,
this herd was estimated to be about 200 animals, an unexplained decline from an estimate of 500–600 individuals earlier in the decade.
Between 1970 and 1977, 71 muskoxen were released on the western
North Slope near Cape Thompson. Although the resulting western herd
is self-sustaining, its growth rate has been low compared with the eastern herd, possibly due to illegal hunting.

15

Human Natural History Through the Mid-Twentieth Century

T he North Slope has a rich record of human occupation dating from the late Pleistocene to the present. Some well-studied areas, such as Galbraith Lake and Atigun Gorge, contain an archeological record of almost continuous occupation for about 13,000 years! The North Slope is of particular interest to archeologists because it remained largely ice-free during the Pleistocene and may contain traces of the first humans colonizing North America as they traveled across the Bering land bridge[1] into North America. Archeological studies, however, have revealed only sparse clues concerning the identity of these first colonizers. To simplify a rich and complex prehistory, we will focus only on occupation sites near the Dalton Highway.

Before beginning the following primer on the archeology of the North Slope, a few terms must be defined. In the context of archeology, *tradition* (with lowercase "t") refers to similar assemblages of artifacts that occur over large geographic areas for substantial periods of time. *Complex* (with uppercase "C") refers to what is basically a mini tradition, being more restricted in duration and geographical range. A comment about dating is also warranted. Prehistoric dates are usually provided in either of two forms: radiocarbon dates derived from the analysis of carbon 14 content and the more familiar calendar dates. Due to technical reasons these date systems are not equivalent, however. For example, a radiocarbon date of 10,000 years before present (BP) is about 12,000 calendar years BP. All dates provided here are calendar dates.

Paleoindian Tradition (~13,700–11,800 Years BP)

The Paleoindian tradition encompasses all North American occupation sites that are older than about 10,000 years. The cultures of this tradition shared an economy based on hunting ice-age megafauna during the last 3,000 years of the Pleistocene. Their major weapon system was the atlatl or spear thrower. The stone points that tipped the spears launched by these devices are used to diagnose different cultures. One of the best-documented Paleoindian cultures of the North Slope is the Mesa Complex,[2] which was active from 13,720 to 11,500 years BP with a brief hiatus during the intense cold and dry conditions of the Younger Dryas period[3] (about 13,300–12,200 years BP). The Mesa Complex is named after an extraordinary archeological site on an isolated promontory (the "mesa") about 260 km west of Atigun Gorge. This site has yielded numerous stone artifacts, including narrow, elongated projectile points, multi-spurred gravers, scrapers, anvil stones, and other assorted tools. Some of these artifacts were associated with fire pits containing charcoal yielding dates as old as about 13,700 years BP. Excavations at three sites near the Dalton Highway have also yielded the distinctive Mesa Complex spear points—Putu, Bedwell, and Hilltop (**Fig. 15.1**). Putu and Bedwell are separated by only 100 m and are on a promontory near the Sagavanirktok River near its confluence with the Atigun River (about 20 km east of the Dalton Highway). Hilltop is in the Atigun Gorge. Humans were thus actively hunting in the vicinity of the present-day Dalton Highway relatively shortly after the Atigun Gorge became ice-free at the end of the Pleistocene.

Putu is particularly well known for two enigmatic fluted points[4] that were found there in the 1970s (**Fig. 15.1**). One of these was manufactured from obsidian originating from a quarry on the Koyukuk River, about 490 km to the south. This indicates either wide-ranging movements or the presence of trading networks as early as 12,250 BP. Until recently, this pair of fluted points from Putu had been the focus of some controversy because of uncertainty about their ages and because fluting was thought to be diagnostic for points produced by Paleoindian complexes in temperate North America rather than the Arctic. A recent discovery of similar points on the far western North Slope near the Kivalina River, however, has provided a firm date of 12,200 years BP, showing that these were indeed manufactured by people of the Paleoindian tradition. The presence of fluted points on the North Slope suggests that the Paleoindian technology responsible for their manufacture migrated northward from the High Plains of the North American

Fig. 15.1. *Upper left:* View of Putu and Bedwell toward north (M. Kunz, Alaska BLM). Bedwell is on the summit of the hill. Putu is on the lower slope in the foreground (yellow tent). Both Bedwell and Putu are Mesa Complex sites (13,720–11,500 years BP). *Upper right:* Fluted projectile points from Putu (D. Gullickson, Alaska BLM). The "flute" is a broad, shallow divot extending along the midline of the point that was apparently a modification to facilitate attachment (hafting) to the spear shaft. The point at left was made from obsidian taken from a quarry near the Koyukuk River about 490 km to the south. Caribou hemoglobin residue was tentatively identified from these points. *Lower left:* Hilltop (Mesa Complex, Atigun Gorge, ADH). *Lower right:* Mesa Complex projectile points, gravers, and a biface from Putu (Dan Gullickson, Alaska BLM).

interior through the Ice-Free Corridor[5] to the North Slope when this route became passable sometime after about 12,500 years BP.

About 20,000 years BP the Arctic Ocean was frozen year-round, resulting in low levels of atmospheric moisture and a relatively dry climate for much of the North Slope. As a consequence, this region was covered by a dry grassland or "mammoth steppe" that supported an assemblage of large herbivorous mammals, including woolly mammoths (*Mammuthus primigenius*), horses (*Equus lambei, E. caballus*), muskoxen (*Bootherium bombifrons, Ovibos moschatus*), steppe bison (*Bison priscus*), and caribou. Following the thawing of the Arctic Ocean (about 15,000 years BP) and the submergence of the Bering land bridge, the climate of the North Slope became wetter, resulting in the replacement of the mammoth steppe with tussock tundra. This occurred relatively rapidly and had a large effect on the prey available to the first humans colonizing this region. As the area of mammoth steppe diminished, the abundance of mammoths and horses rapidly declined. Steppe bison, however, remained relatively numerous and became the major food source for the Mesa Complex people. Promontories such as Mesa, Bedwell, and Hilltop were apparently used by hunters to spot bison (**Fig. 15.1**). While waiting, these hunters produced and repaired tools, explaining the presence of numerous chert flakes and partially formed spear points at these sites. Remarkably, hemoglobin residues tentatively identified as those of caribou have been obtained from the fluted points found at Putu. Caribou were thus hunted by the people of Paleoindian tradition as well as all succeeding cultures using inland habitats of the North Slope through the mid-20th century. The paleontological record, however, suggests that caribou were not sufficiently abundant to provide a reliable regional food source until about 9,000–8,500 years BP, when the transition from steppe to tussock tundra was sufficiently advanced.

American Paleoarctic Tradition (~11,800–8,000 Years BP)

Sites occupied by people of the American Paleoarctic tradition are identified by microblades, the distinctive wedge-shaped cores used in their manufacture, and burins (tools used as engravers). Microblades are small, rectangular to trapezoidal, double-edged blades (about 1–3 cm long and 1–2 cm wide) that were wedged into longitudinal grooves along antler, bone, or ivory cylinders to produce composite tools such as projectile points (**Fig. 15.2**). The manufacture of such tools is thought to be an adaptation for mobility, allowing hunters to efficiently transport lightweight tool kits over long distances. The ability to carry raw materials for tool manufacture is especially important in the Arctic, where quarries remain buried beneath snow and ice for much of the year. The manufacture of lightweight composite projectile points suggests that the American Paleoarctic tradition may have used the bow and arrow, a technology introduced from Eurasia as early as 10,500 years BP. Gallagher Flint Station, strategically located on a large kame northeast of Slope Mountain, is an excellent example of a site near the Dalton Highway that was used by people of the American Paleoarctic tradition (**Fig. 15.3**). Excavations here have yielded microblades, microblade cores, and hearths dated at about 9,400–8,100 years BP.

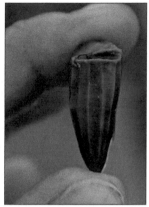

Fig. 15.2. *Left:* Microblades from a site near the Kuna River (Tony Baker, Alaska BLM). Composite projectile points were manufactured by placing microblades into slots gouged into sharpened cylinders of antler or bone. This technology was an important adaptation to the Arctic because it allowed raw materials for tool making to be easily transported during winter when stone quarries were inaccessible. *Right:* Wedge-shaped microblade core from a site near the Utukok River. Cores such as this were held in a split-wood vise while microblades were flaked from them using a bone or antler stylet (Tony Baker, Alaska BLM).

Fig. 15.3. *Upper left:* View of Gallagher Flint Station from Dalton Highway (MP 302, ADH). *Upper right:* Southern view from summit of Gallagher Flint Station toward Slope Mountain (ADH). *Lower left:* Gallagher Flint Station, excavation pit from mid-1990s (ADH). *Lower right:* Mosquito Lake (MP 270, ADH).

Northern Archaic Tradition (~8,000–3,000 Years BP)

Sites once occupied by people of the Northern Archaic tradition are identified by the presence of notched points, which first appear in the archeological record about 7,500 years BP. The basal notches were used to haft points to arrow shafts using sinew. The Northern Archaic tradition was originally described as an interior forest culture ancestral to the modern-day Athapaskans, but recent discoveries of occupation sites on the North Slope indicate that these people ventured onto tundra. Their central activity was probably caribou hunting. The best examples of Northern Archaic tradition occupation sites on the North Slope are Tuktu near Anaktuvuk Pass and the Kuparuk Pingo, about 50 km west of Prudhoe Bay in the Kuparuk River oil field. Excavations at the Kuparuk Pingo site have yielded notched points of local black chert, scrapers, blades, bone tools, hearths, and raw stone material apparently transported from the vicinity of Livengood in central Alaska. Charcoal from hearths unearthed here has established that the camp had been occupied about 5,915 years BP. Isolated notched points have also been found elsewhere on the North Slope, including the vicinity of Prudhoe Bay and the Ribdon River, an eastern tributary of the Sagavanirktok River.

Arctic Small Tool Tradition (~5,000–2,400 Years BP)

The Arctic Small Tool tradition is composed of the Denbigh Flint Complex and its eastern arctic (Canada/Greenland) contemporaries. It marks the beginning of what has been referred to as the Eskimo cultural continuum, which is identified by the development of novel technologies for effectively using regional resources. Occupation sites used by these people are distributed from the Bering Sea to Greenland and are identified by the presence of fine bifacial points, microblades, ground adzes, and other tools suggesting a historical link with Siberian tool industries. The development and spread of the Arctic Small Tool tradition was remarkably rapid, with its expansion from Alaska to Greenland completed in less than 500 years. The Denbigh Flint Complex consisted of numerous small and mobile groups of hunters that used coastal (e.g., seals, birds, fish) and inland (e.g., caribou) resources on a seasonal basis. These people first appeared in the archeological record about 5,000 years BP and soon became widely distributed across the North American Arctic. The Denbigh Flint Complex is the oldest of the cultures comprising the Eskimo continuum and is likely ancestral to the arctic coastal-marine cultures that gave rise to the Iñupiat. Mosquito Lake (about 0.5 km south of the Atigun River 2 Bridge, **Fig. 15.3**) is the best-documented site used by these people along the Dalton Highway. Excavations here have yielded more than 30,000 artifacts (mostly waste flakes or lithic debitage). Given the lack of hearth rings and charcoal, Mosquito Lake probably functioned as a tool workshop. Dates for this site range from 3,800 to 2,600 years BP. Evidence of occupation by people of the Denbigh Flint Complex has also been found at Gallagher Flint Station (**Fig. 15.3**) and Franklin Bluffs.

Kavik Athapaskan (AD 1500–1800)

Although primarily an interior forest culture, several Athapaskan occupation sites have been documented on the North Slope. One of the best known is the Atigun Site on the deep sand and silt deposit near the Atigun 2 Bridge (**Fig. 15.4**). Excavations here have revealed hearths, projectile points of chert, obsidian, bone and antler, waste flakes, bone game pieces, and a roughly fashioned copper ornament. Evidence in the form of hearth construction (paved rather than encircled by stones)

Fig. 15.4. *Upper left:* Atigun Site, view from excavation pit toward south (ADH). *Upper right:* Atigun Site, chert waste flakes ("lithic debitage") produced during manufacture of tools (ADH). *Lower left:* Atigun Site, hearth stones near excavation pit (ADH). *Lower right:* One of two stone walls on summit of Hunter's Hill, a large kame south of Galbraith Lake (ADH). This wall was probably used as a blind by Nunamiut hunters.

and type of projectile points indicates that the people who once camped here were Kavik Athapaskan. Radiocarbon analyses of charcoal indicate that the Atigun Site was used from AD 1500 to 1800. Although hearths are abundant, signs of dwellings (e.g., tent rings, post holes) are conspicuously absent. Also notable is a lack of evidence of butchering. It is probable that the Atigun Site was primarily a workshop with meat occasionally transported to hearths after being butchered at kill sites elsewhere. The Atigun Site was probably visited no more than once a year. It has been suggested that the sandy dunes of this site were visited seasonally by hunters seeking ground squirrel hides for garments.

The Maritime Eskimos: Birnirk, Thule, and Iñupiat (1,600 Years BP to Present)

By about AD 500 the coastal regions of the Beaufort Sea were occupied by the Birnirk, a specialized culture of ringed seal (*Pusa hispida*) hunters. By AD 900 the Birnirk had transitioned to the Thule culture, identified by extensive tool kits, weaponry, and drag floats used for hunting large marine mammals such as bearded seals (*Erignathus barbatus*), walrus (*Odobenus rosmarus*), and bowhead whales (*Balanea mysticetus*). The Thule rapidly dispersed along the coasts of arctic Alaska, Canada, and Greenland, eventually giving rise to the present-day Iñupiat. By AD 1500, the Nunamiut ("mountain") Iñupiat began to hunt caribou in the western Brooks Range, and by 1800 they were year-round residents of the eastern Brooks Range, including the upper Colville, Kuparuk, Sagavanirktok, and Canning River drainages. The abrupt appearance of Nunamiut in the archeological record about 400 years ago is due to rapid cultural evolution related to the development of methods for using dog teams to haul sleds. This had an important effect on their patterns of resource use because it greatly increased their ability to exploit resources over wide areas.

The history of the Nunamiut prior to significant European contact (e.g., 1868–1898) is not well known as they left only traces of their presence. In the Brooks Range the Nunamiut probably never exceeded about 1,400 people distributed among bands of 25–100 individuals. At that time they were a mobile culture, moving among scattered camps while following a seasonal cycle of subsistence activities. During summer and winter they dispersed into small bands of two to four households to hunt Dall sheep, ground squirrels, and ptarmigan. During spring and summer, larger bands hunted caribou. Fishing was apparently a minor activity except when other game were scarce. By the late 19th century, excursions

Fig. 15.5. *Upper left:* Nunamiut tent ring (western shore of Galbraith Lake, ADH). *Lower left:* Nunamiut tent ring (Toolik Field Station, Jen Kostrzewski). *Upper right:* Arrow indicates location of Aniganigaruk, a Nunamiut winter camp, near south bank of Atigun River below Guardhouse Rock (ADH). *Lower right:* Fire ring at Aniganigaruk (ADH).

for trading with the coastal Iñupiat at Barrow, the Colville delta, or Kaktovik had become a regular summer activity and an important source of supplies for winter camps, such as blubber needed to supplement a low-fat winter diet. Typical dwellings were caribou skin tents about 2.5–4.5 m in diameter. These circular to oval tents were formed from a willow frame overlain by caribou skins and weighted down by a ring of stones. When the tent was removed, a characteristic stone tent ring remained as evidence of a Nunamiut encampment (**Fig. 15.5**). Double-layered skin tents and moss houses were used for winter dwellings.

The upper Colville River and the Galbraith Lake regions were used intensively by the Nunamiut (**Figs. 15.4, 15.5**). The following is a quote from Herbert L. Alexander, the archeologist who first studied the history of human occupation of the lower Atigun River and Galbraith Lake: "Whenever we found a piece of dry ground large enough to support a tent, near a willow patch of even modest size, there would be a tent ring, or sometimes twenty tent rings" (Alexander 1967, 23). When exploring Galbraith Lake, Alexander found that "the west side of the lake was an almost continuous site, tent ring after tent ring and almost all of them with some evidence for the use of metal. We also found the pit houses . . . used as meat caches or blinds for hunting ducks" (Alexander 1967, 27). The presence of metal artifacts shows that these camps were used from the late 19th century to possibly as late as 1966, when Alexander explored this region. Surveys of the western shore of Galbraith Lake during 2009 and 2010, however, indicated that few tent rings remain apparent. Other evidence of Nunamiut occupations along the Dalton Highway is found along the south bank of the Atigun River near its entrance into the Atigun Gorge. Here archeologists searching for evidence of human occupation along the proposed route of the Trans-Alaskan Pipeline in the early 1970s uncovered remains of a small winter and occasional summer camp known as Aniganigaruk ("old camp," **Fig. 15.5**). This camp was used from about 1880 to 1890 and contained five winter houses and at least three winter and three summer tents. The rectangular winter houses had stone hearths and willow frames covered with a layer of peat and sphagnum moss. With the exception of a fire ring and a few scattered stones, little evidence of Aniganigaruk remains today.

Although the lower Atigun River and Galbraith Lake were historically used most heavily by the Nunamiut, there is evidence of other high-use sites in the Kuparuk and Sagavanirktok drainages. At least four winter camps occupied during 1898–1909 have been documented along the Kuparuk River (one near Imnavait Mountain and another about 35 km downstream of Imnavait Mountain), the Toolik River (about 20 km north of Slope Mountain), and the confluence of the Ribdon River with the Sagavanirktok River. Tent rings have been found in the Toolik Lake inlet series (**Fig. 15.5**) and Franklin Bluffs, and excavations at Putu (**Fig. 15.1**) have yielded artifacts indicating a Nunamiut presence there as well.

For at least 9,000 to 8,000 years prior to the mid-20th century, caribou were essential for the persistence of humans in the interior of the North Slope. To put it bluntly, "no caribou, no humans." This was painfully demonstrated during the dramatic crash of the Western and Central Arctic caribou herds during the close of the 19th century and the first decade of the 20th century. Between 1890 and 1900 the size of the caribou herd sustaining the Nunamiut was reduced by about 95 percent, from about 300,000 to about 15,000 animals. Consequently, the Nunamiut began to abandon foothills and mountain habitats, and by 1920 there were essentially no human residents in the interior of the North Slope. Following the recovery of the caribou herds in the 1930s, a number of Nunamiut returned to the Brooks Range where they formed several bands, one in the Killik Valley, another in the Itkillik Valley, and a third, very mobile band that used the Chandler, Anaktuvuk, and John River valleys. In 1947 this latter band settled at Tuluaq Lake north of Anaktuvuk Pass. Over the next several years the other groups joined them, and by 1951 their settlement was large enough for a post office to be established. Other than transient camps in support of seasonal subsistence activities, however, the Atigun, Sagavanirktok, and Kuparuk drainages remained essentially unpopulated by humans until the construction of the Dalton Highway in the late 20th century.

Over the centuries, the Nunamiut accumulated a deep and extensive knowledge of the natural history of the North Slope interior. As scientific study of this region accelerated during the mid-20th century, the Nunamiut people graciously shared their knowledge with university and U.S. government scientists. Prominent among those assisting in scientific inquiry was Simon Paneak. Simon Paneak was born in the Killik Valley of the central Brooks Range in 1900. During the starvation years that followed the decline of the caribou herd in this region, he accompanied his family to the coast, where he learned to read and write English. During the 1930s, he returned to the Brooks Range, where he followed a seasonally nomadic lifestyle until about 1960 when he became a semipermanent resident of the village of Anaktuvuk Pass. From 1947 until his death in 1975, Simon Paneak forged active scientific collaborations with many academic and government scientists and scholars who traveled to the North Slope to study its geology, biology, ecology, anthropology, and archeology. He was particularly well known among arctic scientists for his encyclopedic knowledge of geography, geology, archeology, and the distribution and life cycles of birds and mammals. His careful documentation of the annual cycles of the birds and mammals of the Anaktuvuk Pass region in his journals for more than 20 years is renowned. Evidence of the strength of Simon Paneak's collaborations with the scientific community remains today in the form of scholarly journal articles on which he appears as coauthor. Simon Paneak pioneered the modern study of the natural history of the North Slope. It is our hope and intent that this book celebrates his spirit by sharing knowledge of arctic natural history with any and all willing students.

Appendix

Guide to Natural History Along the Dalton Highway: Atigun Pass to Deadhorse

A. D. Huryn, J. E. Hobbie, and J. W. Schas

Introduction

The Dalton Highway provides an excellent opportunity to explore a cross section of the North Slope, including the Brooks Range, Arctic Foothills, and Arctic Coastal Plain. The impressive range of habitats easily accessible from the Dalton Highway includes alpine barrens and meadows, dry heaths, tussock grasslands, sedge wetlands, lakes and ponds, and rivers and streams. The objective of this road log is to provide a hands-on guide to the natural history of the North Slope by linking specific locations of particular interest to the familiar green mile posts (MP)[1] along the Dalton Highway (Maps 2, 3, 4). The information provided is brief and meant to complement rather than supersede information contained in the main text of this book. We urge those using this road log to also consult other excellent sources concerning geology and permafrost features (see Sources).

Four Notes of Caution Before Traveling on the Dalton Highway

1. Never approach large mammals. The behavior of grizzly bears, moose, and muskoxen can be unpredictable. Aggressive encounters between bears and humans on the North Slope are rare. They do happen, however, and human fatalities have resulted. Take the time to learn about bear safety. Less well known is the aggressive nature of moose. Females with calves, in particular, are dangerous. Although we are not aware of moose attacks on the North Slope, elsewhere

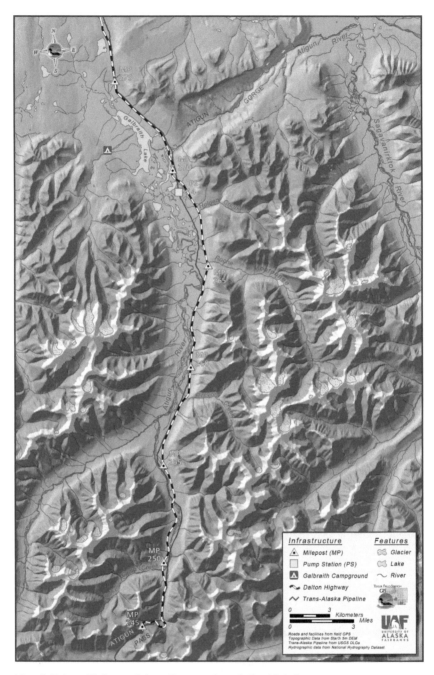

Map 2. Dalton Highway: Atigun Pass north to Galbraith Lake.

female moose have attacked and killed people who have approached their calves.

2. Be alert for trucks. The Dalton Highway was constructed for truckers; it is their road. Carry a CB radio tuned to Channel 19. A CB radio will allow you to communicate with truckers who are very knowledgeable about current road conditions and potential hazards. Drive at a safe speed (50 mph is the posted speed) with your lights on. Slow down and move to the far right of the road for approaching trucks. Check your mirrors frequently for trucks approaching from behind. Slow down while giving them room to pass safely. When stopping or parking, be sure that you are not hindering the safe flow of traffic. If this is not possible, drive to a safe pull-off and return to the location of interest on foot.

3. Wear seatbelts. The chance of dying on the Dalton Highway during a single vehicle accident while not wearing a seatbelt is much higher than that of colliding with another vehicle and much, much higher than being hurt during an aggressive encounter with wildlife.

4. Be self-sufficient. There are no gas stations, motels, or stores along the 390 km (240 mile) stretch of the Dalton Highway between Coldfoot (south of the Brooks Range) and Deadhorse. First-time travelers on the Dalton Highway are often unaware that the Sagwon airstrip, often indicated as a town on maps, is not accessible from the road and has a permanent population of 0.

The Road Log

MP 244.7—Atigun Pass. Here the topographical divide formed by the spine of the Brooks Range marks the beginning of the North Slope. All streams and rivers to the north of this location flow to the Arctic Ocean, and the entire landscape is underlain by continuous permafrost; trees are absent. Although the elevation of the Atigun Pass region is unremarkable (the crest of the pass is only 1,447 m), it is an extremely harsh alpine habitat due to its high latitude (about 68°N). The valleys nearby have supported cirque glaciers (Fig. 3.1) for the past 4,500 years. There is safe parking to the east.[2] Adventurers can reach the Grizzly Glacier by climbing the steep talus slope above the roadside parking area and descending into the cirque on its north side. The large, circular man-made structure to the southeast is a Wyoming snow gauge used to measure snowfall. The slopes and road cut to the west of the parking area are Kanayut Conglomerate (upper Devonian and Lower Mississippian, 385–345 mya, Fig. 2.3).

MP 245.4—Mountain meadow. A mountain meadow is accessible from a pipeline access road and parking area to the east. The meadow is northeast of the parking area and can be reached by walking north about 100 yards along the buried pipeline and crossing a borrow pit toward the east. This meadow contains a lush carpet of *Sphagnum* moss and a network of small streams that drain north towards the Atigun River. Birdwise, this meadow provides habitat for mountain specialists such as semipalmated plovers, rock ptarmigans, willow ptarmigans, snow buntings, gray-crowned rosy finches, and northern wheatears.

MP 245.8—Atigun River valley overlook. An overlook to the west provides a view of the Atigun River valley. Beware of trucks climbing the grade toward Atigun Pass. The view here includes the classic U-shaped Atigun River valley (Fig. 3.6), shaped by the Pleistocene glaciers that were active as recently as 11,000–12,000 years ago, and steep slopes of Hunt Fork Shale (Upper Devonian, 385 mya, Figs. 2.1, 2.2) with talus cones and rock glaciers. From this vantage point, one lobe-like rock glacier can be seen to the northwest and several others are to the northeast. The Hunt Fork Shale is the primary bedrock exposed from Atigun Pass to the Atigun River 1 Bridge (MP 253).

MP 246.3—First crossing of Atigun River.

MP 247—Rock glacier and alpine meadow. A short road to the west provides access to a rock glacier (the steep, flat-topped slope immediately west of the access road) and a good example of an alpine meadow with a diverse plant community. On sunny days in late June and early July this is an excellent habitat for observing alpine butterflies.

MP 248.4—Hunt Fork Shale road cut. A pull-off to the west provides safe access to a road cut and a good opportunity for a hands-on examination of the laminated structure of Hunt Fork Shale (Fig. 2.2). To the east is the braided channel of the Atigun River, talus cones of Hunt Fork Shale, and a rock glacier.

MP 249.4–250—Spike Camp Creek. The large mountain stream passing beneath the road from the west is Spike Camp Creek, a tributary of the Atigun River. Spike Camp Creek provides habitat for arctic grayling. A rock glacier is to the east.

MP 250—Atigun Camp. The Atigun Construction Camp is to the east. It was one of 30 camps active during the pipeline construction and is still used occasionally. There are several safe parking locations here.

MP 253—Atigun River 1 Bridge. This second crossing of the Atigun River provides good views and access to its braided channel and extensive floodplain. There is safe parking north of the bridge. Here the Atigun River provides habitat for arctic grayling, Dolly Varden char, slimy sculpin, and round whitefish. Ravens have used the stanchions of this bridge as a nest support (Fig. 13.21). An active gravel quarry is on the floodplain east of the bridge. The Grizzly Glacier is visible to the south. From MP 253 to Pump Station 4 (MP 269) the bedrock exposures are primarily Kanayut Conglomerate.

MP 256—West Fork of the Atigun River. The West Fork of the Atigun River enters the Atigun River from the west.

MP 256.9—Aufeis and slush flows. A small aufeis is to the west on the Atigun River floodplain. Prior to breakup the aufeis is visible as a blue ice layer within the white snowpack; during early summer it appears white. The broad U-shaped tracks of "slush flows" (water combined with melting snow and ice) are visible on the talus-laden slopes to the east and west.

MP 258.5—Trevor Creek. Trevor Creek is a high-gradient arctic mountain stream. Although it freezes solid during winter, Trevor Creek provides good summer habitat for arctic grayling. Safe parking is available at the bridge, which is an ideal starting point for a hike up the valley to explore alpine habitats.

MP 260.7—Rock quarry. The steep access road here leads to a rock quarry with impressive fresh exposures of Kanayut Conglomerate (Fig. 2.3) and associated strata of soft, reddish shale. The large inclusions of chert (black to maroon) and quartz (white) are clearly evident. This quarry has been in operation since 1974 (during the original road construction). Here Kanayut Conglomerate is "shot" (blasted) into boulder-size pieces and then further crushed and graded to provide road gravel. Be sure to ask permission before exploring if the quarry is in operation.

MP 263.2—Atigun River "transformation." From this approximate location the Atigun River changes from a stream flowing through a broad braided channel composed of cobbles and boulders to a deep, meandering, single-thread channel composed of silt and sand (Fig. 3.5). This transformation marks the southernmost extent of the ancestral Galbraith Lake shoreline (see MP 272). From this point north to Atigun Gorge the floor of the Atigun River valley is a poorly drained sandy plain with frost polygons, string bogs, and thaw ponds.

MP 263.9—Roche Moutonnee Creek. Roche Moutonnee Creek is a high-gradient arctic mountain stream. It freezes solid during winter, but like other mountain streams in this region it provides summer habitat for arctic grayling.

Safe parking is available at the bridge, which is an ideal starting point for a hike up the valley to explore alpine habitats. Golden eagles nest on the headwater cliffs of this stream.

MP 266—Sedge meadow. A good example of a wet *Eriophorum angustifolium* and *Carex bigelowii* meadow is to the west.

MP 267.5—Holden Creek. Holden Creek (also known as China Valley Creek) is a high-gradient arctic mountain stream. Like other streams along this part of the Dalton Highway, it freezes solid during winter but provides habitat for arctic grayling in summer. Safe parking is available near both the northern and southern approaches to the bridge. Common birds found here during summer include American robins, American pipits, northern wheatears, northern shrikes, American tree sparrows, white-crowned sparrows, spotted sandpipers, and wandering tattlers.

Northern shrikes and American robins nest in the willow thickets to the north. During late summer, shrikes hunt fledgling American robins, white-crowned sparrows, and American tree sparrows, which are abundant here prior to migrating south. A hike upstream may reveal wandering tattlers and spotted sandpipers foraging along the braided streambed. Wandering tattlers are relatively large gray-and-white birds that will likely be heard before being seen. If one continues to the upper mountain valley, northern wheatears and American pipits may be found. Wheatears have a diagnostic black inverted T-shaped patch at the tip of their tails. The tail of the smaller American pipit has white outer feathers and black inner feathers. In early summer pipits may forage for invertebrates stranded on snowbanks. Invertebrates are often carried aloft by thermals and eventually deposited on mountain slopes.

MP 268.9—Wet sedge meadow and thaw pond. An extensive pond and sedge wetland to the west below Pump Station 4 provides an opportunity to view a diversity of arctic birds, particularly during late spring and early summer. Red-throated loons, red-necked phalaropes, glaucous gulls, mew gulls, arctic terns, lesser yellowlegs, least sandpipers, western sandpipers, American golden plovers, Savannah sparrows, Lapland longspurs, and Wilson's snipes are common here. Take care when stopping because the road is narrow and truck traffic frequent. Carefully pull off onto the sloping shoulder so traffic can pass unimpeded.

Red-throated loons nest near the margins of the pond. Adults and newly hatched young are conspicuous as they lounge on its surface. Since the pond is too shallow for overwintering fish, young are fed fish captured and transported by adults from nearby lakes and streams. Glaucous and mew gulls also frequently nest here, usually on the islands dotting the pond's surface. Glaucous gulls tend to nest on the south end of the pond and mew gulls on the north end, often with arctic terns. Nesting gulls may harass observers on the road by aggressive diving. Red-necked phalaropes often swim in tight circles to corral zooplankton prey. They are one of only a few species of sandpipers that swim. Also, unlike most bird species, females are brightly colored while males are drab. This is due to reversed nesting roles—eggs are tended by males. Listen for the short whistles of lesser yellowlegs. These long-legged waders nest among sedges. A search near calling adults may reveal young. Western and least sandpipers also nest here. The presence of a nest is indicated by an adult feigning a broken wing to lure would-be predators away from its eggs. Their nests are in the drier areas of the wetland and are almost impossible to find. The least sandpiper has yellow legs and is smaller than the black-legged western sandpiper.

MS 269.2—Access road to Pump Station 4 and Tea Lake. The foundation for Pump Station 4 is on limestone bedrock. Here the permafrost is more than 245 m deep. The wide road allows safe parking. The kettle lake directly to the northwest is Tea Lake. It provides habitat for arctic grayling, lake trout, and burbot. An extensive sedge wetland is east of the road.

MP 270—Lisburne Limestone. This location provides a good view of the Lisburne Limestone (Upper Mississippian to Upper Permian, 326–254 mya, Fig. 2.4) to the northeast. The erosion-resistant Lisburne Limestone forms massive cliffs of limestone (calcium carbonate) and dolomite (magnesium carbonate). Its color ranges from light gray to yellowish when weathered.

MP 270.6—Mosquito Lake. Mosquito Lake is to the east (Fig. 15.3). Its shore was occupied by people of the Denbigh Flint Complex about 3,800–2,600 years ago. Excavations here have yielded more than 30,000 artifacts (mostly waste chert flakes). Mosquito Lake provides habitat for round whitefish. Its maximum depth is 7–8 m.

MP 271—Atigun Bridge 2 and Atigun Gorge. Atigun Bridge 2 is one of two bridges crossing the Atigun River. The boundary of the Arctic National Wildlife Refuge (ANWR) is about 5 km (3 miles) east. On the south side of the bridge there is a parking area that provides a convenient staging point for hikes into the Atigun Gorge and along the Atigun River. The Atigun Gorge is a narrow, 13 km long canyon downstream (east) of the bridge. It is a fault valley bordered by limestone, siltstone, and shale of Mississippian to Permian age (326–254 mya) to the south, and by various siltstones, sandstones, and conglomerates of the Fortress Mountain Formation (Cretaceous, 122–100 mya, Fig. 2.6) to the north. It contains evidence of human occupations dating from the late Pleistocene to the early 1900s (Fig. 15.1). Guardhouse Rock is the castle-like promontory east of the parking area (Fig. 2.4). Its massive yellowish cliffs are Lisburne Limestone. Extreme folding of the bedrock

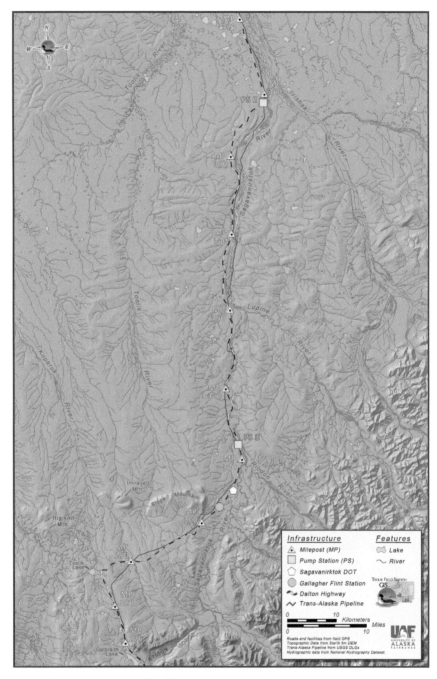

Map 3. Dalton Highway: Galbraith Lake to the Ivishak River.

here has resulted in an inversion of Guardhouse Rock—it's upside down! Consequently, the oldest rock layers are near its summit and the youngest are near its base. Fossilized crinoid stem fragments, brachiopod shells, and other mollusks are found here (Fig. 2.5).

The Galbraith Lake outlet stream (informally known as Fox Creek) enters the Atigun River directly west of the bridge. The sand dunes west and north of the bridge are formed by windblown sediments that once covered the bed of the ancestral Galbraith Lake, which once extended as far as 18 km southward along the Atigun River valley. This well-drained habitat supports a population of arctic ground squirrels that has been subject to physiological and ecological study by scientists from the University of Alaska and the Toolik Field Station for many years. This abundant population attracts predators such as foxes, wolves, and humans. As long as 700 years ago, bands of Athapaskan people routinely crossed the Brooks Range from the Alaskan interior to this location to hunt ground squirrels for pelts (Fig. 15.4). The tracks of foxes and wolves are often found in the soft sediments upstream and downstream of the bridge when water levels are low.

Birds commonly found near the Atigun Bridge 2 include white-crowned sparrows, American tree sparrows, northern shrikes, Savannah sparrows, cliff swallows, golden eagles, Smith's longspurs, white-crowned sparrows, American tree sparrows, and common ravens. Cliff swallows are conspicuous as they fly to and from their jug-shaped mud nests, which are cemented to stanchions beneath the road and pipeline bridges. Golden eagles often soar above the cliffs of the Atigun Gorge, where they seek Alaskan marmot, ground squirrels, and the lambs of Dall sheep. Their nests are deep within the gorge. While at the parking area, take a moment to listen to birdcalls. The buzzy call of a male Smith's longspur indicates the presence of nests near the parking area. A careful search of the tundra on either side the Atigun River downstream of the parking lot may produce several Smith's longspurs. Common ravens often nest within the structure of the pipeline crossing. During spring the presence of a nest may be revealed by the calls of the begging young, particularly when adults arrive with food.

MP 272—Galbraith Lake and mountain glaciers. Galbraith Lake (Fig. 3.5), to the west, is one of the largest lakes in the Arctic Foothills. It has a maximum depth of about 7 m and an area of 417 ha. Its basin was dammed by an end moraine during the retreat of the Itkillik II glacier about 11,500 years ago. Galbraith Lake provides habitat for arctic grayling, lake trout, round whitefish, and burbot. A series of three cirque glaciers can be seen near the summit of the mountains toward the west. These are informally known as the Three Sisters.

MP 274—Frost polygons and Fortress Mountain Formation. There are extensive frost polygons in the wet sedge meadow to the west (Fig. 4.5). The angled troughs indicating the positions of the ice wedges forming their perimeters are clearly visible. Small, shallow thaw ponds formed by melting ice wedges are also found here. To the east are the impressive, dark-brown slopes of the Fortress Mountain Formation (Cretaceous, 122–100 mya, Fig. 2.6), composed of sandstone, conglomerate, and other sedimentary rocks. Look for Dall sheep on the steep cliffs (Fig. 14.8). Alaskan marmot may be found on the upper slopes.

MP 274.7—Galbraith Lake campground. To the west is an access road leading to the Galbraith airstrip (2.1 miles) and a campground (4.3 miles). A large cirque glacier (informally known as Gates glacier, Fig. 3.1) is visible from the campground road south of the airstrip. Galbraith Campground is the only official campground north of the Brooks Range. An outhouse, bearproof food safe, and information kiosk are provided. The campground provides an opportunity to explore mountain and foothills habitat without heavy truck traffic or long hikes. Rock ptarmigans and willow ptarmigans are common in the willow thickets near the campground. Northern shrikes nest in the tall felt-leaf willows along the stream south of the campground.

Two aufeis are accessible here. The first is in a mountain valley directly west of the northern end of the airstrip and is approached using a road to a gravel quarry. This valley is used as nesting habitat by Say's phoebe. The second aufeis is southeast of the campground. This aufeis is actually the result of the fusion of two bodies of overflow ice. The northern half is produced by the upwelling of water from the deep gravel channel of a mountain stream that enters the Atigun River floodplain from the west. The southern half is produced by a tundra spring stream that flows along the base of the low bluffs directly south of the campground. To reach the spring you must walk south from the campground through the felt-leaf willow thicket and across the mountain stream. The spring stream is identified by the abundant aquatic mosses that cover its bottom. It provides habitat for a landlocked population of Dolly Varden char. Although its water temperature may cool to almost 0°C and ice covers most of its length during winter, this spring stream does not freeze solid. By following the spring downstream one will reach a wide gravel plain into which the water of the spring percolates and upon which the aufeis is formed during winter. Depending on summer conditions, this aufeis may persist well into July. While exploring the aufeis be sure to note stones with powdery white deposits of calcium carbonate that precipitated from the spring water as it froze. This material was originally dissolved from limestone upstream and then transported to the aufeis in groundwater. Also note the reddish sediment deposited on the gravel margins of the mountain stream. This is glacial flour carried by the stream from Gates glacier, visible to the south from the campground road.

MP 275.8—Arctic Foothills. Here the Dalton Highway leaves the mountains of the Brooks Range and crosses the Arctic Foothills for the next 80 miles. Extensive areas of moist tussock tundra, well-drained heaths, and snow beds are visible from the road. The heaths are typically on the windward side of hills formed by glacial moraines, moraine-like features, kames, and other glacial deposits.

MP 276.4—Island Lake. Island Lake is the compound kettle lake to the west. It is inhabited by arctic grayling, arctic char, lake trout, and round whitefish. Its maximum depth is 6 m and its area is 62 ha. To the north the road crosses a series of moraines left by the receding Itkillik II glacier.

MP 277.3—Divide between the Sagavanirktok and Colville River drainages. From this approximate location water flowing south enters the Atigun River and eventually reaches the Beaufort Sea through the Sagavanirktok River. Water flowing to the north enters the Itkillik River and eventually reaches the Beaufort Sea via the Colville River. East of the pipeline are abundant dry heaths on moraine-like features and kames (Fig. 3.4). Frost boils and stone stripes are common on the heaths (Fig. 4.8).

MP 279.3—I-Minus Lake. I-Minus Lake is one of many lakes in this area that have been the focus of long-term research by the scientists from the Toolik Field Station (MP 284). The west side of the lake's bank shows extensive slumping that may be due to the ongoing melting of ancient buried ice from the Itkillik II glacier (Fig. 3.5).

MP 278.8—Divide between Colville and Kuparuk River drainages. From this approximate location water flowing south eventually reaches the Arctic Ocean via the Colville River while water flowing north eventually reaches the Arctic Ocean via the Kuparuk River.

MP 280.4—Pipeline utility road. The pipeline utility road to the west provides an opportunity to explore a diversity of foothills habitats, including thaw ponds, tundra streams, tussock tundra, wet sedge meadows, dry heaths, and snow beds.

MP 281.7—Toolik Lake. Directly to the west are several small kettle lakes. These lakes are collectively known as the Inlet Series or the I-Series because they are all drained by a stream that eventually enters Toolik Lake (the Toolik Lake "Inlet Stream"). Toolik Lake is within the Kuparuk River drainage. The I-Series and Toolik Lake have been the focus of intensive ecological research for many years. Toolik Lake and the buildings of the Toolik Field Station are visible to the northwest. Toolik Lake is a large compound kettle lake that was formed by the melting of blocks of ice that were buried as the Itkillik II glacier began to recede about 13,000 years ago. Its maximum depth is 22 m and its total area is 150 ha. Toolik Lake contains arctic grayling, lake trout, round whitefish, burbot, and slimy sculpin. The landscape here has abundant moraines, moraine-like hillocks, kames, erratic boulders, and other evidence of the Pleistocene glaciers.

MP 282.3—Pipeline utility road. The pipeline utility road to the east leads to excellent dry heath and boulder field habitat. These features were formed during the retreat of the Itkillik II glacier. By walking north along the pipeline one can cross a divide into the Kuparuk River valley that shows the stark contrast between the boulder fields of the relatively young Itkillik II age (20,000–11,500 years ago) glaciated landscape and the relatively subdued Sagavanirktok age landscape (see comments for MP 286). Alaskan marmot are common here. While walking up the grade, listen for their sharp, loud warning whistles.

MP 283—Jade Mountain. The low mountain to the west-northwest is Jade Mountain. The cliffs on its eastern flank provide nesting habitat for common ravens, gyrfalcon, and peregrine falcons. Jade Mountain overlooks the hills forming the southern shores of Toolik Lake. The boardwalks and greenhouses on these hills are used by scientists of the Toolik Field Station to study the ecology of tundra plant communities.

MP 284.3—Access road to Toolik Lake. The Toolik Lake Field Station, an ecological research facility managed by the Institute of Arctic Biology at the University of Alaska, is on the southeastern shore of Toolik Lake. Each year more than 100 scientists and their students conduct field studies in the Toolik Lake region. The Toolik Field Station is not open to the public. The northern shore of Toolik Lake, however, can be reached by driving west on the Toolik Lake access road, turning north at the first fork, and following the road to the yellow spill-containment box. There is ample parking here. The dry heath tundra and wet sedge tundra along the road to the north is a good birding area. Bird species here include bluethroats, American golden plovers, horned larks, eastern yellow wagtails, yellow-billed loons, common redpolls, hoary redpolls, horned larks, American golden plovers, Lapland longspurs, Savannah sparrows, common redpolls, hoary redpolls, white-crowned sparrows, American tree sparrows, yellow warblers, and Wilson's warblers.

During summer there is a good chance that a scan of Toolik Lake will reveal yellow-billed loons. These huge birds nest on small brood lakes near large feeding lakes, such as Toolik Lake. A few days after hatching, adults guide their young from the brood lake to the feeding lake. Bluethroats are small thrushes that spend much of their time skulking in thickets. Courting males, however, are conspicuous. Their displays begin with a cricket-like chirping followed by a melodious song produced as males quickly ascend to as high as 47 m and then rapidly descend along spiraling flight paths. Their courtship period begins in late May and lasts until mid-June. The willow thicket along the outlet of Toolik Lake usually contains one or two pairs of nesting bluethroats. Eastern yellow wagtails often nest in the tall willows near the spill-containment box where they may be conspicuous as they "hawk" flying insects. Their "tszee tszee" call is distinctive.

Additional habitat can be explored by walking directly north from the yellow spill-containment box along the abandoned airstrip road. Horned larks, American golden plovers, Lapland longspurs, Savannah sparrows, and redpolls are common here. Look for horned larks and American golden plovers on dry heaths. Be alert for the courtship displays of male horned larks, which fly as high as 250 m during their aerial displays. American golden plovers are large black-and-white birds that can be located by their siren-like calls. Their nests are simple scrapes on dry heaths. When the airstrip road ends at a small lake, take the trail to the right to return south. The riparian wetland habitat along the beginning of the trail contains white-crowned sparrows, American tree sparrows, and possibly yellow and Wilson's warblers.

The most abundant bird at Toolik Lake is the Lapland longspur. This distinctive bird is usually found in wet, shrubby tundra. When they arrive in mid- to late May the tundra becomes alive as singing males begin their aerial courtship displays, which reach elevations as high as 30 m. This activity may continue until mid-June. The Savannah sparrow is also abundant here. It is a "skulker" that spends much of its time on the ground. The unmistakable single-note call is the best way to find concealed birds.

As you explore the Toolik Lake area, pay particular attention to the songbirds overhead. If you hear a noisy "flock" of birds but spot only one or two, you have probably found redpolls. There are two species of redpolls here: common and hoary. Both have the "redpoll" on their heads. The hoary redpoll is a frosty whitish brown with a pale pink wash on its breast. The common redpoll has a dark-red necklace and a deep-pink breast. They nest in tall felt-leaf willow thickets.

MP 284.3—Lake E1.[3] Lake E1 is directly east of the entrance to the Toolik Lake access road. During summer it usually hosts a pair of nesting glaucous gulls and provides good habitat for ducks and shorebirds. Lake E1 contains arctic grayling and slimy sculpin.

MP 285.6—Itkillik I age glacial moraine. Proceeding north, the Dalton Highway climbs the lateral moraines of the Itkillik I glacier (less than 12,500 years ago, Fig. 3.2). Toward both the east and the west is a steep, dry boulder field deposited by the receding glacier. There is a good view of Toolik Lake to the southwest as the summit of the moraine crest is approached.

MP 286.1—Itkillik I moraine crest. Abundant rock debris deposited by the Itkillik I age glacier (glacial drift) is evident as a dense boulder field to the southwest (Fig. 3.2). The numerous lakes also visible to the southwest form a "lake district," a characteristic of young postglacial landscapes. The view to the southwest contrasts sharply with the view to the northeast, where few boulders and lakes are apparent on the rolling, tussock-covered terrain formed from the significantly older Sagavanirktok age drift (800,000 years ago, Fig. 3.2). From this location there are also good views of Slope, Imnavait, and Itigaknit Mountains to the northwest (Fig. 2.7) and Lake E5 and the Kuparuk River valley to the north and northeast. A truck park provides safe parking to the east.

MP 287—Lake E5. Lake E5 is visible directly to the north-northeast. This lake can be visited by taking a short hike east of MP 287.6 (the lake is not visible from the roadside at this location). Lake E5 is deep (maximum depth = 12 m) for such a small lake and provides habitat for arctic char. Arctic char rarely coexist with lake trout, an aggressive and dominant competitor. Lake E5 has provided a refuge for arctic char since the Pleistocene because its outlet stream is impassable to lake trout due to its steep gradient and lack of surface water during much of the summer. Its outlet stream crosses beneath the highway and eventually flows into the Kuparuk River.

MP 288.8—Kuparuk River. The grade that descends into the Kuparuk River valley provides an excellent view of the river's meandering channel and gravel point bars with associated riffle habitats. Several fishless floodplain ponds are also visible. These provide habitat for fairy shrimp during summer. Fairy shrimp are fascinating animals that are easily captured with an aquarium dip net. Here the Kuparuk River is a large tundra stream that eventually flows directly into the Beaufort Sea west of Prudhoe Bay. Parking is available at the bridge. The pipeline maintenance road at the north side of the bridge provides access to excellent examples of wet sedge, moist tussock, shrub, and dry heath habitats. The Kuparuk River freezes during winter, but in summer it contains a population of arctic grayling that has been the focus of study by scientists from the Toolik Field Station for more than two decades. During late summer these fish migrate upstream to Green Cabin Lake (about 14 km from the bridge as the crow flies), where they overwinter. The Kuparuk River provides the best opportunity to observe harlequin ducks along the Dalton Highway. Breeding pairs or small flocks of males are occasionally observed here. *Kuparuk* is an Iñupiat word meaning "rather large river."

MP 290.6—Imnavait Creek. This location is the divide between the Kuparuk River valley to the south and the relatively small Imnavait Creek valley to the north. There is good parking here. The beaded channel of Imnavait Creek, a small tundra stream, is visible to the north at the bottom of the descending road grade. Horsetail watertracks (e.g., Fig. 4.7) are visible on the hillslopes to the northwest. Imnavait Creek eventually drains into the Kuparuk River. There is an excellent view of the meandering channel of Kuparuk River to the southeast. The gated road to the east provides access to dry heath habitat and is a good staging point for hikes into the upper Kuparuk and Oksrukuyik River drainages.

MP 291.3—Headwaters of the Toolik River. The Toolik River is a fine example of a beaded tundra stream (e.g., Fig. 4.7). A short hike along its channel from the Dalton Highway west to the pipeline provides an opportunity to explore a beaded stream. Toolik River, a tributary of the Kuparuk River, provides habitat for arctic grayling.

MP 294–297—Divide between Kuparuk and Sagavanirktok drainages. From approximately MP 294 to MP 297 streams flowing west of the road eventually drain into the Kuparuk River, while streams flowing east drain into the Sagavanirktok River. From MP 297 to Deadhorse, the Dalton Highway is in the Sagavanirktok River drainage. Horsetail watertracks are visible on the hillslopes west of MP 295 to 297.

MP 297.7—First Oksrukuyik Creek bridge. Oksrukuyik Creek is a tundra stream that drains into the Sagavanirktok River. It freezes solid during winter but provides summer habitat for arctic grayling and round whitefish, which overwinter in the deeper waters of the Sagavanirktok River. Oksrukuyik Creek drains Itkillik I–age terrain and consequently contains many kettle lakes (not visible from the road but can be accessed by foot from the Imnavait Creek utility road). These lakes contain arctic grayling, arctic char, lake trout, round whitefish, and sculpin.

MP 298.4—Fog Lakes. A group of five small kettle lakes (not visible from the road) known collectively as the Fog Lakes is located a short hike east of the road. One of these (Fog 2, 68°40′44.76″N, 149°05′27.45″W) is quite deep (17 m) relative to its size (3.1 ha) and provides habitat for arctic char. Presumably this population of arctic char has occupied Fog 2 since the Pleistocene. Lake trout are unable to enter this lake because of the steep gradient of its outlet to the Sagavanirktok River.

MP 299—Sagavanirktok River. The Sagavanirktok River, which can be seen to the east, provides habitat for arctic grayling, Dolly Varden char, burbot, and round whitefish. The numerous kettle lakes visible to the east and northeast comprise a lake district formed on the relatively young landscape exposed by the recession of the Itkillik II–age glacier that once extended north along the Sagavanirktok River valley. *Sagavanirktok* is an Iñupiat word meaning "strong current."

MP 301—Slope Mountain access road. Slope Mountain consists primarily of sandstones of the Nanushuk Group (Cretaceous, 122–100 mya, Fig. 2.7). The upper layers were deposited in a riverine environment. The lower layers were deposited in a marine environment. Raptors often nest on cliffs below its summit and Alaskan marmot can be found on its western slopes. Dall mountain sheep are usually visible on the steep cliffs facing the road (look for clusters of white dots). There is a salt lick near the bottom of these cliffs that the sheep use as a source of dietary minerals. Accomplishment Creek enters the Sagavanirktok from the east and is visible from the summit of the mountain.

MP 302.9—Gallagher Flint Station. The large kame directly to the west of the road is Gallagher Flint Station, an important archeological site (Fig. 15.3). Gallagher Flint Station was occupied by members of the American Paleoarctic tradition about 9,400–8,100 years BP. This site was apparently used to spot game on the surrounding tundra—experience the view yourself—and for the production of stone tools (thus its designation as a flint station). Sites occupied by the American Paleoarctic tradition are identified by distinctive stone tools indicating possible cultural ties with Eurasia. Excavations here have yielded microblades, microblade cores, and hearths.

MP 305.6—Oksrukuyik Creek and Sag River Station. The turnoff to the east leads to the Sag River Station of the Alaska Department of Transportation. The turnoff to the west provides access to the lower part of Oksrukuyik Creek (this stream was first crossed at MP 297.7). There is ample space for parking here but be sure to pull off onto the roadside so the gate remains unobstructed. Hiking along the channel of lower Oksrukuyik Creek is an excellent way to explore foothills habitats. To access the lower reaches of Oksrukuyik Creek, walk west along the road, cross the pipeline, and continue toward the dense willows that mark its riparian zone. Here the streambed is wide and rocky with banks that are covered with tall felt-leaf willows near the streambed and diamond-leaved willows farther away. There is also a dense understory of grasses, wild roses (Fig. 9d.10), and many other shrubs. This reach has "intermittent" flow (i.e., flows for only a portion of the year) and is usually dry by early July. Bird species found here are gray-cheeked thrushes, American robins, Wilson's warblers, yellow warblers, gray jays, and fox sparrows.

The most effective birding strategies are to walk along the tussock tundra at the outer edge of the riparian shrub line or slowly meander along the streambed when it is dry. Gray-cheeked thrushes nest in the riparian willows, where they are regularly observed. Listen for their song and then carefully make your way to the bird's location. Wilson's and yellow warblers are also regularly found here. If you hear an animal loudly scratching the ground, you have probably located a fox sparrow. These sparrows spend much of their time skulking on the ground. In early summer, however, they may be found singing near the tops of willows. A final "special" bird that can usually be found along this reach of Oksrukuyik Creek is the gray jay. Although abundant in the interior of Alaska, gray jays are uncommon on the North Slope. They have been observed here in February and are one of the few species of birds that overwinter on the North Slope.

Finally, the riparian willow thicket of Oksrukuyik Creek is a good spot to search for mammals. In some years snowshoe hares may be abundant. Search for scats, girdled willows, and other signs of their presence. They are most active at dusk. Moose are also abundant here, with herds of as many as 18 individuals observed in winter. Be sure to note their trackways, scats, and the broomed branches of willow shrubs that are caused by browsing. *Beware of grizzly bears and moose, especially when moving quietly in search of birds in willow thickets. Be vigilant at all times. Carry bear spray. Never approach moose—be particularly wary of cows with calves.*

MP 307—Poplar grove. A poplar grove is in the gully east of the road, indicating the presence of either unfrozen groundwater year-round or a sheltered south-facing slope (Fig. 9d.6). Poplars are uncommon on the North Slope.

MP 309—View of Sagavanirktok River floodplain. From the bluffs to the east there is an excellent view of the Sagavanirktok River floodplain. The Ribdon River, one of the major tributaries of the Sagavanirktok River, can also be seen to the east.

MP 309.6—Sagavanirktok River floodplain. Here the road abruptly descends through a bench composed of Itkillik-age drift and enters the Sagavanirktok River floodplain for the next 10 miles. Abundant wet sedge, dry heath, and stony floodplain habitats are accessible from numerous pull-offs.

MP 311.9—Access road to Pump Station 3. The access road to Pump Station 3 is to the west. Unlike Pump Station 4, which rests on limestone bedrock, the foundation for Pump Station 3 must be refrigerated to keep the underlying permafrost from thawing.

MP 313.7—Second bridge over Oksrukuyik Creek. From Pump Station 3 to here the roadbed has been raised to form a causeway that keeps it above overflow ice and floodwaters from the Sagavanirktok River during breakup.

MP 317.9—"Yellow warbler" creek. The informally named yellow warbler creek is a tiny, unassuming tributary of the Sagavanirktok River. Parking at MP 317.9 is difficult, and we suggest that visitors park at the access road about 200 yards north to the east and walk south along the road to the creek. Make your way to its rocky bottom and then walk downstream thorough the tall thicket of felt-leaf willows until you cross an access road that terminates at the bank of the Sagavanirktok River. Follow this road west to return to your vehicle. Bird species found here include the yellow warblers, Wilson's warblers, American tree sparrows, and—historically—alder flycatchers.

Yellow warbler creek is an excellent location for observing warblers and the American tree sparrow because its steep banks provide an un-impeded view of the canopy of the riparian willow thicket when viewed from the road. From such a vantage point yellow warblers are conspicu-ous to both eye and ear, being bright yellow with orange streaks on their breasts and extraordinarily vocal. Wilson's warblers are olive green with small black caps. Locate these secretive birds by searching locations from which they are singing. Alder flycatchers have also been found here, al-though there have been none reported in recent years.

MP 319.6—Oil Spill Hill. At this point the Dalton Highway leaves the Sagavanirk-tok River floodplain and ascends a gentle grade up Oil Spill Hill. There is safe parking to the east at the crest of the hill. Alternate parking is on a pipeline maintenance road to the west at the northern base of the hill (MP 320.4). The summit of Oil Spill Hill is an excellent place for observing arc-tic butterflies. Males of several hilltopping species congregate at the summit to mate with passing females. After descending Oil Spill Hill and crossing Gustafson Gulch the highway once again enters the Sagavanirktok River floodplain.

MP321.5—Horsetail watertracks. Horsetail watertracks are visible on the hill-slopes to the northwest.

MP 322—String bogs. Wet sedge "string bog" habitat, characterized by numer-ous long, sinuous, and raised string-like hummocks, is abundant between the road and the pipeline. String bogs form on relatively flat wetland terrain. Water flowing across the wetland's surface rolls tangles of dead grasses into linear hummocks, or "strings." These provide topographical relief that, although only a few tens of centimeters high, is important in determining the diversity of wetland plant communities. Take a moment to examine the different plants on the strings versus those between strings. Thaw pools in this area provide habitat for buckbean and other aquatic vascular plants.

MP 324.6–325.2—Ice Cut area. The Ice Cut area is the approximate northern limit of the Itkillik-age glaciers and can be explored from two excellent parking places. The first is the access road at MP 324.6. The second (MP 325.2) is a large turnaround area on the eastern side of the highway at the "Ice Cut" sign near the base of the grade up Ice Cut. Bird species often observed here include gyrfalcons, peregrine falcons, rough-legged hawks, cackling geese, white-crowned sparrows, American tree sparrows, Savannah sparrows, Lapland longspurs, Smith's longspurs, yellow warblers, Wilson's warblers, and arctic warblers.

Driving north, the first Ice Cut stop is the access road at MP 324.6. From here steep cliffs (Nanushuk sandstone) can be seen above the eastern bank of the Sagavanirktok River. A close examination of these cliffs (a spotting scope is helpful) will show numerous nesting sites used by gyrfalcons (white and dark morphs), peregrine falcons, and rough-legged hawks among natural hollows and ledges. Splashes of white guano indicate nest sites. The bulky nests are built by rough-legged hawks; falcons nest either in an abandoned hawk nest or directly on a ledge. Although all three species may be found here, there is usually only a single pair of nesting raptors in a given summer. The sandy banks of the western channels of the Sagavanirktok River are used as burrow sites for bank swallows. The ponds directly south of the access road provide habitat for larvae of both damselflies and dragonflies.

The parking area at the base of Ice Cut (MP 325.2) provides access to extensive willow thickets and riparian herb and grass fields. Cackling geese nest here, as do numerous songbirds, including white-crowned sparrows, American tree sparrows, Savannah sparrows, Lapland longspurs, Smith's longspurs, yellow warblers, and Wilson's warblers. The tall felt-leaf willow thicket north of the Ice Cut sign is a good place to find arctic warblers. These active birds greet intruders with loud, continuous chattering and vigorous wing displays.

MP 325.2–325.7—Ascent of Ice Cut. The 0.8 km (0.5 mile) grade up Ice Cut provides excellent views of the Sagavanirktok River and floodplain. Ice Cut is named for a large volume of ground ice uncovered during construction of the road cut.

MP 330.8—Dan Creek. Here the Dalton Highway crosses Dan Creek, a good example of a tundra stream. Dan Creek freezes solid during winter but provides summer habitat for arctic grayling and burbot, which migrate from the Sagavanirktok River. There is an excellent view of the Sagavanirktok River floodplain to the east. Lupine River, a major tributary, enters the

Sagavanirktok River from the east about 4.8 km (3 miles) upstream of this location.

MP 334.4—Happy Valley. Happy Valley is the site of a former pipeline construction camp. This site is currently used for an airstrip, gravel extraction, and a staging camp for geological exploration. The stream that crosses beneath the road near the turnoff to Happy Valley is a tundra stream known as Happy Valley Creek. This stream provides habitat for arctic grayling. A raven nest has been constructed between the antlers of a moose skull mounted near the buildings along the bank of the Sagavanirktok River (Fig. 13.21).

MP 339—End moraines of the Sagavanirktok glaciation. Sagavanirktok-age glaciers extended north from the Brooks Range to this approximate location.

MP 341.5—Horsetail watertracks. Horsetail watertracks are visible on the hillslopes to the west.

MP 347.7—Sagavanirktok River and floodplain overlook. This spot provides one of the best panoramas of the braided Sagavanirktok River and its floodplain. The Sagwon Bluffs are visible to the north-northwest. An aufeis here usually persists into early summer. An information kiosk nearby provides vignettes of arctic natural history.

MP 348—Sagwon Uplands. Here the Dalton Highway ascends to the Sagwon Uplands. This location marks the northernmost limit of the ancient Anaktuvuk-age glaciers (less than 2.5 mya) as well as the northern limit of alder along the Dalton Highway. Although evidence is sparse, it is probable that the older Gunsight Mountain glaciers (more than 2.6 mya) extended farther north. To the east, near the eastern bank of the Sagavanirktok River, is Sagwon, an abandoned camp and airstrip. Sagwon was an important logistical center for geological exploration in the 1960s.

MP 351—Horsetail watertracks. Horsetail watertracks are visible on the hillslopes to the northeast.

MP 352.3—Prince Creek Formation. To the east is a low outcrop of siltstones and sandstones of Prince Creek Formation (Late Cretaceous, 86–66 mya, Fig. 2.7). Outcrops of this formation along the Colville River (about 145 km [90 miles] to the northwest) contain abundant dinosaur fossils. The habitat in which these dinosaurs lived was located even farther north than the present location of the Prince Creek Formation, showing that dinosaurs were capable of living under conditions of alternating periods of nearly continuous daylight and darkness.

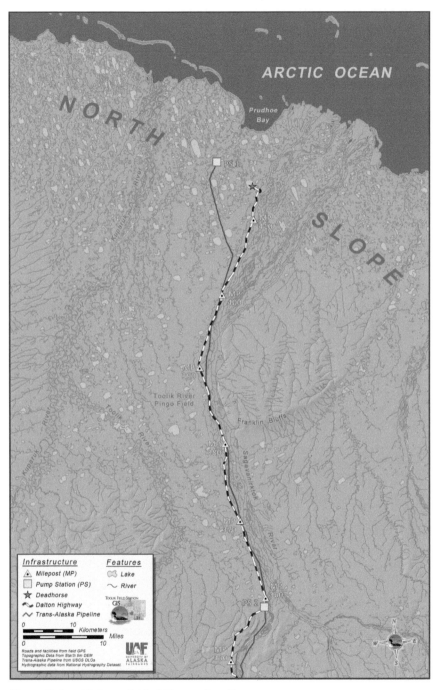

Map 4. Dalton Highway: Ivishak River to Deadhorse.

MP 354.5—View of Arctic Coastal Plain. The "355 Wayside" rest stop is to the west just before the crest of the long grade that descends to the coastal plain. By climbing the low hill to the northwest of the parking lot, one will find excellent examples of dry heath and a stunning view of the Arctic Coastal Plain to the north. The Franklin Bluffs are visible to the northeast; the White Hills are visible to the northwest.

MP 355.1–358.1—Descent to coastal plain. A 4.8 km (3 mile) grade descends from the Sagwon Uplands to the Arctic Coastal Plain.

MP 359—Pump Station 2. Pump Station 2 has been ramped down (i.e., out of effective service) since 1997. This location is the northern limit of dwarf birch along the Dalton Highway.

MP 361—Ivishak River. Here the Ivishak River (not visible from the road) enters the Sagavanirktok River from the east. The Ivishak River is the largest tributary of the Sagavanirktok River. *Ivishak* is an Iñupiat word meaning "red earth," apparently a reference to abundant deposits of iron pyrites in some of its headwater tributaries. Both the Ivishak and the Echooka (a northern tributary of the Ivishak River) Rivers contain numerous springs and large areas of open water during winter. As a consequence they are critical habitat for Dolly Varden char. The Ivishak River contains the largest population of breeding Dolly Varden on the North Slope. Interestingly, Simon Paneak—a prominent Nunamiut elder from Anaktuvuk Pass—once pointed out that the Nunamiut concept of the Sagavanirktok River requires the switching of the Ivishak River and the Sagavanirktok River as indicated on USGS maps. In other words, the Nunamiut concept of the Sagavanirktok River would include the Ivishak River as its headwaters rather than the present-day Sagavanirktok River upstream of MP 361.

MP 363–370—Patterned ground and thaw ponds. Frost polygons, string bogs, and thaw ponds are evident from the road. The extensive pond near MP 367 provides excellent birding, particularly in late spring and early summer. From here to Deadhorse, the coastal plain is a relatively uniform habitat mosaic composed of wet grass and sedge meadows, string bogs, frost polygons, and thaw ponds. *These habitats cannot be properly appreciated from a vehicle. Stop often to hike on the tundra.*

MP 365—White Hills. The low hills forming the western horizon are the White Hills.

MP 368.6–369.5—Stone revetments. The raised stone structures extending into the Sagavanirktok River from the west are river training devices that protect the road by reducing bank erosion.

MP 371–374—Patterned ground. Frost polygons and string bogs are evident near the road.

MP 373–376—Pingos. To the west-northwest is the first of several pingos visible from the Dalton Highway. The large pingo west of MP 376 is the easternmost member of the Toolik River pingo field and is about 8 km (about 5 miles) from the road. Given their elevation and good drainage, pingos provide habitats for plant communities that are more similar to foothills habitats than those of the coastal plain. The largest pingos of this region may contain ice cores as high as 25 m.

MP 376–380—Patterned ground. String bogs and frost polygons are evident from the road. Small pingos can be seen toward the west.

MP 380—Franklin Bluffs. Here the Franklin Bluffs (Fig. 2.8) rise along the eastern bank of the Sagavanirktok River (they are most spectacular from approximately MP 385 to 390). These white-and-orange-stained bluffs are composed of siltstone, sandstone, and conglomerate. The orange staining is due to iron oxidation. The Franklin Bluffs are members of the Sagavanirktok Formation, which was deposited during the Eocene (56–34 mya).

MP 382.5—Pingo. A collapsing pingo is to the west.

MP 385–389—Thaw ponds. Along this section of the highway, numerous thaw ponds are accessible to the west. We recommend the exploration of several ponds to experience differences among their animal communities. Shallow, unconnected thaw ponds will be fishless. As a consequence they will have dense populations of *Daphnia middendorffiana,* which appear as clouds of tiny, dark swimmers near the water's surface. Their dark color is due to pigments protecting them from UV radiation. Other common invertebrates in fishless ponds are fairy shrimp, amphipods, and tadpole shrimp. Tadpole shrimp will likely be seen only in late summer. Deep ponds (3+ m) and ponds connected to streams may contain fish (usually ninespine sticklebacks) and therefore few large-bodied crustaceans.

MP 394.8—"Deadhorse 20 Miles" sign. Perhaps the best opportunity for successful birding on the coastal plain is the stretch of highway from MP 394.8 (the "Deadhorse 20 Miles" sign) to Deadhorse. The highway is wide here so stopping and parking is relatively safe. The tundra adjacent to the road provides many easily accessible lakes, ponds, and wetlands that provide excellent habitat for waterfowl. The seasonal distribution of birds here is influenced by the "dust effect." The dark dust that settles on the snow along the margins of the road absorbs solar radiation and causes this area to become snow-free much more rapidly than the surrounding tundra. The dust effect produces an important loafing habitat for early migrants that must wait for lakes and ponds to thaw. Because of this, birding along the road in mid- to late May may be spectacular in some years. Birds often spotted on the northern coastal plain include greater white-fronted geese, snow geese, blue geese, king eiders, spectacled eiders, tundra swans, northern harriers, and snowy and long-eared owls.

The greater white-fronted goose is the most common goose species likely encountered. Its name refers to the white band between the bill and the forehead. As the only all brown-gray goose in North America, it blends well into the early-spring tundra. Another species commonly observed is the snow goose, which is large and white with black wing tips. Snow geese migrate at relatively high elevations and flocks of migrants appear as loose strings accompanied by faint calls. Look carefully for dark "blue geese," or Ross's geese, when scanning flocks of snow geese. The "blue goose" is an uncommon morph (same species but showing a variation of the usual white plumage) of the snow goose distinguished by dark, gray-brown bodies and white heads. Ross's goose, an Alaskan rarity that has been occasionally reported from the northern coastal plain, is a smaller version of the snow goose that is distinguished by its small bill and the absence of the black longitudinal "grin" patch found on snow geese. Like the snow goose, Ross's goose also has a dark morph. In addition to the various species of geese, tundra swans are also often found on ponds adjacent to the road.

The opportunity to see a snowy owl on the coastal plain depends on the cycle of lemming abundance. Patterns of lemming abundance throughout the North Slope will affect the occurrence of snowy owls at any one location. For example, during years of high lemming abundance at Barrow, snowy owls will be numerous there. In years of low lemming abundance, however, they will disperse to other regions where prey abundance is more favorable. Snowy owls are most likely to be seen on the ground. Be sure to take a second look at any white bird on the tundra. What might appear to be a glaucous gull or a lone snow goose may actually be a snowy owl. Short-eared owls also show cycles of abundance that are linked to those of their prey. Unlike snowy owls, however, they are usually spotted flying in search of prey. Be aware that short-eared owls and northern harriers are often mistaken for one another. Northern harriers are easily identified by their white rump.

MP 396–398—Patterned ground. Frost polygons can be seen from the road.

MP 397.5—Franklin Bluffs. This location is the approximate northern limit of the Franklin Bluffs.

MP 398—Percy pingo. Percy pingo, an excellent example of a mature, conical pingo, is about 3 km (1.8 miles) west of the road (Fig. 4.2). It is approximately 15 m high. Two other collapsed pingos are visible toward the west-northwest.

MP 398–400—Thaw ponds. Good examples of thaw ponds are directly to the west and east.

MP 409–412—Patterned ground and thaw ponds. Good examples of frost polygons and thaw ponds can be seen from the road. Frost polygons are particularly well developed from MP 411 to Deadhorse.

MP 410.5—Thermokarst. Thermokarsting, massive sinking of the tundra's surface due to the thawing of the ground ice wedges that form frost polygons, is evident directly east of the road.

MP 412–414—Sagavanirktok River. Sagavanirktok River is easily accessible from the road here. Use a spotting scope to search the extensive gravel flats for resting snowy owls.

MP 415—Deadhorse. Deadhorse provides numerous outstanding examples of both low-center and high-center frost polygons. There are also good examples of thermokarsting, the massive slumping of soil caused by the rapid melting of the ice wedges that provide structure to frost polygons. With a little luck, a trip to Deadhorse may provide an opportunity to see king and spectacled eiders and arctic fox. The larger lakes, such as Lake Colleen and Lake Olivia, and the numerous ponds of Deadhorse provide excellent waterfowl habitat. Be aware that there is heavy truck traffic in and around Deadhorse, so plan stops with safety in mind.

Endnotes

Notes to Chapter 1

1. Many factors interact to determine the position of the tree line. Because temperature is just one of them, the "10°C July mean-temperature rule" should be considered a rough rule of thumb rather than a precise predictor of the boundary of the tree line.

2. Permafrost is a layer of earth (including ice, soil, and bedrock) that is permanently frozen. The North Slope is underlain by a continuous layer of permafrost 90–600 m thick. Because permafrost may or may not contain ice, it "thaws" rather than "melts" when warmed. Permafrost is discussed in detail elsewhere in this book (see "Permafrost and Patterned Ground").

3. The "uncoupling of air and ground temperatures" refers to a lack of a relationship between air and ground temperatures.

4. Another factor contributing to the relatively moderate temperatures occurring beneath the snow is the release of heat as soil water freezes (an "exothermic" or "heat-releasing" process). In the case of water-saturated soils, the continuous release of heat that occurs as pore water freezes can result in soil temperatures that remain above 0°C until mid-December even though air temperatures have been consistently well below zero since at least early October.

5. Sublimation is the conversion of ice to vapor without an intervening liquid state.

Notes to Chapter 2

1. Alaska and many other landmasses are composed of distinct blocks of continental crust that have become fused. These blocks, or "terranes," may have geographical and geological origins that are very different from one another. As a consequence, neighboring terranes may show large differences in bedrock structure (e.g., rock type, age, sequence of rock layers, types of fossils) that allow their delimitation. To simplify things, picture Alaska as a jigsaw puzzle made up of many pieces (terranes) of different sizes, shapes, and geographical and geological origins. The processes that are involved in moving terranes about the Earth's surface and fusing some together to form compound terranes are related to the concepts of plate tectonics and continental drift.

2. Overthrusting is the folding and eventual overlapping of bedrock strata, or layers. Overthrusting has resulted in a general north–south contraction of the North Slope terrain.

3. Bedrock often consists of layers of different rock types, with the oldest near the bottom and the youngest near the top—like a many-layered cake. In the case of the North Slope, however, the cake has been "dipped" or tilted to the north and then planed nearly flat by erosion, resulting in the oldest layers being exposed in the south and the youngest being exposed in the north.

4. The names of major geological formations are usually based on a geographical location where exposures were first encountered or are particularly

apparent. The name of the Hunt Fork Shale, for example, is based upon the Hunt Fork of the John River, which arises on the south slope of the Brooks Range near Anaktuvuk Pass.

5. Talus refers to the eroded stones that accumulate at the base of a cliff or a mountain slope.

6. Ice-cored rock glaciers are formed by the combination of a deep talus slope and ice-rich permafrost. The ice cements the talus particles together to form a massive, solid structure called an ice core. Over time, the ice core slowly creeps downslope under the control of gravity. This process results in a distinctive lobe-like structure that distinguishes ice-cored rock glaciers.

7. Stratigraphy refers to the sequence of bedrock strata that appear in a cross section of a bedrock exposure. The oldest strata are usually at the bottom and the youngest are near the top. In cases of deformation, however, this can be altered. In cases of extreme deformation the stratigraphy of a bedrock layer can be inverted so that the oldest layers are near the top. A stratigraphical mirror image occurs when a single bedrock layer is folded over onto itself to form two layers that are mirror images—the lower layer has normal stratigraphy while that of the upper layer is inverted.

8. Geologists use a system of classification that organizes bedrock types into units called formations and groups. Formations consist of one or more rock types that together form a distinctive unit that is regional in size. Groups contain one or more formations.

Notes to Chapter 3

1. Outwash refers to sand and gravels deposited by water flowing from melting glaciers.

2. Erratics are boulders carried from their source bedrock by glaciers and deposited in seemingly random locations.

3. During periods of widespread glaciation sea levels are significantly lower and the area of the Arctic Coastal Plain substantially greater, so the land remaining ice free when the Kuparuk gravels and Gunsight Mountain erratics were deposited was much broader than 30 km.

4. Cirques are distinctive, bowl-shaped mountain valleys formed by small alpine glaciers.

5. Moraines are linear or crescent-shaped mounds of rocks, sand, and soils that have been transported and deposited by a glacier. Lateral moraines are formed along the sides of a glacier. End moraines are formed along the front of a glacier and mark the location of its farthest advance. End moraines often dam valleys following a glacier's retreat, resulting in the formation of lakes.

6. Kames are discrete hills formed from piles of sand and gravel deposited during the recession of a glacier. Compound kames have irregular shapes and multiple hilltops due to the coalescence of two or more kames.

7. Kettle lakes are formed when buried blocks of glacial ice melt to produce open basins.

Note to Chapter 4

1. In the cold and relatively dry climate of the Arctic, carbonate rocks such as the Lisburne Limestone resist erosion. This is unlikely the case in warmer, wetter climates.

Notes to Chapter 5

1. Although often a correlate of temperature, shrub height is by no means determined solely by temperature.

2. Plant biomass is usually measured as the total mass of dried plant tissue harvested from one-square-meter plots.

3. Fellfields are habitats composed primarily of frost-heaved rocks.

4. Whether a lake or river provides suitable habitat for overwintering fish is not simply a matter of whether the body of water freezes solid or not. There must also be a sufficient volume of oxygenated water beneath a 1.7–2.0 m thick ice layer to support the respiratory demands of the fish population.

5. Midges are true flies (Diptera) of the family Chironomidae. Their tiny, legless larvae may be extremely abundant in freshwater sediments where they are important prey. Adults resemble mosquitoes but do not bite.

6. Precise coordinates are given for some geographic features to assist readers in locating them using Google Earth.

7. A compound lake has a basin formed by the coalescence of several basins that were previously independent.

8. Kettle lakes are formed by the melting of large blocks of buried glacier ice.

9. Rotifers are tiny multicellular organisms that appear similar to protozoa when viewed through a microscope.

10. Diatoms are photosynthetic algae enclosed in telescoping silica cases.

11. Distributaries are parallel divisions of what was once a single river channel.

12. Braided rivers have multiple channels that are divided into roughly parallel distributaries in such a way that, when viewed from above, they resemble loosely braided ropes.

13. The discharge of a river refers to the volume of water flowing through its channel. Discharge is reported in units such as cubic meters per second.

14. Rock flour or glacial flour is fine rock powder produced by the grinding action of a glacier on underlying bedrock.

15. Biofilms are thin films of algal cells and other microorganisms such as bacteria and fungi that are all bound together by a layer of a mucous-like substance. Biofilms coat the surfaces of essentially all objects in aquatic habitats and are of critical importance to aquatic food-webs.

16. Aufeis is a German word that translates to "ice on top" and refers to the buildup of layers of ice by the freezing of sheets of flowing water.

17. The amount of heat released by 1 g of water as it is cooled by 1°C is 4.2 joules (1 calorie). The amount of heat released (latent heat of fusion) during the conversion of 1 g of water at 0°C to 1 g of ice is 334 joules (about 80 calories).

Note to Chapter 7

1. The lichen thallus is a flattened lobe-like or tube-like structure formed by fungal hyphae. The lichen thallus is the structure visible to the naked eye.

Notes to Chapter 9

1. Vegetative reproduction is an asexual process by which new individuals are formed without production of seeds.

2. Trees are plants with a single trunk attaining heights of 3 m or more.

3. A rhizome is essentially a horizontal, underground plant stem. Rhizomes often produce roots and shoots at intervals along their length. A bulbil or bulblet is a small

bulb produced in association with flowers or on other parts of a plant's stem. Bulblets are dispersed like seeds but are actually a mode of asexual vegetative reproduction.

4. Stomata are tiny pores on the surface of leaves that can be opened and closed to control the rate of gas and water vapor exchange with the atmosphere.

5. Sepals are modified leaves that form the cup-like flower base that usually encloses the petals.

6. Taxonomic synonyms occur when a single species receives two or more scientific names. When such a situation is discovered, the first assigned name takes precedence. The first assigned name, or oldest name, is known as the senior synonym and the other names are junior synonyms. This situation has occurred many times in the Arctic, where European and North American taxonomists have often worked in isolation.

7. Nitrogen fixation is a process by which atmospheric nitrogen (N_2) is converted to a form (e.g., NOx) that can be used to construct biological tissues. This process is usually carried out by specialized bacteria, often in association with higher plants.

8. The Nunamiut are members of the greater Iñupiat culture that migrated from the arctic coast to the foothills and mountains of the North Slope about 400 years ago.

9. Bracts are modified leaves that support the base of the flower.

10. Leaf stipules are tiny leaf-like structures borne at the base of the leaf stalk or petiole.

11. The gray-headed chickadee is primarily a Eurasian bird whose easternmost range includes the Sagavanirktok River drainage.

12. Vegetative layering is a form of vegetative propagation during which new stems arise from buried branches.

13. Adventitious roots originate from structures other than a seed.

14. Many—but not all—species of the Rosaceae are shrubs. To simplify presentation we include all species of this family among the "trees and shrubs," whether shrubby or herbaceous.

15. Subfossils are the remains of plants and animals that have been preserved without being completely or partially mineralized (fossilized) by postmortem processes. Commonly, preservation without mineralization is due to lack of sufficient time for true fossilization and the conditions of burial (e.g., frozen in permafrost or anoxic sediments).

Notes to Chapter 10

1. Beringia was a grassland-steppe habitat that encompassed eastern Siberia, the Bering land bridge, and much of present-day Alaska and the Yukon Territory during most of the Pleistocene. During this time, Beringia remained largely glacier-free, other than the relatively small glaciers originating in mountain cirques of the Brooks Range, and provided a refuge for numerous plants and animals that were extirpated elsewhere.

2. To ensure that one doesn't get the impression that only invertebrates supercool during the North Slope winter, one should be aware that hibernating arctic ground squirrels (*Urocitellus parryi*) tolerate body core temperatures as low as -2.9°C without freezing. Since no specialized cryoprotectants are synthesized, this state of supercooling is attained with normal concentrations of body fluid solutes. Also, some arctic plants such as willows are capable of supercooling their tissues (see "Trees and Shrubs").

3. Larvae of the Alaskan beetle *Cucujus clavipes* (Cucujidae) are able to avoid freezing at temperatures as low as -100°C by converting supercooled fluids to a glass-like state (vitrification) as temperatures decline below -40° to -58°C. Although yet to be reported from the North Slope, this beetle occurs as far north as Wiseman (Dalton Highway MP 188.5).

4. Ice nuclei are tiny ice crystals, dust particles, or other objects that enhance the rate of ice formation.

5. Unlike insects which have a single pair of antennae, crustaceans have two pairs of antennae.

6. Seed banks are assemblages of viable buried seeds that provide a source of colonists when a habitat is disturbed. Zooplankton "egg banks" play an essentially identical ecological role.

Notes to Chapter 11

1. Cycloid scales are simple oval scales with flexible margins.

2. The lateral line is a line of sensory pores extending along the middle of the flank of the body.

3. The adipose fin is a small, fleshy dorsal fin near the tail.

4. Parr marks are a series of distinct dark vertical bars along flanks of young salmonids.

5. Anadromous fish species migrate from marine to freshwater habitats to spawn.

6. Diadromous fish species migrate between marine and freshwater habitats to spawn. This generalized category includes both anadromous (marine to freshwater) and catadromous (freshwater to marine) species.

Notes to Chapter 13

1. Staging refers to the congregation of migrating birds in resting and feeding areas prior to arrival at their ultimate destination.

2. Polynyas are areas of perennially open water in seas that normally freeze during winter.

3. Precocial young are able to walk and forage independently for food shortly after hatching. By contrast, altricial young are relatively helpless after hatching and depend on parents for food and heat.

4. Kleptoparasites are animals that steal food from other individuals.

5. Owl pellets are regurgitated boluses of undigestible prey remnants, usually bones, fur, and feathers (Fig. 13.19). They are usually found near roosts. Although the regurgitation of pellets is usually associated with owls, other species of birds—such as the common raven—show similar behavior.

6. Barrow's Iñupiat name is *Ukpiaġvik,* or the "place where owls sit."

Notes to Chapter 14

1. Estimates of the number of species occurring in a given region are usually somewhat subjective due to how rarities are treated. The count of 26 mammal species provided here is based on the number of species that we believe can be reasonably considered residents of the North Slope.

2. The abundance statistics provided here are scaled to km^2 to produce comparable values between very common and very rare species. These must be treated with a heathy skepticism, however. For example, singing voles may occur in densities as high as 50 animals per hectare, or about 5,000 animals per km^2, in optimal habitat patches. Such patches, however, are probably always much less than one km^2.

3. Population estimates of lemmings at Barrow are averages across all habitats. Brown lemmings may be much more abundant in specific habitats.

4. Although an apparent population irruption occurred for snowshoe hares in the vicinity of the Dalton Highway during 2007–2009, long-term records are

required to establish whether a given population shows regular cycles in abundance. Such records are not available for the North Slope.

5. The dusky shrew occurs in the Brooks Range near the Continental Divide. The tiny shrew is known from a handful of locations, all from Alaska, including a record from the shore of the Canning River near the Beaufort Sea.

6. Scatter-hoarding refers to the storing of single food items in numerous, spatially scattered caches.

7. Dew claws are digits of mammalian feet that do not normally come in contact with the ground when walking. They are most conspicuous among species that walk on their toes, such as the hoofed mammals. The caribou foot consists of a pair of hooves (toes) that make contact with the ground with every step and a pair of conspicuous raised dew claws that may not.

Notes to Chapter 15

1. During much of the Pleistocene, the Bering land bridge provided a terrestrial route between present-day Siberia (western Beringia) and Alaska (eastern Beringia). At its greatest extent, this land bridge was huge, roughly equivalent to the area of present-day Alaska. Humans are thought to have used it to enter North America as early as 18,000 years BP. The Bering land bridge was exposed and available to migrating humans and animals as late as 13,000 years BP.

2. The Mesa Complex was not the only significant Paleoindian culture of the North Slope. The Sluiceway Complex includes a number of occupation sites from the mountains and foothills of the western North Slope. The people of this complex were contemporaneous with the Mesa Complex from which they can be distinguished by differences between their weapon points.

3. The Younger Dryas period was a brief but dramatic reversal of the warming trend that signaled the end of the Pleistocene.

4. Fluting refers to the removal of a shallow, longitudinally oriented flake from either face of a stone spear point.

5. The Ice-Free Corridor was a north–south route through the continental Pleistocene ice sheets of the North American interior. It was located along the eastern flank of the Rocky Mountains in the current-day province of Alberta and the Northwest Territories of Canada.

Notes to the Appendix

1. We provide most locations as decimal fractions measured from the closest mile post to the south. For one reason or another, however, mile posts along the Dalton Highway are sometimes more or less than one mile apart, which may cause our locations to be inaccurate when approached from the north (e.g., MP 324.6 measured from the south is not equivalent to MP 225.4 measured from the north).

2. Throughout this road log we use "east" and "west" to designate the sides of the Dalton Highway rather than specific compass directions. This reduces problems with using "left" or "right" when driving north (i.e., left is west) or south (i.e., left is east).

3. Lakes that are used for long-term ecological studies by scientists at the Toolik Field Station are given alphanumeric designations depending on compass direction from Toolik Lake. Lakes to the east are designated E#, lakes to the north are designated N#, and so on.

Sources

Introduction

Marchand, P.J. 1991. *Life in the cold: An introduction to winter ecology*, 2nd ed. University Press of New England, Hanover.

Olsson, P.Q., L.D. Hinzman, M. Sturm, G.E. Liston, & D.L. Kane. 2002. *Surface climate and snow-weather relationships of the Kuparuk Basin on Alaska's Arctic Slope*. U.S. Army Corps of Engineers, Cold Regions Research and Engineering Laboratory. ERDC/CRREL TR-02-10.

Olsson, P.Q, M. Sturm, C.H. Racine, V. Romanovsky, & G.E. Liston. 2003. "Five stages of the Alaskan Arctic cold season with ecosystem implications." *Arctic, Antarctic, and Alpine Research* 35:74–81.

Pielou, E.C. 1994. *A naturalist's guide to the Arctic*. University of Chicago Press, Chicago.

Polunin, N. 1951. "The real Arctic: Suggestions for its delimitation, subdivision and characterization." *Journal of Ecology* 39:308–315.

Sturm, M., J. Schimel, G. Michaelson, J.M. Welker, S.F. Oberbauer, G.E. Liston, J. Fahnestock, & V.E. Romanovsky. 2005. "Winter biological processes could help convert arctic tundra to shrubland." *BioScience* 55:17–26.

Wendler, G., & M. Shulski. 2007. *The climate of Alaska*. University of Alaska Press, Fairbanks.

Bedrock Geology

Bureau of Land Management. 1993. *Riches from the earth: A geologic tour along the Dalton Highway, Alaska*. Alaska Natural History Association, Anchorage, Alaska.

Moore, T.E., W.K. Wallace, K.J. Bird, S.M. Karl, C.G. Mull, & J.T. Dillon. 1994. "Geology of northern Alaska." Pp. 49–140 *in* Plafker, G. and H.C. Berg (*eds.*), *The geology of Alaska. The geology of North America*, Volume G-1, Geological Society of America, Boulder, Colorado.

Mull, C.G., & K.E. Adams (*eds.*), 1989. *Dalton Highway, Yukon River to Prudhoe Bay, Alaska*. Guidebook 7. Alaska Division of Geological and Geophysical Survey, Anchorage, Alaska.

Glacial Geology

Hamilton, T.D. 1994. "Late Cenozoic glaciation of Alaska." Pp. 813–844 *in* Plafker, G., and H.C. Berg (*eds.*), *The geology of Alaska. The geology of North America*, Volume G-1, Geological Society of America, Boulder, Colorado.

———. 2003. *Glacial geology of the Toolik Lake and Upper Kuparuk River Regions.* Institute of Arctic Biology, Biological Papers of the University of Alaska, Number 26.

Permafrost and Patterned Ground

Brown, J., & R.A. Kreig (*eds.*). 1983. *Elliot and Dalton Highways, Fox to Prudhoe Bay, Alaska: Guidebook to permafrost and related features, Guidebook 4.* Fourth International Conference on Permafrost, Fairbanks, Alaska. Alaska Division of Geological and Geophysical Surveys, Anchorage.

Davis, N. 2001. *Permafrost: A guide to frozen ground in transition.* University of Alaska Press, Fairbanks.

Pielou, E.C. 1994. *A naturalist's guide to the Arctic.* University of Chicago Press, Chicago.

Habitat and Ecology

Brown, J., K.R. Everett, P.J. Webber, S.F. MacLean, Jr., & D.F. Murray. 1980. "The coastal tundra at Barrow." Pp. 1–29 *in* Brown, J., P.C. Miller, L.L. Tieszen, & F.L. Bunnell (*eds.*), *An arctic ecosystem: The coastal tundra at Barrow, Alaska.* US/IBP Synthesis Series 12. Dowden, Hutchinson & Ross, Inc., Stroudsburg, Pennsylvania.

Carson, C.E. 2001. "The oriented thaw lakes: A retrospective." Pp. 129–138 *in* Norton, D.W. (*ed.*), *Fifty more years below zero.* University of Alaska Press, Fairbanks.

Hall, D.K. 1980. "Mineral precipitation in North Slope river icings." *Arctic* 33:343–348.

Hershey, A.E., G.M. Gettel, M.E. McDonald, M.C. Miller, H. Mooers, W.J. O'Brien, J. Pastor, C. Richards, & J.A. Schuldt. 1999. "A geomorphic-trophic model for landscape control of arctic lake food webs." *BioScience* 49:887–897.

Hinkel, K.M., R.C. Frohn, F.E. Nelson, W.R. Eisner, & R.A. Beck. 2005. "Morphometric and spatial analysis of thaw lakes and drained thaw basins in the western Arctic Coastal Plain, Alaska." *Permafrost and Periglacial Processes* 16:327–341.

Hobbie, J.E. (*ed.*). 1980. *Limnology of tundra ponds.* US/IBP Synthesis Series 13. Dowden, Hutchinson & Ross, Inc., Stroudsburg, Pennsylvania.

Hobbie, J.E., A.E. Hershey, P.P.W. Lienesch, M.E. McDonald, G.W. Kling, & W.J. O'Brien. 2001. "Studies of freshwaters on the North Slope." Pp. 123–128 *in* Norton, D.W. (*ed.*), *Fifty more years below zero.* University of Alaska Press, Fairbanks.

Li, S., C. Benson, L. Shapiro, & K. Dean. 1997. "Aufeis in the Ivishak River, Alaska, mapped from satellite radar interferometry." *Remote Sensing of the Environment* 60:131–139.

Markon, C.J., & D.V. Derksen. 1994. "Identification of tundra land cover near Teshekpuk Lake, Alaska, using SPOT satellite data." *Arctic* 47:222–231.

Moulton, L.L., W.A. Morris, C. George, J. Bacon, J.R. Rose, & M. Whitman. 2007. *Surveys of fish habitats in the Teshekpuk Lake region, 2003–2005.* North Slope Borough, Department of Wildlife Management, PO Box 69, Barrow, Alaska.

O'Brien, W.J. (*ed.*). 1992. *Toolik Lake: Ecology of an aquatic ecosystem in Arctic Alaska.* Kluwer Academic Publishers, Boston.

Raynolds, M.K., D.A. Walker, & H.A. Maier. 2006. Alaska Arctic tundra vegetation map. Scale 1:4,000,000. Conservation of arctic flora and fauna (CAFF) Map No. 2. U.S. Fish and Wildlife Service, Anchorage, Alaska. http://www.arcticatlas.org/maps/themes/ak/.

Sloan, C.E., C. Zenone, & L.R. Mayo. 1976. *Icings along the Trans-Alaska Pipeline road*. United States Geological Survey Professional Paper 979.

Thomas, D.N., G.E. Fogg, P. Convey, C.H. Fritsen, J.-M. Gili, R. Gradinger, J. Laybourn-Parry, K. Reid, & D.W.H. Walton. 2008. *The biology of polar regions*. Oxford University Press, Oxford, England.

Vincent, W.F., & J. Laybourn-Parry. 2008. *Polar lakes and rivers: limnology of arctic and antarctic aquatic ecosystems*. Oxford University Press, Oxford, England.

Walker, D.A., J.G. Bockheim, F.S. Chapin III, W. Eugster, F.E. Nelson, & C.L. Ping. 2001. "Calcium-rich tundra, wildlife, and the 'mammoth steppe.'" *Quaternary Science Reviews* 20:149–163.

Walker, H.J., & P.F. Hudson. 2003. "Hydrologic and geomorphic processes in the Colville River delta, Alaska." *Geomorphology* 56:291–303.

Weller, M.W., & D.V. Derksen. 1979. "The geomorphology of Teshekpuk Lake in relation to coastline configuration of Alaska's coastal plain." *Arctic* 32:152–160.

Mushroom Madness

Hobbie, J.E., & E.A. Hobbie. 2006. "15N in symbiotic fungi and plants estimates nitrogen and carbon flux rates in Arctic tundra." *Ecology* 87(4): 816–822.

———. 2008. "Natural abundance of 15N in nitrogen-limited forests and tundra can estimate nitrogen cycling through mycorrhizal fungi: A review." *Ecosystems* 11:815–830.

Laursen, G.A., & R.D. Seppelt. 2009. *Common interior Alaska cryptogams: Fungi, lichenicolous fungi, lichenized fungi, slime molds, mosses, and liverworts*, 2nd ed. University of Alaska Press, Fairbanks.

Lincoff, G.H. 1997. *National Audubon Society field guide to North American mushrooms*. Alfred A. Knopf, New York.

Parker, H. 1994. *Alaska's mushrooms: A practical guide*. Alaska Northwest Books. Anchorage, Alaska.

Lichens

Brodo, I.M., S.D. Sharnoff, & S. Sharnoff. 2001. *Lichens of North America*. Yale University Press, New Haven.

Burt, P. 2000. *Barrenland beauties: Showy plants of the Canadian Arctic*. The Northern Publishers, Yellowknife, Northwest Territories.

Calkin, P.E., & J.M. Ellis. 1980. "A lichenometric dating curve and its application to Holocene glacier studies in the central Brooks Range, Alaska." *Arctic and Alpine Research* 12:245–264.

Jandt, R., K. Joly, C.R. Meyers, & C. Racine. 2008. "Slow recovery of lichen on burned caribou winter range in Alaska tundra: Potential influences of climate warming and other disturbance factors." *Arctic, Antarctic, and Alpine Research* 40:89–95.

Jandt, R.R., & C.R. Meyers. 1982. *Recovery of lichen in tussock tundra following fire in northwestern Alaska.* BLM-Alaska Open File Report 82, U.S. Department of the Interior, Bureau of Land Management, Anchorage, Alaska.

Moser, T.J., T.H. Nash III, & J.W. Thomson. 1979. "Lichens of Anaktuvuk Pass, Alaska, with emphasis on the impact of caribou grazing." *The Bryologist* 82:393–408.

Thomson, J.W. 1979. *Lichens of the Alaskan Arctic Slope.* University of Toronto Press, Toronto.

Vitt, D.H., J.E. Marsh, & R.B. Bovey. 1988. *Mosses, lichens and ferns of northwest North America.* Lone Pine Publishing, Vancouver.

Mosses and Liverworts

Köckinger, H., J. Kučera, & A. Stebel. 2005. "*Pohlia nutans* subsp. *schimperi* (Müll.Hal.) Nyholm, a neglected Nordic moss in Central Europe." *Journal of Bryology* 27:351–355.

Longton, R.E. 1988. *Biology of polar bryophytes and lichens.* Studies in Polar Research, Cambridge University Press, New York.

Marino, P.C. 1991. "Competition between mosses (Splachnaceae) in patchy habitats." *Journal of Ecology* 79:1031–1046.

Pearce, I.S.K., S.J. Woodin, & R. van der Wal. 2003. "Physiological and growth responses of the montane bryophyte *Racomitrium lanuginosum* to atmospheric nitrogen deposition." *New Phytologist* 160:145–155.

Steere, W.C., & B.M. Murray. 1974. "The geographical distribution of *Bryum wrightii* in arctic and boreal North America." *Bryologist* 77:172–178.

Vitt, D.H., J.E. Marsh, & R.B. Bovey. 1988. *Mosses, lichens, and ferns of northwest North America.* Lone Pine Publishing, Vancouver.

Grasses, Sedges, and Forbs

Burt, P. 2000. *Barrenland beauties: Showy plants of the Canadian Arctic.* The Northern Publishers, Yellowknife, Northwest Territories.

Hultén, E. 1968. *Flora of Alaska and neighboring territories: A manual of the vascular plants.* Stanford University Press, Stanford, California.

Johnson, D., L. Kershaw, A. MacKinnon, & J. Pojar. 1995. *Plants of the western boreal forest & aspen parkland.* Lone Pine Publishing, Edmonton, Alberta.

Pielou, E.C. 1994. *A naturalist's guide to the Arctic.* University of Chicago Press, Chicago.

Trelawny, J.G. 1988. *Wild flowers of the Yukon, Alaska and northwestern Canada.* Harbour Publishing, Madeira Park, British Columbia.

Trees and Shrubs

Argus, G.W. 2007. "*Salix* (Salicaceae) distribution maps and a synopsis of their classification in North America, North of Mexico." *Harvard Papers in Botany* 12:335–368.

Colet, D.M. 2004. "Willows of interior Alaska." U.S. Fish and Wildlife Service. Available at http://alaska.fws.gov/nwr/yukonflats/pdf/willowsfinal.pdf.

De Groot, W.J., P.A. Thomas, & R.W. Wein. 1997. "*Betula nana* L. and *Betula glandulosa* Michx." *Journal of Ecology* 85:241–264.

Edwards, M.E., & P.W. Dunwiddie. 1985. "Dendrochronological and palynological observations on *Populus balsamifera* in northern Alaska." *Arctic and Alpine Research* 17:271–277.

Elsner, W.K., & J.C. Jorgenson. 2009. "White spruce seedling (*Picea glauca*) discovered north of the Brooks Range along Alaska's Dalton Highway." *Arctic* 62:342–344.

Hultén, E. 1968. *Flora of Alaska and neighboring territories: A manual of the vascular plants.* Stanford University Press, Stanford, California.

Lennartsson, M. 2003. "Cold hardening and dehardening in *Salix*." Doctoral thesis, Swedish University of Agricultural Sciences, Umeå.

Sibley, D.A. 2009. *The Sibley guide to trees.* Knopf, New York.

Viereck, L.A., & E.L. Little, Jr. 2007. *Alaska trees and shrubs,* 2nd ed. University of Alaska Press and Snowy Owl Books, Fairbanks.

Zalatan, R., & K. Gajewski. 2006. "Dendrochronological potential of *Salix alaxensis* from the Kuujja River area, western Canadian arctic." *Tree-Ring Research* 62:75–82.

Invertebrates

Adler, P.H., D.C. Currie, & D.M. Wood. 2004. *The black flies (Simuliidae) of North America.* Cornell University Press, Ithaca.

Barnes, B.M. 1989. "Freeze avoidance in a mammal: body temperatures below 0°C in an arctic hibernator." *Science* 244:1593–1595.

Barnes, B.M., J.L. Barger, J. Seares, P.C. Tacquard, & G.L. Zuercher. 1996. "Overwintering in yellowjacket queens (*Vespula vulgaris*) and green stinkbugs (*Elasmostethus interstinctus*) in subarctic Alaska." *Physiological Zoology* 69:1469–1480.

Belk, D. "Key to Anostraca (fairy shrimps) of North America." *Southwestern Naturalist* 20:91–103.

Bennet, V.A., O. Kukal, & R.E. Lee, Jr. 1999. "Metabolic opportunists: Feeding and temperature influence the rate and pattern of respiration in the high arctic woollybear caterpillar *Gynaephora groenlandica* (Lymantriidae)." *Journal of Experimental Biology* 202:47–53.

Brock, J.P., & K. Kaufman. 2003. *Field guide to butterflies of North America.* Houghton Mifflin, New York.

Brtek, J., & G. Mura. 2000. "Revised key to families and genera of the Anostraca with notes on their geographical distribution." *Crustaceana* 73:1037–1088.

Chernov, T.I., & A.G. Tatarinov. 2006. "Butterflies (Lepidoptera, Rhopalocera) in the arctic fauna." *Entomological Review* 86:760–786.

Clarke, A.H. 1981. *The freshwater molluscs of Canada.* National Museum of Natural Sciences/National Museums of Canada, Ottawa.

Clements, A.N. 1992. *The biology of mosquitoes. Volume I: Development, nutrition and reproduction.* Chapman & Hall, London.

Corbet, P.S. 1964. "Autogeny and oviposition in arctic mosquitoes." *Nature* 212:669.

———. 1967. "Facultative autogeny in arctic mosquitoes." *Nature* 215:662–663.

Danks, H.V., O. Kukal, & R.A. Ring. 1994. "Insect cold-hardiness: Insights from the Arctic." *Arctic* 47:391–404.

Dodson, S.I., & D.L. Egger. 1980. "Selective feeding of red phalaropes on zooplankton of arctic ponds." *Ecology* 61:755–763.

Ellers, J., & C.L. Boggs. 2004. "Functional ecological implications of intraspecific differences in wing melanization in *Colias* butterflies." *Biological Journal of the Linnaean Society* 82:79–87.

Fauchald, P., et al. 2007. "Escaping parasitism in the selfish herd: Age, size and density-dependent warble fly infestation in reindeer." *Oikos* 116:491–499.

Frohne, W.C. 1953. "Natural history of *Culiseta impatiens* (Wlk.), (Diptera, Culicidae), in Alaska." *Transactions of the American Microscopical Society* 72:103–118.

———. 1954. "Mosquito distribution in Alaska with especial reference to a new type of life cycle." *Mosquito News* 14:10–13.

———. 1956. "The biology of northern mosquitoes." *Public Health Reports* 71:616–622.

Gjullin, C.M., R.I. Sailer, A. Stone, & B.V. Travis. 1961. *The mosquitoes of Alaska.* Agricultural Handbook No. 182, Agricultural Research Service, United States Department of Agriculture.

Goulson, D. 2010. *Bumblebees: Behaviour, ecology, and conservation,* 2nd ed. Oxford University Press, Oxford, England.

Green, A.J., & J. Figuerola. 2005. "Recent advances in the study of long-distance dispersal of aquatic invertebrates via birds." *Diversity and Distributions* 11:149–156.

Guppy, C.S. 1986. "The adaptive significance of alpine melanism in the butterfly *Parnassius phoebus* F. (Lepidoptera: Paplionidae)." *Oecologia* 70:205–213.

Hanna, G.D. 1956. "Land and freshwater mollusks of the Arctic Slope of Alaska." *Nautilus* 70:4–10.

Heinrich, B. 1990. "Is 'reflectance' basking real?" *Journal of Experimental Biology* 154:31–43.

———. 1996. *The thermal warriors.* Harvard University Press, Cambridge, Massachusetts.

———. 2004. *Bumblebee economics.* Harvard University Press, Cambridge, Massachusetts.

Hudson, J., & R.H. Armstrong. 2005. *Dragonflies of Alaska.* Todd Communications, Anchorage, Alaska.

Kevan, P.G., T.S. Jensen, & J.D. Shorthouse. 1982. "Body temperatures and behavioral thermoregulation of high arctic woolly-bear caterpillars and pupae (*Gynaephora rossi*, Lymantriidae: Lepidoptera) and the importance of sunshine." *Arctic and Alpine Research* 14:125–136.

Kevan, P.G., & J.D. Shorthouse. 1970. "Behavioral thermoregulation by high arctic butterflies." *Arctic* 23:268–279.

Kearns, C.A., & J.D. Thomson. 2001. *The natural history of bumblebees: A sourcebook for investigators.* University Press of Colorado, Boulder, Colorado.

Kukal, O. 1993. "Biotic and abiotic constraints on foraging of arctic caterpillars." Pp. 509–533 *in* Stamp, N.E., and T.M. Casey (*eds.*), *Caterpillars: Ecological and evolutionary constraints on foraging.* Chapman & Hall, New York.

Kukal, O., & T.E. Dawson. 1989. "Temperature and food quality influences feeding behavior, assimilation efficiency and growth rate of arctic woolly-bear caterpillars." *Oecologia* 79:526–532.

Kukal, O., B. Heinrich & J.G. Duman. 1988. "Behavioural thermoregulation in the freeze-tolerant arctic caterpillar *Gynaephora groenlandica*." *Journal of Experimental Biology* 138:181–193.

Kutz, S.J., E.P. Holberg, L. Polley, & E.J. Jenkins. 2005. "Global warming is changing the dynamics of arctic host-parasite systems." *Proceedings of the Royal Society* B 272:2571–2576.

Layberry, R.A., P.W. Hall, & J.D. Lafontaine. 1998. *The butterflies of Canada.* University of Toronto Press, Toronto.

Litzenberger, G., & W. Chapco. 2001. "A molecular phylogeographic perspective on a fifty-year-old taxonomic issue in grasshopper systematic." *Heredity* 86:54–59.

Lyon, B.E., & R.V. Cartar. 1996. "Functional significance of the cocoon in two arctic *Gynaephora* moth species." *Proceedings of the Royal Society of London* B 263:1159–1163.

Maynard, S.S. 1976. "*Branchinecta paludosa* (Müller) (Crustacea: Anostraca) in northern Utah with some notes on its ecology." *The Southwestern Naturalist* 20:582–585.

McLean, D.M. 1975. "Mosquito-borne arboviruses in arctic America." *Medical Biology* 53:264–270.

Miller, M.C. 1980. "Tadpole shrimp." Pp. 323–335 *in* Hobbie, J.E. (*ed.*), *Limnology of tundra ponds: Barrow, Alaska.* US/IBP Synthesis Aeries 13. Dowden, Hutchinson & Ross, Inc., Stroudsburg, Pennsylvania.

Moore, M.V., & R.E. Lee, Jr. 1991. "Surviving the big chill: Overwintering strategies of aquatic and terrestrial insects." *American Entomologist* Summer 1991:111–118.

Morefield, W.D. & P. Lang. 1995. "Immature stages of high arctic *Gynaephora* species (Lymantriidae) and notes on their biology at Alexandra Fiord, Ellesmere Island." *Journal of Research on the Lepidoptera* 34:119–141.

Morewood, W.D., & R.A. Ring. 1998. "Revision of the life history of the high arctic moth *Gynaeophora groenlandica* (Wocke) (Lepidoptera: Lymantriidae)." *Canadian Journal of Zoology* 76:1371–1381.

Morewood, W.D., & D.M. Wood. 2002. "Host utilization by *Exorista thula* Wood (sp. nov.) and *Chetogena gelida* (Coquillett) (Diptera: Tachinidae), parasitoids of arctic species of *Gynaephora* species (Lepidoptera: Lymantriidae)." *Polar Biology* 25:575–582.

Newfoundland and Labrador Agriculture Wildlife Diseases Factsheet. 2004. "Parasites of caribou (2): Fly larvae infestations." Publication AP010, July 27, 2004. Government of Newfoundland and Labrador, Department of Natural Resources.

Nilssen, A.C., J.R. Anderson, & R. Bergersen. 2000. "The reindeer oestrids *Hypoderma tarandi* and *Cephenemyia trompe* (Diptera: Oestridae): Batesian mimics of bumblebees (Hymenoptera: Apidae: *Bombus* spp.)?" *Journal of Insect Behavior* 13:307–320.

Pollard, R.H., W.B. Ballard, L.E. Noel, & M.A. Cronin. 1996. "Parasitic insect abundance and microclimate of gravel pads and tundra within the Prudhoe Bay Oil Field, Alaska, in relation to use by caribou, *Rangifer tarandus granti.*" *Canadian Field Naturalist* 110:649–658.

Powell, J.A., & P.A. Opler. 2009. *Moths of western North America.* University of California Press, Berkeley.

Randolph, R.P., & W.P. McCafferty. 2005. "The mayflies (Ephemeroptera) of Alaska, including a new species of Heptageniidae." *Proceedings of the Entomological Society of Washington* 107:190–199.

Reed, E.B. 1962. "Freshwater planktonic crustacea of the Colville River area, Northern Alaska." *Arctic* 15:27–50.

Richards, K.W. 1973. "Biology of *Bombus polaris* Curtis and *B. hyperboreus* Schön-herr at Lake Hazen, Northwest Territories (Hymenoptera: Bombini)." *Quaestiones entomologicae* 9:115–157.

Roland, J. 1982. "Melanism and diel activity of alpine *Colias* (Lepidoptera: Pieridae)." *Oecologia* 53:214–221.

——. 2006. "Effect of melanism of alpine *Colias nastes* butterflies (Lepidoptera: Pieridae) on activity and predation." *Canadian Entomologist* 138:52–58.

Saunders, J.F. III, D. Belk, & R. Dufford. 1993. "Persistance of *Branchinecta paludosa* (Anostraca) in southern Wyoming, with notes on zoogeography." *Journal of Crustacean Biology* 13:184–189.

Schmid, F. 1998. *Genera of the Trichoptera of Canada and adjoining or adjacent United States: The insects and arachnids of Canada*, Part 7. NRC Research Press, Ottawa, Ontario.

Sformo, T., K. Walters, K. Jeannet, B. Wowk, G.M. Fahy, B.M. Barnes, & J.G. Duman. 2010. "Deep supercolling, vitrification and limited survival to –100°C in the Alaskan beetle *Cucujus clavipes puniceus* (Coleoptera: Cucujidae) larvae." *Journal of Experimental Biology* 213:502–509.

Sinclair, B.J. 1999. "Insect cold tolerance: How many kinds of frozen?" *European Journal of Entomology* 96:157–164.

Sinclair, B.J., A. Addo-Bediako, & S.L. Chown. 2003. "Climatic variability and the evolution of insect freeze tolerance." *Biological Review* 78:181–195.

Stewart, K.W., & M.W. Oswood. 2006. *The stoneflies (Plecoptera) of Alaska and western Canada*. Caddis Press, Columbus, Ohio.

Teskey, H.J. 1990. "The horse flies and deer flies of Canada and Alaska." *The insects and arachnids of Canada*, Part 16. Publication 1838. Agriculture Canada, Ottawa.

Vickery, V.R., & D.K.M. Kevan. 1985. *The grasshoppers, crickets, and related insects of Canada and adjacent regions: The insects and arachnids of Canada*, Part 14. Publication 1777. Agriculture Canada, Ottawa.

Vogt, F.D., B. Heinrich, T.O. Dabolt, & H.L. McBath. 1994. "Ovary development and colony founding in subarctic and temperate-zone bumblebee queens." *Canadian Journal of Zoology* 72:1551–1556.

Walters, L.L., S.J. Tirrell, & R.E. Shope. 1999. "Seroepidemiology of California and Bunyamwera serogroup (Bunyaviridae) virus infections in native populations of Alaska." *American Journal of Tropical Medicine and Hygiene* 60:806–821.

Watt, W.B. 1968. "Adaptive significance of pigment polymorphisms in *Colias* butterflies. I. variation of melanin pigment in relation to thermoregulation." *Evolution* 22:437–458.

Wiggins, G.B. 1996. *Larvae of the North American caddisfly genera (Trichoptera)*, 2nd ed. University of Toronto Press, Toronto, Ontario.

Williams, P.H. 1998. "An annotated checklist of bumble bees with an analysis of patterns of description (Hymenoptera: Apidae, Bombini)." *Bulletin of the Natural History Museum of London (Entomology)* 67:79–152. Updated at http://www.nhm.ac.uk/research-curation/research/projects/bombus/.

——. 2008. "A simplified subgeneric classification of the bumblebees (genus *Bombus*)." *Apidologie* 39:46–74.

——. 2008. "Do the parasitic *Psithyrus* resemble their host bumblebees in colour pattern?" *Apidologie* 39:637–649.

Wood, D.M., P.T. Dang & R.A. Ellis. 1979. "The mosquitoes of Canada." *The insects and arachnids of Canada*, Part 6. Publication 1686. Agriculture Canada, Ottawa.

Fish

George, J.C, L. Moulton, & M.J. Deering. 2009. *A field guide to the common fishes of the North Slope of Alaska*, Version 1.5. North Slope Borough, Department of Wildlife Management, Barrow, Alaska. Available at http://www.co.north-slope.ak.us/departments/wildlife/Fish.php#IdentificationofNSfish.

Hemming, C.R. 1993. *Tundra stream fish habitat investigations in the North Slope oilfields*. Technical Report 93-1. Alaska Department of Fish and Game, Habitat and Restoration Division, Juneau, Alaska.

Johnson, J., & P. Blanche. 2010. *Catalogue of waters important for spawning, rearing, or migration of anadromous—Arctic region, effective June 1, 2010*. Special Publication No. 10-04. Alaska Department of Fish and Game, Divisions of Sport Fish and Habitat.

Mecklenburg, C.W., T.A. Mecklenburg, & L.K. Thorsteinson. 2002. *Fishes of Alaska*. American Fisheries Society, Bethesda, Maryland.

Morrow, J.E. 1980. *The freshwater fishes of Alaska*. Alaska Northwest Publishing Company, Anchorage, Alaska.

Moulton, L.L., B. Seavey, & J. Pausanna. 2010. "History of an under-ice subsistence fishery for arctic cisco and least cisco in the Colville River, Alaska." *Arctic* 63:381–390.

Page, L.M., & B.M. Burr. 1991. *Freshwater fishes*. Houghton Mifflin, Boston.

Truett, J.C., & S.R. Johnson (eds.). 2000. *The natural history of an arctic oil field*. Academic Press, San Diego.

Winters, J.F. 1992. *Fisheries investigations in the upper Atigun River drainage in relation to the Alyeska Atigun mainline pipe replacement project*. Technical Report No. 92-2. Alaska Department of Fish and Game, Division of Habitat, Juneau, Alaska.

Woodford, R. 2008. *Alaska wildlife notebook series*. Alaska Department of Fish and Game, Division of Wildlife Conservation, Juneau, Alaska.

Reptiles and Amphibians

Alaska Wood Frog Monitoring Project, Alaska Citizen Science Program. Available at http://aknhp.uaa.alaska.edu/zoology/zoology_frogs.htm (accessed September 16, 2010).

Brouwers, E.M., W.A. Clemens, R.A. Spicer, T.A. Ager, L.D. Carter, & W.V. Sliter. 1987. "Dinosaurs on the North Slope, Alaska: High latitude, latest Cretaceous environments." *Science* 237:1608–1610.

Gangloff, R.A. 1992. "The record of Cretaceous dinosaurs in Alaska: An overview." *ICAM Proceedings* pp. 399–404.

Gangloff, R.A., A.R. Fiorillo, & D.W. Norton. 2005. "The first pachycephalosaurine (Dinosauria) from the paleo-arctic of Alaska and its paleogeographic implications." *Journal of Paleontology* 79:997–1001.

Hodge, R.P. 1976. *Amphibians and reptiles in Alaska, the Yukon and Northwest Territories*. Alaska Northwest Publishing Company, Anchorage.

Licht, L.E. 1991. "Habitat selection of *Rana pipiens* and *Rana sylvatica* during exposure to warm and cold temperatures." *American Midland Naturalist* 125:259–268.

Storey, K.B., & J.M. Storey. 1990. "Frozen and alive." *Scientific American*, December, pp. 92–97.

Birds

Bowman, T.D. 2004. *Field guide to bird nests and eggs of Alaska's coastal tundra*. Alaska Sea Grant College Program, University of Alaska, Fairbanks.

Brown, S. (*ed.*). 2006. *Arctic wings: Birds of the Arctic National Wildlife Refuge*. The Mountaineers, Seattle.

Elbroch, M., & E. Marks. 2001. *Bird tracks and sign: A guide to North American species*. Stackpole Books, Mechanicsburg, Pennsylvania.

Heath, J.E., J.E. Hobbie, T.J. Cade, J. Davis, A.H. Miller, R.G. McCaskie, J.R. Northern, G.G. Robinson, W.N. Goodall, & H. Howard. 1962. "Observations on the breeding of golden eagles at Lake Peters in northern Alaska." *Condor* 64:234–242.

Hohenberger, C.J., W.C. Hanson & E.E. Burroughs. 1994. "Birds of the Prudhoe Bay region, Northern Alaska." *Western Birds* 25:73–103.

Johnson, J.A., R.B. Lanctot, B.A. Andres, J.R. Bart, S.C. Brown, S.J. Kendall, & D.C. Payer. 2007. "Distribution of breeding shorebirds on the Arctic Coastal Plain of Alaska." *Arctic* 60:277–293.

Johnson, S.R., & D.R. Herter. 1989. *The birds of the Beaufort Sea*. BP Exploration, Inc., Anchorage, Alaska.

Powell, A.N., & S. Backensto. 2009. *Common ravens* (Corvus corvax) *nesting on Alaska's North Slope oil fields*. Coastal Marine Institute, University of Alaska, Fairbanks.

Ritchie, R.J. 1978. "Probable common flicker nest on the North Slope of the Brooks Range, Alaska." *Murrelet* 59:31–33.

Schorger, A.W. 1947. "The deep diving of the loon and old-squaw and its mechanism." *Wilson Bulletin* 59:151–159.

Sibley, D.A. 2000. *The Sibley guide to birds*. Alfred A. Knopf, New York.

———. 2004. "Distinguishing Cackling and Canada Goose." http://www.sibley guides.com/2007/07/identification-of-cackling-and-canada-goose/. Last edited October 4, 2010. Accessed August 28, 2011.

Sinclair, P.H., W.A. Nixon, C.D. Exkert, & N.L. Hughes. 2003. *Birds of the Yukon Territory*. University of British Columbia Press, Vancouver.

Swem, T.R., C.M. White, & R.J. Ritchie. 1992. "Comments on the status of certain birds on the North Slope of Alaska." *Northwestern Naturalist* 73:84–87.

Terres, J.K. 1980. *The Audubon Society encyclopedia of North American birds*. Alfred A. Knopf, New York.

Truett, J.C., & S.R. Johnson (*eds.*). 2000. *The natural history of an arctic oil field*. Academic Press, San Diego.

Woodford, R. 2008. *Alaska wildlife notebook series*. Alaska Department of Fish and Game, Juneau, Division of Wildlife Conservation, Alaska.

Mammals

Batzli, G.O., R.G. White, S.F. MacLean, Jr., F.A. Pitelka, & B.D. Collier. 1980. "The herbivore-based trophic system." Pp. 335–410 *in* Brown J., P.C. Miller,

L.L. Tieszen, & F.L. Bunnell (*eds.*), *An arctic ecosystem: The coastal tundra at Barrow, Alaska.* US/IBP Aynthesis Aeries 12. Dowden, Hutchinson & Ross, Inc., Stroudsburg, Pennsylvania.

Carroll, G. 2007. "Unit 26A furbearer." Pp. 335–343 *in* Harper, P. (*ed.*), *Furbearer management report of survey and inventory activities 1 July 2003–30 June 2006.* Alaska Department of Fish and Game, Juneau, Alaska.

———. 2009. "Unit 26A wolf management report." Pp. 265–278 in Harper, P. (*ed.*), *Wolf management report of survey and inventory activities 1 July 2005–30 June 2008.* Alaska Department of Fish and Game, Juneau, Alaska.

Elbroch, M. 2003. *Mammal tracks and sign: A guide to North American species.* Stackpole Books, Mechanicsburg, Pennsylvania.

Feldhammer, G.A., B.C. Thompson, & J.A. Chapman. 2003. *Wild mammals of North America: Biology, management, and conservation,* 2nd ed. John Hopkins University Press, Baltimore, Maryland.

Fuglesteg, B.N., Ø.E. Haga, L.P. Folkow, E. Fuglei, & A.S. Blix. 2006. "Seasonal variations in basal metabolic rate, lower critical temperature and responses to temporary starvation in the arctic fox (*Alopex lagopus*) from Svalbard." *Polar Biology* 29:308–319.

Kays, R.W., & D.E. Wilson. 2002. *Mammals of North America.* Princeton Field Guides, Princeton, New Jersey.

Lenart, E.A. 2009. "Unit 26B and 26C muskox." Pp. 48–69 in Harper, P. (*ed.*). *Muskox management report of survey and inventory activities 1 July 2005–30 June 2008.* Alaska Department of Fish and Game, Juneau, Alaska.

Lent, P.C. 1999. *Muskoxen and their hunters.* University of Oklahoma Press, Norman, Oklahoma.

MacDonald, S.O., & J.A. Cook. 2009. *Recent mammals of Alaska.* University of Alaska Press, Fairbanks.

Pamperin, N.J. 2008. "Winter movements of arctic foxes in northern Alaska measured by satellite telemetry." M.Sc. thesis, University of Alaska Fairbanks.

Pitelka, F.A., & G.O. Batzli. 2007. "Population cycles of lemmings near Barrow, Alaska: A historical review." *Acta Theriologica* 52:323–336.

Pruitt, W.O. 1959. "Snow as a factor in the winter ecology of the barren-ground caribou." *Arctic* 12:159–179.

Reid, F.A. 2006. *Mammals of North America,* 4th ed. Houghton Mifflin, Boston.

Telfer, E.S., & J.P. Kelsall. 1984. "Adaptation of some large North American mammals for survival in snow." *Ecology* 65:1828–1834.

Truett, J.C., & S.R. Johnson (*eds.*). 2000. *The natural history of an arctic oil field.* Academic Press, San Diego.

Woodford, R. 2008. *Alaska wildlife notebook series.* Alaska Department of Fish and Game, Division of Wildlife Conservation, Juneau, Alaska.

Human Natural History Through the Mid-Twentieth Century

Alexander, H.L., Jr. 1967. "Alaskan survey." *Expeditions,* Spring 1967:20–29.

———. 1969. "Prehistory of the central Brooks Range—an archeological analysis." Ph.D. dissertation, University of Oregon.

Amsden, C.W. 1977. "A quantitative analysis of Nunamiut Eskimo settlement dynamics: 1898 to 1969." Ph.D. dissertation, University of New Mexico.

Bever, M.R. 2001. "An overview of Alaskan Late Pleistocene archaeology: Historical themes and current perspectives." *Journal of World Prehistory* 15:125–191.

———. 2001. "Stone tool technology and the Mesa Complex: Developing a framework of Alaskan Paleoindian prehistory." *Arctic Anthropology* 38:98–118.

———. 2006. "Rethinking the Putu Site: Results of a spatial analysis of a fluted point site in northern Alaska." *Arctic Anthropology* 43:20–39.

———. 2006. "Too little, too late? The radiocarbon chronology of Alaska and the peopling of the New World." *American Antiquity* 71:595–620.

Corbin, J.E. 1975. "Aniganigaruk: A study in Nunamiut Eskimo archeology." Ph.D. dissertation, Washington State University, Pullman, Washington.

Dixon, E.J., Jr. 1973. The Gallagher Flint Station: An early man site on the North Slope, Arctic Alaska." Master's thesis, M-3973, University of Alaska.

———. 1999. *Bones, boats & bison: Archeology and the first colonization of western North America*. University of New Mexico Press, Albuquerque, New Mexico.

Guthrie, R.D. 1990. *Frozen fauna of the mammoth steppe: The story of blue babe*. University of Chicago Press, Chicago.

Irving, L. 1976. "Simon Paneak." *Arctic* 29:58–59.

Kunz, M., M. Bever, & C. Adkins. 2003. *The Mesa Site: Paleoindians above the Arctic Circle*. Bureau of Land Management Alaska Open File Report 86/U.S. Department of the Interior, Anchorage, Alaska.

Langdon, S.J. 2002. *The native people of Alaska: Traditional living in a northern land*, 4th ed. Greatland Graphics, Anchorage, Alaska.

Lobdell, J.E. 1986. "The Kuparuk Pingo Site: A Northern Archaic hunting camp of the Arctic Coastal Plain, North Alaska." *Arctic* 39:47–51.

Mason, O.K., P.M. Bowers, & D.M. Hopkins. 2001. "The early Holocene Milankovitch thermal maximum and humans: Adverse conditions for the Denali complex of eastern Beringea." *Quaternary Science Reviews* 20:525–548.

Rasic, J.T. 2008. "Paleoalaskan adaptive strategies viewed from northwestern Alaska." Ph.D. dissertation, Department of Anthropology, Washington State University, Pullman, Washington.

Solecki, R.S., B. Salwen, & J. Jacobson. 1973. *Archaeological reconnaissances north of the Brooks Range in northeastern Alaska*. Occasional Papers No. 1, Department of Archeology, University of Calgary, Alberta.

Wenzel, K.E., & P.H. Shelley. 2001. "What put the small in the Arctic Small Tool Tradition: Raw material constraints on lithic technology at the Mosquito Lake Site, Alaska." Pp. 106–123 *in* Andrefsky, W. (*ed.*), *Lithic debitage: Context, form, meaning*. University of Utah Press, Salt Lake City, Utah.

Wilson, I.R. 1978. *Archeological investigations at the Atigun Site, Central Brooks Range, Alaska*. Archeological Survey of Canada, Paper No. 78. National Museums of Canada, Ottawa, Ontario.

Appendix

Brown, J., & R.A. Kreig (*eds.*). 1983. *Elliot and Dalton Highways, Fox to Prudhoe Bay, Alaska: Guidebook to permafrost and related features, Guidebook 4*. Fourth International Conference on Permafrost, Fairbanks Alaska. Alaska Division of Geological and Geophysical Surveys, Anchorage.

Bureau of Land Management. 1993. *Riches from the earth: A geologic tour along the Dalton Highway, Alaska*. Alaska Natural History Association, Anchorage.

Mull, C.G., & K.E. Adams (*eds.*). 1989. *Dalton Highway, Yukon River to Prudhoe Bay, Alaska, Guidebook 7*. Alaska Division of Geological and Geophysical Surveys, Anchorage.

Walker, D.A., T.D. Hamilton, C.L. Ping, R.P. Daanen, & W.W. Streever. 2009. *Dalton Highway field trip guide for the ninth international conference on permafrost*. Guidebook 9. State of Alaska, Department of Natural Resources, Division of Geology and Geophysical Surveys. Available at http://www.geobotany.org/nicop/docs/gb009.pdf.

Index

Note: *Italicized* page numbers indicate illustrations. Page numbers followed by (log) refer to the Road Log. Plant and animal names are indexed as follows: common name (scientific name for family or order).

calendar dates, 243
Campsite Lake, 159
camus (Liliaceae), 79, *81*
Canadian lynx (Felidae), 222
caribou (Cervidae)
  abundance on North Slope, 211
  aufeis and, 51
  bot flies and, 126–128
  diet and digestive systems of, 59
  and human survival, 252
  lichen grazing system, 59–61
  migrating to calving grounds, *237*
  migration pathways, 237–238
  mosquitoes and, 121
  North Slope herds, 236–237
  Rangifer tarandus (barren-ground
    caribou), *235,* 235–238
  snow craters and tracks, *236*
cell dehydration, controlled, in invertebrates, 114
centipedes (Chilenophilidae, Lithobiidae), *149,* 150
chars (Salmonidae), 48, 151, 156–
  158, *157,* 158–159
chert, 11, *249*
chickadees (Paridae), 101, 199,
  284n11 (ch. 9)
chickweed (Caryophyllaceae), 80–81,
  81
cinquefoil (Rosaceae), *106*
circles, sorted, 28–29, *29*
cirque glaciers, *18–19,* 58
cirques, defined, 282n4 (ch. 3)
ciscoes (Coregininae), 41, 152, *152,*
  152–155
clams, fingernail, *148*
climate, 4–5. *See also* temperatures
cloudberry (Rosaceae), *105,* 106
clubmosses (Lycopodiaceae), *73,* 73–74
cold hardening, invertebrates and,
  114–115
cold season, 5
coltsfoot (Ranunculaceae), *95*
Colville River
  area used by Nunamiut people,
    251–252
  divide between drainages of
    Kuparuk River and, 265 (log)
  divide between drainages of
    Sagavanirktok River and, 265
    (log)

drainage of, 44
exposures of Prince Creek
  Formation, 16
Complex, defined, 243
composites (Compositae, Asteraceae),
  95, 95–97, *96*
compound kames, 282n6 (ch. 3)
compound kettle lakes, 42
compound lakes, 283n7 (ch. 5)
conglomerates (pudding stones), 11
copepods (Copepoda), *147,* 147–148
corydalus (Fumariaceae), *83*
cottongrass (Cyperaceae), 74, *75,* 76
coyotes (Canidae), 223
crane flies (Tipulidae), 118, 124, *124*
cranes (Gruidae), 184, *184*
crinoid stem fossil, *13*
crowberry (Empetraceae), 107, *108*
crustaceans
  antenna of, 285n5 (ch. 10)
  copepods (Copepoda), *147,* 147–148
  fairy shrimp (Anostraca), *94,* 144,
    145, 145–146
  tadpole shrimp (Notostraca), 144–
    145, *145*
  water fleas (Cladocera), 144, 146–
    147, *147,* 147–148
cryoprotectants, in freeze-avoiding
  invertebrates, 113–115
cycloid scales, 285n1 (ch. 11)

D
Dall sheep (Bovidae), 239–240, *240*
Dalton Highway, *2* (map), *44, 256*
  (map), *262* (map), *275* (map)
  Arctic Circle crossing monument, 3
  bedrock along cross section, 10–16
  cautionary notes for travelers,
    255–257
  human settlement and, 253
  natural history guide, 255–280
damselflies (Odonata), 115–116, *117*
dance flies (Empididae), *70*
Dan Creek, 273–274 (log)
dates, prehistoric and calendar, 243
Deadhorse, *275* (map), *279* (log)
"Deadhorse 20 Miles" sign, 277–278
  (log)
Denbigh Flint Complex, 248–249
depth hoar, *7, 8*
deserts, common definition, 5